9

The Diary of a Season

THE DIARY OF A SEASON

Lawrie McMenemy's account of the 1978–9 season as manager of Southampton Football Club

Introduced and edited by
Brian Scovell

ARTHUR BARKER LIMITED · LONDON

A subsidiary of Weidenfeld (Publishers) Limited

ISBN 0 213 16724 7
Printed in Great Britain by
Butler & Tanner Ltd
Frome and London

Contents

Illustrations

*To Brian, who helped me write it, and
Anne, who helped me keep it right.*

Introduction

by Brian Scovell of the *Daily Mail*

Lawrence McMenemy, manager of Southampton Football Club, is one of the best known men in Britain. His face is so familiar that he can't walk down a street without being stopped. He appears on television more frequently than the Prime Minister.

There are only ninety-two Football League club managers in England and Wales and many of them are more famed for being sacked than anything else. McMenemy is one of the successful ones along with Brian Clough of Nottingham Forest, Bob Paisley of Liverpool and Bobby Robson of Ipswich.

All these men are Geordies, people who have had a tough up-bringing in one of England's less wealthy areas. Their breeding and background seem to have given them the mental capacity to withstand the strains of one of the hardest jobs in sport.

The football manager is utterly dependent on eleven men winning a game of football. He is a managing-director, a finder of talent, a coach, a publicist, a psychologist and a headmaster rolled into one. Yet he can be proficient in all those functions and still fail.

There is one quality the football manager needs above all others, the ruthlessness to make decisions that can affect the livelihoods of other people. He is running a business and can't afford to be sentimental. It is a job that calls for a considerable personality and strength of character.

This book is a chronicle of a ten-month season in the life of Lawrie McMenemy, the season 1978–9 which started for him in Los Angeles and ended in Cairo. In the intervening time, he travelled 100,000 miles, spoke at more than a hundred functions, attended over 150 games of football and moved house five times. He had just three days off.

The name McMenemy is Irish and his ancestors were gentlemen farmers. Early in this century, the family migrated across the Irish Channel, four settling in England and four in Scotland. McMenemy's father, a caretaker at a community centre among other unskilled jobs, went to live in Gateshead in a terraced house which had an outside toilet and just two bedrooms.

Lawrie was the eldest of the family of eight, two sisters and five brothers. He was born on 26 July 1936, and his pre-school years were spent in Bournemouth, where the family moved after his father took a job on the South Coast. 'They panicked a bit when the War started and went back to Gateshead,' he recalled. 'My mother always said Bournemouth was a nice place to live because she didn't need to wash the curtains so frequently.'

Until he was eleven, McMenemy went to Corpus Christi School in Gateshead before qualifying to attend the St Cuthbert's Grammar School in Newcastle. His ambition, he said, was to become a journalist, prophetic in view of his many appearances in print and on television after becoming a famous football manager.

He passed four subjects at 'O' Level in the GCE, including English, but he was never destined to be an academic. He spent too much time in the street playing football with his friends. The cobbled streets around his house were called avenues though there wasn't a tree in sight. They used a tennis ball and the lamp posts were the goals. There was no spare money in the McMenemy household for football kit and the local Catholic priest, Father Parker, contributed occasionally towards the cost of his outfits.

His grandfather had been a musician and one uncle played the violin in the London Symphony Orchestra and another in George Melachrino's Orchestra. He himself also trained with the violin.

He left school at sixteen and worked as a £5-a-week junior clerk in the Education Department at Gateshead but really wanted to be a footballer. Newcastle signed him on schoolboy forms, unpaid, along with scores of other teenagers and loaned him out to Gateshead, who were then in the Third Division North. He was tall and skinny, a natural centre-half.

His period of National Service was spent with the Coldstream Guards. While serving with the Guards – he is six feet four inches tall and has the ideal physique – he served on public duties, standing on guard duty outside Buckingham Palace, St James and the Bank of England, two hours on and four hours off.

Back in civilian life, he combined his job with the Education Authority with a coaching appointment at Gateshead FC. He passed his preliminary FA Coaching Badge, then the full Badge. Famous ex-Newcastle players like Jack Fairbrother and Bobby Mitchell came and went and he was left virtually running the side for £6 a week.

He was married by this time to Anne, a secretary in the local Council offices; she used to invite the players' wives round for supper while their husbands were away training and playing. His next coaching job was with the amateur side Bishop Auckland and he was so successful that they set a record by winning the League, the Cup and the County Cup in the same season.

His secondary ambition in life was to earn £1,000 a year and he achieved it at Bishop Auckland. He was mixing with Football League managers at coaching courses and in 1966 Alan Brown, manager of Sheffield Wednesday, persuaded him to join Wednesday as a coach.

'Anne was the decisive influence there,' he said. 'She said she was happy to go anywhere for my career and I left the Education Department and moved house to Sheffield.'

Brown quit to join Sunderland and in 1968–9 McMenemy, struggling to raise a family on £35 a week, became manager of Fourth Division Doncaster, the club's thirteenth manager in thirteen years. In his first season Doncaster won the Fourth Division championship. Their second season was uneventful and the third saw them relegated.

McMenemy was sacked and for the first time in his life he signed on the dole. 'I made one visit,' he said. 'I told them I wouldn't be back. It was too humiliating.'

Not long afterwards, he joined another Fourth Division club, Grimsby Town, and the pattern was similar: promotion in the first season, a second championship in four seasons. Attendances which were down to 2,000 rose to 24,000. The BBC sent John Motson up to interview him. He was, as they say in professional football, being talked about.

In 1973 he was approached by a First Division club, Southampton, who wanted a young track-suit manager to succeed Ted Bates. He got the job and in his first season at the Dell he admitted he couldn't handle it. There were too many old professionals in the club, too many drinkers and what he calls 'high fliers'.

Southampton were relegated with thirty-six points, an abnormally high number of points. The crowd that applauded him on his arrival now booed and hissed. 'Fortunately the directors stood by me,' he said.

He rebuilt the side and in 1976 they achieved one of the major surprises in the history of the FA Cup by beating Manchester United 1–0 in the Final. In 1977–8, he brought Southampton back into the First Division and when the 1978–9 season started he faced what could be a difficult season with a largely young, inexperienced side.

His greatest strength as a manager, he once said, was his ability to handle problem players. In a game where players sneer at managers – 'how many caps did you win?' – he faced a grave disadvantage because he was one of the few managers who had never played a single League game, let alone an international game. But he overcame that by force of character and earned the respect of players of international reputation like Alan Ball, Mike Channon, Peter Osgood and Ted MacDougall.

The story starts with him pondering over an offer to join Leeds as their manager. The world of the football manager is like the centre of an active volcano, always bubbling and fermenting, sometimes erupting.

The pressures from within are immense. Few managers can withstand them for long. But by the end of the season McMenemy had taken his team to the League Cup Final and a respectable position in the First Division table.

He once told a young reporter: 'Stick with me, son, and you'll be with a winner.' After eleven years as a manager in the Football League, Lawrie McMenemy has won three championships, won the FA Cup once, reached the Final of the League Cup, visited Wembley as a manager of a competing club three times, taken his team to the quarter-final of the European Cup Winners Cup, had two clubs relegated and been sacked once. He's won more than he's lost.

1. Pre season

At the end of the 1977–8 season, when Southampton were promoted back to the First Division, McMenemy arranged a part business, part holiday trip to the United States with his family.

While there, he was asked whether he would be interested in becoming manager of Leeds United, the club that Don Revie had made into one of Europe's leading sides. There was a certain amount of irony in that. When George Reader, the then Southampton chairman, wanted to check McMenemy's credentials before offering him the Southampton post in 1973, he rang Revie for advice. Revie said McMenemy had the qualities to succeed in the First Division. He had the right apprenticeship, he said.

Now McMenemy was poised to move into the seat at Elland Road which Revie vacated in 1974 to become England manager.

Tuesday, 18 July.

On the plane coming home I wasn't thinking so much about pre-season training as about what was happening with the Leeds job. I was linked with it at the end of the previous season but Jimmy Armfield was kept on. Now with Jimmy out it was mine if I wanted it.

Before I left on holiday, I discussed renewing my contract with Southampton. Money wasn't important – I was already one of the best paid managers in the country – but always you think of the challenge of going to a big club. I didn't want to be known as a manager who was frightened of the big one.

It's a dehumanizing business being a football manager. You have to fight hard to keep your self-respect and not end up being a rat. The system of hiring and firing makes managers want to get in first and move on when it suits them. Loyalty suffers. You soon learn to be cunning. I've tried to be above that.

One of the troubles is that the Secretaries and Managers Association is so weak. The last annual meeting was rushed through because everyone had to get dressed for a dinner in the evening. I once made a speech telling them that their stature wasn't high enough and they should do something about it. The Association should be able to get on to the chairman of a football club when he has just fired the manager and say, 'Has your manager been properly paid up?' If the club chairman says 'Mind your own business,' we should say, 'We are blacklegging your job.' If necessary, our members should be withdrawn.

A high proportion of managers who are sacked don't have their contracts paid up. The club keeps them on the payroll, hoping they will soon get another job and relieve them of their financial responsibilities. It's humiliating. The fellow has to creep round to collect his cheque. Often he cheats, taking on a job abroad and saying he is on holiday. Football League regulations are watertight in almost every way but amazingly they can let this happen. It takes away a man's pride and you can understand why managers pull the strokes some of them do, like Tommy Docherty when he agreed to join a Norwegian club and then, when Derby came in, changed his mind.

I wanted to be fair to the Southampton directors. This was to be one projected move that was going to be handled properly. I first heard about Leeds wanting me when, in San Francisco, several journalists, Doug Weatherall of the *Daily Mail*, Peter Cooper of the *Daily Mirror*, Vince Wilson of the *Sunday Mirror* and David Bobin of Southern Television, managed to find my telephone number and reach me. The first call came at half past midnight when I was downstairs having a drink with some friends. We were travelling in a foursome and both rooms were booked in my name. The call was put through to a room occupied by the children and one of them had to get dressed and come downstairs to tell me I was wanted. I also had a call from someone connected with the Leeds club so I knew it wasn't just newspaper speculation. They did want me. I tried not to let it disrupt the holiday but it did.

All sorts of things go through your mind. I've always thought five years is about the right time to be manager of a club. If you haven't done it then, it's time to go somewhere else. I'd been at Southampton five years, five happy years, and was just in the process of building another team both on and off the field.

My assistant, Jim Clunie, had left to become manager of St Mirren, Keith Honey, the secretary, had resigned to be replaced by Brian Truscott and Ted Bates, my predecessor, was about to go on to the board. Bill Ellerington, the chief scout, had retired. A lot of changes were being made in a short space of time.

And on my first day back, my secretary, Valerie Gardner, was on holiday and the physio, Don Taylor, was still recovering from an operation. That left George Horsfall and John McGrath to help me with the first day back at training. While I had been away there had also been speculation that Bob Wilson, a fellow panellist on the BBC World Cup team, was possibly going to become my number two. I knew Bob hankered after a management position. He'd done some coaching with his old club Arsenal and I had offered him the chance to gain experience under me. I wasn't sure how the players would react but I was prepared to do it.

All these problems were small ones alongside the Leeds business. How could you talk to players about loyalty if you were the first person to walk out? Players were tied by their contracts but managers could usually get out of theirs. I wouldn't have any qualms about taking the Leeds job because of the size and scope of the task. There are only half-a-dozen clubs in that class.

I ran the Southampton club. No-one interfered with me and I could virtually do what I liked. I knew I would be under more pressure at Leeds but that didn't worry me. I was confident I could handle it. Leeds had a slightly shady image but I was sure I could put that right.

In the talks I had had with the Southampton directors the subject of a testimonial match came up. Brian Clough had one at Nottingham Forest after fourteen years as a manager, why shouldn't I have one after eleven years? It didn't cost the directors anything. It was a decision only on their part, a gesture.

After bringing the club up from the Second Division, I was in a strong position, very different to the position I was in at the start when some of the Saints fans used to boo me as I walked along the running track to the bench before matches. I'd had peaks in my eleven years of management, like winning the FA Cup in 1976. But I'd also had lows, like the time I was on the dole at Doncaster after being sacked. In those years, I'd worked in every Division. I'd served my apprenticeship and I knew I was good enough to take the best jobs in the land. I'd been interviewed for the England job. Not many managers make it that far.

All these things went through my mind as we arrived at London Airport from Philadelphia at half-past eight in the morning. You don't sleep much on these night-time West–East flights. I had less chance to sleep than normal.

We drove home to Chandlers Ford and I changed and went to the Dell to welcome the players at midday. The first day is always a happy occasion, full of banter about suntans and why some people haven't got suntans. The chief joker, Alan Ball, wasn't there. He was over in America acting as player-manager of Philadelphia Furies. It's always livelier when Bally is about.

The day's first task was to weigh the players. If they are over-weight, they've got to work hard and get it off. The previous January–February, we'd had a problem with one of the goalkeepers, Peter Wells, whom I signed from Nottingham Forest. We were away on a mid-season break when the manager is closer to the players than usual and can watch them and get to know more about them. Peter seemed to be taking our advice to relax too literally. He looked too bulky and his dress was sloppy.

I'm not a tyrant who goes around ordering players to change their life-style to suit mine but I do believe in certain standards. I don't really approve of players perming their hair but as long as it doesn't look too unruly, I won't interfere. I prefer to make half-serious remarks like 'when is the barber going to give you the second half of that hair cut?' With Peter Wells, I'd said, 'When are you going to get that lion's mane tamed?' His style of dress wasn't too clever either and I said, 'Did you get those clothes from Oxfam?' He didn't improve, as I had hoped, and I had him in for a talking to. I told him he was sloppy and scruffy and was letting himself and the club down. I asked him if he had anything to say and he replied, 'No, I can't argue with what you say.' I fined him £50 and told him I would cancel his contract if he didn't pull himself together. He was drinking too much. I don't mean alcohol but milk and orange and he wasn't realizing that milk contains a lot of calories and is weight producing. It's fine drinking milk when you want to build up but

Wells was twenty-one and didn't need any more building up. When we weighed him on the first day back he was half a stone overweight and I told him to get stuck into it in the next week and get it off. He said he would.

Ted MacDougall made everyone laugh when he said, 'You want to get off milk and get on to lager.' If that crack had been made when I first went to the Dell, or before the 1976 Cup Final, it wouldn't have been so funny. We had some really high fliers in those days. Big drinkers. Fellows like Jim Steele, Peter Osgood, Jim McCalliog. You could fill the bath with champagne and they'd get through it. This lot were different. There wasn't a real drinker among them.

After the players left, I went to my office to look at a few letters. Guy Askham, one of the younger directors, a fellow I could identify with because he was about my age, came in to tell me what had happened at board level while I was away. I was beginning to wilt. It had been a long night and an even longer day.

Outside, my seventeen-year-old son Chris, who is a Southampton apprentice, was fast asleep in the car! When we arrived home, Anne unpacked a few cases and by ten we were in bed just about to drop off when the phone rang. It was Jock Wallace. I'd written to him urging him to keep going when he was having his troubles at Glasgow Rangers. Under his management Rangers had won virtually everything but he was still looked on as the trainer not the manager. He was so frustrated that his wife had started a course in pub management because they were toying with the idea of leaving the game altogether.

Unless you've worked in Scotland, you don't know the different pressures a manager has to face there. The game is full of politics, much more so than in England. I had known for some time that Jock was very unhappy. It was good to hear him now saying that he was settling into his new job at Leicester.

I was just getting back to sleep again when the telephone went again. Jimmy Armfield was on the line. Earlier I'd rung his home and left a message with his wife for him to call me if he wanted any help. There is a great camaraderie among managers. As men under constant pressure, they like having people to talk to. Jimmy wasn't saying 'hey don't go to Leeds' or anything like that. He said he thought the dressing room was just right and it was a good time for a new man to go there. If I wanted any help, he would willingly oblige. He was the man out of a job, and was volunteering help. He's a fine man.

Wednesday, 19 July.

I woke up at seven. That's early for me. I'm never moving much before eight. But I had one or two calls to make, including one to the acting chairman, Alan Woodford, to tell him I was back. I was flying up to Newcastle at midday to sign an apprentice, a lad of sixteen named Stephen Baker. I always make a point of going to the boy's house and meeting his parents myself. I wanted to see his environment, and I believe the parents want to see me because I'm going to take on the role of the boy's father for the next year or so and it's important we get on and understand each other.

My Daimler 4.2, a club-owned car, knew the way to London Airport by itself it had made the journey so many times. I was met at Newcastle by our chief scout, Jack Hixon, who is a part-timer. We have two other scouts on Wearside and Teesside, Gerry Jordan and Jack Robson. They are important people to a club. The North East is still a productive area for producing talent and you need good scouts to find the best young players.

Jack Hixon had arranged for a picture of our little signing ceremony to appear in that night's *Evening Chronicle*. It was first-class publicity, getting more space than the wrangles on the Newcastle United board. There was a meeting about the Newcastle boardroom crisis that night but news of it was given less prominence than our little story.

While I was at the airport, George House from the local BBC tracked me down and asked me in to record a four-minute piece. I was happy to oblige. This is my country and these are my people.

Before going on to my other engagement that night, presenting the sports prizes at Greenwell Comprehensive School in Gateshead, I popped in to see Bill McGarry, the Newcastle manager. I asked him about his full-back Irving Nattrass. He said Leeds had offered £300,000 but he'd knocked it back. Newcastle didn't want to sell him but if another club offered a silly sum – he said £350,000 – they could talk to him. That was big money by Southampton standards but not for Leeds. It started me thinking again about my dilemma. At Leeds I could go out and compete with the richest clubs in the country. At Southampton I had to be more careful with money.

It was a nostalgic evening at the school. In the audience I recognized many faces I had been to school with almost thirty years previously and here I was presenting prizes to their teenage children!

Thursday, 20 July.

Back to London Airport and on to the new training ground, owned by the Trojans club in Southampton. The first few days are spent going on runs, not so much with the ball. It's a boring ritual but there are squash courts at the club and some of the players like a game.

At two o'clock there was a board meeting at the Dell. Mr Woodford said Leeds had phoned while I was away asking permission to approach me and he'd asked them to put it in writing. The letter arrived that morning. As there were only three directors present, the matter wasn't discussed at length.

Just before I got back from America, the chairman, George Reader, died and things were in a turmoil. Mr Reader was a lovely, lovely man, an uncomplicated person. He was a headmaster but he never tried to dictate to me. He'd appointed me and had confidence in my ability. In the early days, he gave me the odd bollocking when he thought I was getting too uppity. He helped me polish up. I was from the North and when I first arrived some of the Southerners didn't appreciate my bluntness. George wasn't a Hampshire Hog as many people thought. He came from Nuneaton and could understand me because he was on the blunt side himself. He would quote this Latin phrase about making haste slowly. He was the kind of chairman you saw more of when you were losing than when you were winning. Often it is the reverse. I'd seen him the night before we went away. He was in his eighties and though his eyes were as sharp as needles his body was fading away. He refereed the 1950 World Cup Final and I loved it when he told stories of his refereeing days.

When I arrived home Anne told me our daughter Alison had been knocked off her bicycle by a car. She wasn't hurt but it was a shock all the same. For the first time in my life, I took the phone off the hook. I wanted some peace. The calls from the press were starting. Was I going to Leeds or wasn't I?

Friday, 21 July.

Mr Reader's funeral was at eleven o'clock at St Mary's Church. Ironically, that was the church Southampton Football Club was named after when it was formed in 1885. I organized training for nine o'clock so that the players could attend if they wanted to. Footballers in the main aren't great churchgoers but there was a good turn-out – David Peach, my first signing, Chris Nicholl, Malcolm Waldron, John Sharp and young Steve Williams among them. The directors were pleased that so many came along. I'm a Catholic but I was impressed with the Church of England service. It was more of a memorial thanksgiving for his life than a funeral. His daughter, a nursing sister, was dressed in blue and white with a pink hat. She was an agnostic and at first I thought her dress was a gesture of defiance. It didn't appear right to me. But as the service went on, I realized that it was in keeping with the tone of the event.

Denis Hill-Wood, the Arsenal chairman and long-time friend of Mr Reader, gave the address. He had a sheaf of notes but didn't look at them. It was a beautiful speech and it brought tears to my eyes. There was a reception at the Royal Hotel but I had time only for a tomato juice before going back to the ground to meet Fred Scott, our new chief scout who was taking over the work of Bill Ellerington and Ted Bates.

Some of the apprentices were still there and they were needed for a television commercial I had to make for a new soccer monthly. I told them they could share my fee and that pleased them. The television people said they were pleased at how quickly we did it. I think my experience in front of cameras speeded it up.

At home that night an old journalist friend, Vince Wilson of the *Sunday Mirror*, came round to discuss an article his newspaper wanted to feature on Sunday on 'would I join Leeds or would I stay with Southampton?' I told him I honestly hadn't decided anything and the piece would have to be inconclusive. I needed time to speak to my wife and family and you couldn't do that in five minutes. They were all involved. It was no use my rushing off to Leeds because it suited my career prospects only to find it had disrupted my children's lives. I am a family man and always have been. Many managers who flit about from job to job aren't family men but most of the successful ones are men who have a solid base at home, someone to go home to for a cup of tea when the world appears to be falling apart. There are a number of top managers in this category: Don Revie, Bill Shankly, Bob Paisley, Brian Clough among them. That night we went out to dinner with Vince and it was a long night. It was half past three before we got to bed.

Saturday, 22 July.

Training again. Peter Wells took six pounds off in training. We worked him hard but he was still overweight. I had a chat with Ted MacDougall about what I was going to do. Someone once said to me, 'It must be a hard job handling Ted MacDougall.' Ted has been around a lot but I treated him like a responsible thirty-two-year-old adult. When the pressure is on he can be very short-tempered and hasty but a lot of that stemmed from people telling him he couldn't play. He's a person who's had his back to the wall. I told him from the start I thought he could play and we liked each other. When we parted after training, he tapped me on the shoulder and said, 'All the best.' Several people around the club had said, 'I hope you don't go,' and you weren't sure that they meant it. But Ted's gesture meant something to me. He wanted me to stay, that was clear, but he knew what was involved and was leaving it to me to decide. I appreciated that. I had a young side and there weren't many players I could talk to in a meaningful way, only Bally, David Peach and Ted.

Back in my office I went through the *Sunday Mirror* article with Vince and he had to ring Brian Clough in the middle of it. I spoke to Cloughie and we talked about Leeds. He couldn't be expected to speak up for them but he didn't try to put me off. The year Forest came up from the Second Division Southampton played them five times and we were the better side, putting them out of the FA Cup. They went on to win the championship and we gained promotion the following season. I'd always got on well with Cloughie. We were from the same part of the world and our ideas weren't dissimilar. He generalized about how important happiness was in a manager's life. I agreed. I said I couldn't wish for a better lot of directors than I had at the Dell. As for handling players – which had caused him his problems in his forty-four days at Leeds – he said I'd proved I could handle the difficult ones in my earlier days at Southampton. Ted MacDougall's name came up and he said, 'Tell him I've got

Kenny Burns waiting for him.' When we play Forest I'll tell Ted about that conversation. It will motivate him. That's one fixture that's going to be a bit special.

I had another telephone call. It was from the former MP Jeffrey Archer, inviting me out to lunch; but I couldn't make it. He advised me to sit down and write out all the reasons for and against going to Leeds and award marks; 'phasing' the Americans call it. That's not a bad idea but I'm not a statistics man myself. I had an argument with Jimmy Hill during the World Cup when he said that one team had thirteen goal attempts. 'Who's worried about goal attempts?' I said. They could be shots from the halfway line. 'How many times have they scored?' After talking to the family and giving it plenty of thought, I shall know what I have to do. I told Mr Woodford that I had yet to decide. He said, 'Please don't go. There's still a lot to be done here.' Leeds have had a reputation but I feel Jimmy Armfield did much to change their image. The club was right for a challenge for the major honours. At Southampton I'd be establishing a club back in the First Division and it would be hard work. I still didn't know what to do.

Sunday, 23 July.

When I woke up I felt as though the whole nation was waiting on my verdict. The Sunday papers were full of it. But my piece in the *Sunday Mirror* hadn't come out too well. The best bits were left out. That wasn't the fault of the journalist. Something bigger had come in, the Alan Minter fight fatality. It was disappointing all the same.

I was in bed when the first calls from the national reporters came. They were trying to pump me. Outside it was raining which squashed any idea of wandering about in the garden.

I said to Anne, 'Let's jump in the car and drive over to see your parents at Bournemouth.' Anne's parents were staying in a boarding house there but by the time we arrived, we'd missed them. We went to the West Chine and I said, 'Let's have a walk.' My daughter wasn't too happy. 'Have we got to walk in this weather?' she asked. There were lots of people around, most of whom recognized me. We'd just come back from places like San Francisco, Las Vegas and before that on the club tour Barbados. I told my daughter, 'Don't forget. This is their holiday.' People were coming up to me all the time. One man in a tam-o'-shanter-type hat shouted, 'Are you going or aren't you? I'm from Leeds!'

It wasn't helping us to come to a decision. 'Let's get back in the car and go home,' I said. I knew what my decision had to be. 'I'm not going to go,' I said. It was all over in a few seconds. I jotted down on an envelope a few points I would make to the press the next day, like being flattered by the Leeds offer, the five happy years I'd had at Southampton, the big void which would be left if I went.

Monday, 24 July.

I rang Bob Roberts, the Leeds vice-chairman, before nine to tell him the news. He said, 'We are very disappointed to hear that.' I said, 'I appreciate that. I hope you get fixed up very quickly.' Next I called Mr Woodford at his home but he'd already left for his office. I managed to catch him before he caught a train to Coventry. He was delighted. When I got to the ground, there was a large turnout of television people, photographers and reporters. Fans were buying tickets and there were lots of workmen around. I had to pop inside briefly before coming out to face the cameras. I realized that none of them knew what I had decided. The interviewer asked me and I replied, 'The bad news is that I am staying.' There was a big cheer.

One of the things that pleased me most was the reported comment of Manny Cussins, the Leeds chairman. It was quite unsolicited! He said, 'Mr McMenemy is a good type. He is the kind of employee who responds to kindness with loyalty. There are still such people about.'

Now it was time to get down to work. I drove to the training ground to take the training but first I had to tell the players that I was staying. They didn't show much emotion. Footballers don't clap and cheer. They don't want anyone to think they're creeping or crawling but I could tell they were happy about it.

I took a bottle of champagne with me to open at lunchtime. David Peach didn't have much. 'What's up with you?' I said. I'm not having any now but I'll have a bottle myself to celebrate tonight,' he said. That's all you need. 'You can sort out my contract now,' he said. He was one of four or five players whose contracts hadn't been finalized. If you look after people, they respond. He's solid, Peachy.

The first week it had been physical stuff. Now we started the ball work. This is what the players enjoy. We're away from the public. It's our world and they love it. I took the first group, the midfield players and forwards, and it was one of the best sessions I've ever done.

Later in the day, I confirmed that Lew Chatterley, one of my ex-players, was to succeed Jim Clunie as my assistant. I'd known Lew since I was at Doncaster, when I borrowed him from Aston Villa. We were facing relegation and though only a loan player he put in more effort than the players who were on the staff. And when we went down, he was more upset than they were. I was green in those days. Some of the players weren't working and I should have had them out. I went on to Grimsby and Lew joined Northampton. I bought him from Northampton for £8,000 and he did a good job for me. I also took him down to Southampton. This happens frequently in football, a manager will take a player around with him if he trusts him and likes him. It didn't work out so well at the Dell. I kept him in the side too long and he didn't go with the public. He left to join Torquay, where he bought a boarding house. Lew is a honest, dependable type of person, not afraid to speak his mind. Jim Clunie was similar. You could set your clock by him. But Lew is sharper and a better mixer. He'll add to it because he's been in the First Division. He thought Jim was barmy to go to St Mirren. Time will tell about that.

I'd turned over in my mind the names of those people I would have taken to Leeds if I'd gone. One of them was Lew. Another was Ian Branfoot, a Geordie I knew at Sheffield Wednesday when I was on the coaching staff. By chance, he rang me up late in the evening to recommend two players. He was at Lincoln and wasn't too happy.

There was a little bit of aggravation over Lew's appointment. Before I left on holiday he joined Malcolm Musgrove, the former Torquay manager, at Chicago Stings but Malcolm got the sack and Lew was out. The previous season in England, Lew played for Barnstaple, the Western League side, and I had a call from someone at Barnstaple saying that I'd made an illegal approach to one of their players! I didn't want him as a player but as a coach so it didn't arise, but the cheek of it! If someone down there wanted to take me on, there was only one winner. Normally, when a big club signs someone from a small, non-League club, you make a donation, or promise to play a match but I wasn't going to do either after that.

Before going home, I had a haircut. Getting a haircut is difficult for me. Everyone knows you and wants to talk and, without being rude, there are times when you don't want to talk. When I was at Newcastle, the barber there used to sit me down in an upstairs washroom to cut my hair. He always apologized but I loved the privacy. If I could find someone to come to my house and cut my hair I would hire him. Television has done this. You're a household face and everyone wants to know you. I dread going shopping, not that I go often. It's autographs all the time and it's worse for the family. No-one wants to know them. Every time it happens, I feel a little more sorry for George Best. My nature is outgoing and I like talking to people but there's a limit. The only times I've ever had harsh words with Anne were at functions. People talk to me and ignore her. These days, I never go to anywhere there's dancing, and beauty contests are right out.

Wednesday, 26 July.

Meeting of the players about contracts, bonuses and behaviour. I told them the new higher figures and there weren't too many difficulties. You always get the odd old timer who says something – usually the same people every time – and Ted MacDougall got up and raised a few points. I thought they were quite petty and said so. It didn't do any harm. It pricked his bubble in front of the others.

I told them how important it was to look tidy and be aware of their responsibilities. It might sound old-womanish these days, but if they're going to places like Barbados, they've got to dress right and not appear scruffy.

I also spoke to them about taking pills. Since the Willie Johnston business in Argentina, the FA are tightening up and there could be spot checks. I told them that if they had a cold or flu or anything else, they've got to check with us first before they take anything. I gave them an official warning: if anyone was taking pills by themselves they'd be for it. Once or twice I've known a player take a strong type of aspirin to settle his stomach and footballers being what they are, very superstitious, if they had a good game they might be tempted to do it again. I also gave them a warning about using too much strapping. You get players with a slight strain strapping up their ankle and they'd keep it on for days, long after it was necessary, costing the club a fortune in strapping. Some players tend to mollycoddle themselves and are always in the treatment room. I told them I didn't want to see so many of them there.

The discussion on contracts went quite well but there were still three of four of the seniors who hadn't signed. They will.

Tony Sealy, a forward who played a couple of games in the first team the previous season, cracked a bone in training, the same bone he broke last season. It's not too bad. He'll be out five weeks, that's all.

After the meeting, I dashed home, changed, and drove to London with Anne for a television show, arriving back about a quarter to ten. It was a pleasant way to round off my birthday.

Saturday, 29 July.

First of the pre-season friendlies was against Sunderland at Roker Park. Friendlies are an extension of training. We'd done a week and a half's training and this was the first match. Ideally, you want to start off with easy opposition and work up. Sunderland weren't easy.

The North East is a depressed part of the football world, and it hurts. In the morning I answered questions at a local store. I could tell from the questioning how much the locals feel it. Football is part of their life. The questions were good ones, particularly from women and youngsters. They were concerned about violence, hooliganism and the state of the game. At night, I was on the local commercial radio and it was just the same. As I arrived at the studios there were two typical Geordies standing outside wearing cloth caps. One took his cap off, held it out towards me and said, 'Help the poor.' That's pure Geordie humour.

The match at Roker wasn't a classic. We won by the only goal. I was pleased with Ivan Golac, the Yugoslav defender who was on trial. He showed composure, was good going forward and distributed the ball well. I noticed one or two weaknesses in his play but they were 'coachable' ones, things you could coach out of him. When the players came in at the end of the game I had to be a bit careful. Lads like Manny Andruszewski and John Sharp, who might have played at full-back if Golac hadn't been there, were in the dressing room. I had to take account of their feelings too. I congratulated Golac and said quietly, 'You're one of us now.' He nearly cried. One thing you dread about friendlies is getting a player in-

jured. Steve Williams, our England Under-21 international, was injured and that upset me. It looked bad, either knee ligaments or
a cartilage, and I made arrangements to send him home.

Monday, 31 July.

I rang the club to see what the news was about Steve. Don Taylor,
the club physio, is a good medical man – he was an Army RSM – but
he seemed to be dithering. It happens all the time in the game: the
manager wants an instant decision, it's urgent for him; the medical
people want time to be sure of the right diagnosis.

Dr Lawrence, the club doctor, was on holiday and so they had
to get the lad round to the hospital. I asked Don if he'd done that.
He said he hadn't. There was a strike at the hospital switchboard
and he hadn't been able to get through. That made me mad. 'Get
the car out and take him round,' I said. 'I hadn't thought of that,'
said Don. People sometimes say to me, 'You'll be dead by the time
you're fifty,' and when things like this happen I tend to agree with
them. You have to think of everything yourself! There was another
doctor, a Dr Fitzgerald, who could see Steve. I hoped it wasn't a
cartilage. That would mean six weeks out and he's a very good
player.

Tuesday, 1 August.

Better news about Steve. The doctor doesn't think it is an injured
cartilage. He advised us to wait a couple of weeks until the swelling
goes down and he can restart training. So it is a fingers-crossed job.

The two Yugoslav trialists had been back in Yugoslavia. Golac
is due here at the weekend but Lorinc, the winger, is in Turkey
and we've lost him. But my contact has another winger lined up
for us, a Yugoslav who has been playing in West Germany.

Before going on to Glasgow to join up with the team I opened
the Tyneside Summer Exhibition. Princess Anne opened it the previous year. She couldn't have looked any nicer than my Anne with
her new hat and all. The Exhibition is a big thing in Newcastle and
despite the rain there was a big crowd in the streets to watch the
procession. We rode in the leading coach with the Mayor, a seventy-
eight-year-old grandmother, half the size of Bally, who insisted on
having her two grandchildren with her. She waved like the Queen

but I think the punters were waving at me, not her! I answered them through the window. It was a wonderful feeling.

The car which was laid on for me arrived at St Mirren's ground half an hour before the start of the second pre-season game. Jim Clunie was pleased with the result, a 1–0 win for his team, but it was a poor match. I was well received by everyone most likely because of my television appearances during the World Cup. They liked what I said about Scotland. I couldn't move without someone coming up to me.

Norwich, whom we were due to meet on the opening day of the English season, were well represented at the match. John Bond, their manager, was there with Ken Brown, his assistant, and Basil Hayward, the chief scout. It was a long way to come just to watch their opponents. I suspected there was more in it than that but Bondy didn't let on. He came back to the hotel with us for the buffet and stood by the bar chatting to Ted MacDougall and Phil Boyer, former players of his, for a couple of hours. He was making it up with Ted. They'd been great mates at Bournemouth and Norwich but in the past two years Bondy hadn't rung him once. Jock Stein was also there so that meant with Bondy we had three members of the BBC World Cup panel in the same room.

Wednesday, 2 August.

Jock came to lunch. He's going through a limbo period. For the first time in his life he has no job in football and doesn't know what to do with himself. He doesn't want to go to the club [Celtic] too much in case he's in the way. It is a difficult role. Bill Shankly had the same trouble at Liverpool.

After lunch, we went for a walk and decided to have a sauna. The staff were falling over themselves at having two such famous clients but unfortunately it was ladies day and even for us they couldn't stretch the rules that far.

That night we went to see a game, Stenhousemuir *v.* Dundee. There was hardly anyone there and one of the papers said the high-light was seeing Lawrie McMenemy and Jock Stein sitting in the stand. I had Jock on one side and Bob Shankly, Bill's brother, on the other. Bob was general manager of Stirling Albion. He and Jock were in a car crash together a year or two previously. Bob said, 'I've got a great job. I have to sit on my ass all day.' He said it with feeling and didn't smile. These two fellows still had a lot to offer but if they went back into management full time at their age they'd soon be exhausted.

Thursday, 3 August.

We got stuck into the training. We needed to. It had been such a shambles at St Mirren. I had a quiet word with some of the players. Mike Pickering, the centre-half, obviously had something on his mind and hadn't played well. He was worried about playing in the First Division when most of his career had been spent in the Third. I told him that it doesn't come overnight and worrying doesn't make it any easier.

I had to keep an eye on MacDougall. He gets bored easily and can say something out loud which can be off-putting to the younger players. I told him that without Steve, Bally and Golac we weren't a full side and it was no use getting upset about the way we were playing.

That night we went to see Motherwell *v.* West Bromwich Albion and Albion, our opponents on Saturday, won 8–1. Laurie Cunningham and Cyrille Regis tore them apart. They were so cocky. Willie Johnston, the winger in the World Cup drugs affair, had a fine game and was in good spirits because the crowd were clearly on his side. Afterwards I saw Paddy Mulligan sitting in the stand and spoke to him. Paddy is a good type, an experienced defender nearing the end of his career. Atkinson had bought Brendon Batson from Cambridge, the club he used to manage, and Paddy was out of the side. It's something all players have to face but it's not easy to bear.

The Motherwell officials were very hospitable. One of their committeemen wanted to announce my entry into the room. 'Hey,' I said, 'you can't do that. It wouldn't be right because you've already got Ron Atkinson [the Albion manager] in there and you didn't announce him.'

'Aye,' said the man, 'but you're a big man up here.' Anyway, I persuaded him to introduce Ron and managed to slip in while he was saying it. Some of the players were laughing.

I got into a lively discussion with Ron. He's like John Bond, an extrovert, bubbly type. He was very bouncy. 'That's two good results in our last two away games,' he said. 'Eight goals here tonight and six in the previous game in Canton.' He said he was recommending that Southampton should be the next side to go to China. Albion were the first English club to tour there the previous May. 'We could never follow anyone like you,' I said. I was winding him up gently and for a while it was cut and thrust. The people around us were enjoying it. 'All right,' said Ron. 'Put your semi-finals on the table.' Albion had been in the semi-final of the FA Cup the previous season. It was a kind of boasting, like one player saying to another, 'Show us your medals.'

Football-wise Ron's got a lot to offer but he was showing his in-experience. He had 'bitten' as we say. He must have forgotten Southampton had won the Cup. Everyone knew that he'd laid him-self open and I could have knocked him down with a feather if I'd wanted to. I said nothing.

Friday, 4 August.

After training we had a good talk for an hour. The players needed it and it went well. The match against Albion was our first competitive match of the season and we'd need to do much better than we'd been doing to hold them.

Things would get better. Bally would be bouncing back. Steve Williams wouldn't be out too long with any luck. Golac would be returning and if the other winger wasn't good enough, I'd be redoubling my efforts to sign a forward.

Saturday, 5 August.

The organizers of the Tennant-Caledonian Cup wanted a foreign side to make up the four competing clubs: Glasgow Rangers, on whose Ibrox pitch the matches were played; Hearts, promoted from the Scottish First Division; WBA and a club from abroad. But the organizers were let down and they invited us to make another visit, our third in three years.

It was a double-header as they say in the States. Saints v. WBA at two o'clock and Rangers v. Hearts at four. Cyrille Regis put Albion ahead with a shot from the edge of the box which he bent round the keeper and Phil Boyer equalized near the end with another fine shot, a chip over the keeper's head. Two bad mistakes and two goals. At First Division level, they punish you for your mistakes.

In the penalty competition afterwards we won because Regis, who had showed he could do the difficult thing by bending the ball, couldn't shoot straight. He was the first one to miss, striking a post.

Sunday, 6 August.

Nick Holmes was injured but I had to play him in the Final against Rangers. Golac was back, this time with his family, but the travelling had obviously tired him and he had to be replaced at half-time. It wasn't very satisfactory and Rangers walloped us 4–1 in front of a very partisan crowd. We had three goals disallowed. It was John Greig's first competitive match as Rangers' manager. His predecessor, Jock Wallace, had won the Treble the season before so he had a lot to do. John was roaring and shouting from the bench. If he could have heard a tape recording of his antics, I'm sure he'd never open his mouth again. But young managers who have just stopped playing are like that : they don't know what to do with their energy. Afterwards I skipped the celebrations in the lounges and went backstage to the kitchen where I usually have a cup of tea with Lizzie, the old tea woman. We had a nice little chat and halfway through, Greig came in. I like him as a man. 'You'll never last if you keep that noise up,' I said. He smiled.

Monday, 7 August.

Golac had a slight muscle strain. It was also a niggling worry that the Government had imposed a temporary ban on work permits. I felt Ivan should have been a special case. He'd played for us before Osvaldo Ardiles and Ricardo Villa, the Argentinian World Cup players, had played for Spurs and they had been given permits. The lad was heartbroken. He'd severed his links with home and now they were stopping him playing. We booked him and his family, his wife and children aged two and seven months, in the Wessex, a hotel near the Dell where we usually accommodate new players. But his wife had been unhappy about the stairs. She thought the children might fall down them so we moved the family to the Post House.

I was concerned about Wells. I thought he'd let in a goal or two in Scotland which he might have stopped had he been fitter so I asked Lew Chatterley to get him in for extra work.

Tuesday, 8 August.

We played a match at Gloucester against the local Southern League side. The proceeds were for the family of a local referee who had died. I set out by car but forgot it was a seven o'clock kick-off and arrived at half-time. We had a young side out and lost. The crowd shouted, 'That stuffed you,' and a few uncomplimentary things like that. You feel like saying something back but it doesn't pay. 'Yes, your lot did well,' I said. 'I hope you have a good season.' I arrived home about midnight, tired out as usual.

Wednesday, 9 August.

A friendly at Oxford, who are a good, mobile type of side, the kind of opposition you want at this stage. Just before we left the Dell there was a cloudburst and as Oxford had a League Cup tie with Cardiff on Saturday, they rang to try and cancel our game in case the pitch was spoilt. I rang Mick Brown, the Oxford manager, and pleaded with him to let us play. He said come on up and when we got there, the pitch had dried out pretty well and we won 1–0.

Thursday, 10 August.

I expected Alan Ball back from Philadelphia today but he didn't show. Late at night the phone rang and a little voice piped up: Bally, of course. He was more bubbly than usual because he'd been drinking champagne at Salisbury Races to celebrate a 7–1 winner. He had a score on it and had spent most of it on other people, no doubt, as he usually does.

He said he was glad to be back but added, 'I don't think we're going to be good enough. We ought to sign a couple of players. I don't want to struggle at the wrong end of the table you know.' He said he hadn't been too impressed by what he'd heard about the new signing, Golac. 'The hotel wasn't good enough for him was it?' he said. I knew he had been talking to a few hangers on at the races. One who owned a hotel near the ground thought he knew it all.

Bally was trying to get me going but was out of order. I had to weigh it up. He'd had a drink or two and his tongue was loose but that was no way to talk to his manager. 'It's nice to have you back but don't try to tell me what to do,' I said. 'You may be manager of Philadelphia Furies but I'm the manager here.' He said he might go to the races again tomorrow. I spoke to him sharply, more sharply than I'd ever spoken to him before except in the heat of the moment in the middle of matches. 'You get in here in the morning,' I said. 'We've got a game in Belgium at the weekend and you're playing in it.' I put the phone down. I needed Bally to be positive not negative. If he was going to start off like that, it wouldn't take much to get the club's other high flier, MacDougall, at it and before long the morale of the whole side would be affected. I needed the senior players to be confident not doubting. There were enough doubters around among the younger players.

Friday, 11 August.

The Ball incident had got me going. I was up earlier than usual and was in my kit at the ground by nine. I was aware that Lew would be put to the test by Bally. Lew was in my office when we heard a commotion outside among the kids who always hang around at football clubs in the school holidays. It was Ball driving in.

Bally came in and shook hands and said, 'I've come to apologize about last night. I was completely out of order.' I smiled with relief. That's him. If he's in the wrong, he'll admit it. 'That's great because I was going to hammer you,' I said. 'I've got a present for you.' His eyes lit up. He was like a kid at Christmas. I turned to the cabinet and he was straining to see what it was. I handed him a bottle of champagne I had there. He has all the cunning and artfulness that's needed in professional football but he loves the game and needs to be loved himself.

There was a lot of happy noise from the dressing room after Bally went in. Lew took the training session and at the end of it, Bally said to him, 'I enjoyed that.' Lew had passed his test.

Saturday, 12 August.

To Wembley for the Charity Shield between Nottingham Forest and Ipswich. But we went for another reason, the six-a-side youth tournament that preceded it. Saints had a team in. I was determined that it should be an unforgettable day for our youngsters. They travelled in the executive coach used by the first team and stayed at the same four-star hotel, the Royal Garden in Kensington.

My son Chris was a member of the team. I made him sub but gave instructions that he should be brought on at half-time. There is no experience in English football comparable to playing at Wembley and I wanted each apprentice to have it. Oldham, with three players with first-team experience, beat us and it was disappointing.

I bumped into Cliff Lloyd, secretary of the Professional Footballers Association, and talked to him about the PFA opposition to foreign players. I told him we had enough English players playing abroad, why did he fear having some overseas players here? He said the PFA thought a club might go to court over the restriction of two per club and, if successful, that would give clubs licence to play as many as five and six players in their first teams. I raised Golac's case. 'The lad's heartbroken,' I said. 'He's severed his connections with home and has his wife and two youngsters here. Surely he's a special case?' In a few days, Lloyd and Derek Dougan were due to present their case to the Department of Employment.

Forest annihilated Ipswich 5–0, showing that Cloughie was going to start off where he finished the previous season. What a manager!

I was due to fly out to Belgium to join the team but when I arrived at London Airport the flight was cancelled so I stayed at the Post House.

Sunday, 13 August.

Terminal 3, half-past-ten flight and I was in Brussels in just over half an hour. On the way over it struck me that managers are going to have to flit over to the Continent much more in the near future. It beats travelling to Hartlepool.

Monday, 14 August.

We beat FC Malines, a Belgian club, 2–1, and it was a good workout. The local club was managed by John Talbot, the ex-WBA centre-half, and playing together in defence were Keith Coleman, ex-West Ham, and Stan Brookes, a lad I once signed at Doncaster.

Foreign players have added something to Belgian football; why can't we be allowed to reap the same benefits?

Bally was impressed by Golac. That was typical of Bally. His attitude about the new player had changed completely. If he can play, he's a good bloke. Austin Hayes was back from Los Angeles Aztecs and played on the left. He looked sharp.

We had a look at another Yugoslav from FC Nuremburg. He was so keen he drove through the night to get there but he didn't look the part. I needed a winger urgently but it didn't look as though I would get one on the Continent.

Tuesday, 15 August.

Back at the club, I had the apprentices in and I brought them back to earth after Wembley. The previous Friday I noticed that the newly built boot room was filthy. The sink was caked with dirt and there was mud all over the floor.

John McGrath, the youth team coach, should really have sorted it out himself but hadn't managed to do so this time. In the past four years at the club standards had risen and progress had been too quick for some people.

I told the apprentices, 'You did well to get to Wembley but I'm not having this. I'll throw you out of the club if this happens again.' I took them in training myself after that. The first team were off.

In my office later I rang round a few managers about buying a winger. The younger players I had weren't ready yet. I needed someone with experience to lift the team. Williams would probably be fit to play at Norwich on Saturday. Holmes probably wouldn't be but I'd keep him in because you've always got to surprise John Bond with a change or two. It's a tactical battle with Bondy.

I called Ron Atkinson and he said he was in the market for players himself. He'd just had a bid of £300,000 turned down for Kevin Reeves of Norwich and another one of £340,000 for Aston Villa's John Deehan. These prices raised my eyebrows.

At Wembley, I'd met Bob Lord, chairman of Burnley, and I asked him about a winger. 'Which one, lad, Morley or Cochrane?' he asked. I said, 'Cochrane.' He said they might be interested if the price was right. I never like talking to chairmen. Transfer business should be done through the manager and I told him I would ring Harry Potts.

Potts was evasive when I rang him. 'We'd want a few bob,' he said. 'What about thirty bob?' I said. The figure of £100,000 was mentioned. 'No, more than £200,000,' he said. I couldn't pin him down. Harry is one of the old school.

Tommy Docherty was completely different when I spoke to him at Derby. There was no messing. He's like Cloughie when it comes to transfers. 'I've got two you can have,' he said. 'Gerry Ryan and Terry Curran, both at £60,000. We need the money.' Ryan was an Irishman, very skilful, and Curran, ex-Forest, I knew from Doncaster. Curran could be the one. I wanted someone who could get the ball over to MacDougall. I told Tommy I would speak to him later. Tommy was so keen on clinching the deal that he rang me from half-time in a pre-season friendly Derby were playing in Bangor!

I am fascinated by the wheeling and dealing of football transfers. It's exciting and the object is to keep it quiet until everything has been settled. But that's not so easy. Someone will drop a word and then the job becomes hard. I don't think my record in buying is too bad. Wells cost £8,000 from Forest and that's dirt cheap by First Division standards. David Peach at £50,000 becomes a bargain as time goes by. Chris Nicholl, only £90,000, was good business. Bally at £60,000, MacDougall at £50,000, Mike Pickering at £40,000 and Phil Boyer at £130,000 were all good investments. As I said to a director once, 'Tell me a bad one I've bought.' He couldn't think of one.

If I could get a useful winger for £60,000 I would still have £300,000 to splash on one really good player if I could get him.

That night, Jock Stein's testimonial dinner was taking place in Glasgow and I was one of the speakers along with Sean Connery, the former James Bond, and the Secretary of State for Scotland. Anne and I drove up to London Airport to catch the half-past-four flight.

The dinner was in the Civic Chambers in Glasgow, a magnificent room crowded by 550 people from all walks of life. It could have been held in Hampden Park and the place would still have been sold out. It was Anne's birthday and someone found out and announced it and the company rose to sing 'Happy Birthday'. She's a modest lass and it was very embarrassing for her.

The night before, Jock's testimonial match had raised £80,000 for him, tax-free, and in my speech I said: 'It's not often you get James Bond and Goldfinger on the same table!' Jock told me the latest news about the offer he had had from Leeds. Celtic were trying to keep him by offering a directorship and a job on the commercial side, helping to build up the pools. As he told me, 'I'm a football man, not a ticket salesman.' I told him he ought to take the Leeds job if the conditions were right.

I understood only too well the position he was in at Celtic, the club which he had led to so many triumphs over the years. After returning from the road accident which nearly killed him, he was happy to let Billy McNeill take over as manager. He was determined not to get in Billy's way but it wasn't easy. I faced the same problem when I first took over at Southampton and Ted Bates, my predecessor, was still around. When things didn't go so well, and they went badly in my earlier days, people were bound to speak to Ted and say 'what would you have done?' Ted weathered it and I weathered it but only because the directors backed me and I had six years experience. I'm now probably Ted's best friend but I think he will agree that in those days he was sometimes a bit of a hindrance.

Jock's energy and enthusiasm were back and he didn't want to hang around Parkhead in a Ted Bates role. But nor was he keen to leave Scotland. His roots were there and his wife Jean didn't want to live anywhere else. The ideal job for him would have been general manager of the Scottish team with Ally MacLeod as team manager. Jock would have taken care of all those off-field problems which wrecked Scotland's attempt to win the World Cup in Argentina. Jock would soon have sorted it out.

Wednesday, 16 August.

On the way back I arranged to meet Terry Curran and his wife at the Post House, near London Airport. The business end of the deal had been concluded with Tommy Docherty and when we had finished, Tom said, 'See you in the tunnel at Wembley at the end of the season.' He was referring to our appearance in the 1976 FA Cup Final.

The Currans seemed a nice couple. They both come from a small village in Yorkshire near Fitzwilliam, home of the cricketer Geoff Boycott. I wondered how they would settle down in Hampshire. Terry said he would enjoy the change, but that's always the way in football. All new players say it's great when they come to a new club. You aren't kidded by that.

Thursday, 17 August.

Board meeting at the club. By tradition the players assemble in the boardroom and have a drink with the directors and staff. The acting chairman apologized for the fact that only he and Mr Bowyer were there, along with Ted Bates, who had just been made a director. 'Sir George Meyrick is shooting grouse,' he said. 'Mr Corbett is looking after his sheep and probably shooting grouse too and Guy Askham is at lunch.' I couldn't resist interrupting, ' . . . eating grouse!' I thanked the chairman for his best wishes and reminded them of the importance of keeping up standards and the need for the players to compete.

Bally replied on behalf of the players, thanking the club for all they had done for him and the rest of the players. He said they would work hard to get good results. It was a pleasant little occasion. Later, Mr Woodford told me, 'You're the biggest problem here. You're working too hard.' He was right. There wasn't a single minute in the day when I could relax. People were ringing me at home from seven in the morning to twelve at night. I always said I had the capacity to handle it but in recent months it had snowballed and now it was affecting my family and they needed a break as much as I did.

They weren't the kind of family who would answer the phone and say, 'He's not here.' The press were on to me from all over the country, people wanted things opened and speeches made and besides the showbiz side of it I had to run a football club. Perhaps I should have been delegating more but I didn't see anyone at the club strong enough to take over many of my responsibilities. Some of the offers were incredible, like a fee of £500 to open a supermarket. I couldn't take it because it clashed with something else. Another offer was £150 a week to write a newspaper column. That clashed as well and I couldn't do that, either.

I was considering changing my telephone number which was ex-directory. Cloughie gave no-one his number and it didn't seem to harm him in the eyes of the media. I realized it was against my instincts because I have always talked to the press and everyone who wanted me, but, since the World Cup and my appearances on television, it was just too much.

I couldn't sit down and eat a meal in peace. The only time we could have a quiet moment was when we went out for a drive in the car. The club had been good to me over the car. They provided me with a couple of Jags and when we were negotiating my new contract in the close season, they said I could have a new car if I wanted one though the second Jag was less than two years old. I had done 31,000 miles in it. If I waited until later in the season we might be having a bad time and it might be harder to get a new one. I fancied a Mercedes. Managers spend so much of their time driving up and down motorways at high speeds that they've got to have a decent vehicle. Jock Stein and Jack Taylor both had crashes in a Mercedes and survived. They said they felt much safer in a Mercedes.

Southampton's financial director gave me the go-ahead to get one and I contacted a supplier in Woking. He had one lined up for the the husband of Florence Desmond, the actress, but he didn't want it so I could have it. It was a 450 SEL and, when I brought it into the club, Bally and MacDougall were very impressed. 'Now you're in the First Division, that's what you deserve,' said Bally.

As Mr Woodford left after the board meeting, he said, 'See you at the stewards' meeting tonight.' Every year we get two hundred or so stewards and stile men in with the local police for a meeting. 'You're a bright bugger,' I thought. 'Just now you were talking about me working too hard and now you want me to come back tonight.' But I knew I had to go; as I told the stewards, most of whom don't get much more than £2 a man for their Saturday stint, 'You're important people.'

Friday, 18 August.

There was an extra buzz about the place when the players came in for the last day's training before the start of the season. The arrival of Curran was greeted with enthusiasm. Ted MacDougall was particularly pleased for he'd been pressing me about getting a winger. It was as if Christmas Day had come four months early for him.

Malcolm Waldron, one of the back four players, had a twisted ankle but said he was fit to play at Norwich. That pleased me. Normally an ankle takes about a week but the lad obviously wanted to play. Too many footballers will use an injury as an excuse not to play, especially when they're not doing so well. He's never going to be a world-class player but his attitude is right, he's quick and he's getting better all the time. His nature isn't aggressive and I'd been on at him about getting more competitive, a bit more ruthless and, he was coming round to it. All good defenders need to be a bit ruthless. It's part of a defender's game. We need it in our side because the three midfield players aren't markers and there is more responsibility on the back four.

Before leaving the ground, I called Ken Friar, the Arsenal secretary, and arranged four stand seats for Jock and his party for the Arsenal *v.* Leeds game. Jock wanted to have a look at Leeds but he didn't want the press and everyone else to know.

In the train to Norwich the players were more noisy than usual. MacDougall, who was once a Norwich player, said, 'The whole city will be turning out to meet me.' He hadn't been too popular there and I warned him about over-reacting if the crowd baited him, as they were sure to do.

2. The kick off

Norwich finished the 1977–8 season in thirteenth position in the First Division, only three places below their highest-ever position two years earlier. Without the financial resources of the big clubs, they are unlikely ever to win the championship. Their manager, John Bond, has made them into a respectable, middle-order side by good husbandry and sound coaching. Bond is a Ron Greenwood disciple: an exponent of attacking methods. That makes him unusual among English managers because those with weaker sides tend to try and survive by safety-first tactics, packing the defence and relying on breaks. Bond could never afford to buy a £500,000 player. His range is much lower. For the new season, he bought the former Spurs and England centre-forward Martin Chivers from the Swiss club Servette for £25,000 and the defender Phil Hoadley from Orient for £125,000. He had just turned down an offer of £300,000 for his centre-forward Kevin Reeves, who had cost only £50,000 from Bournemouth.

Despite their excellent home record at Carrow Road – only three defeats the previous season – any visiting side with pretensions to a middling season would expect to draw there. Some of the newspapers billed the Southampton v. Norwich match as a battle of wits between Bond and Lawrie McMenemy, two of the most publicized figures in the game. Neither man announced his line-up in advance, both saying that they were selecting from thirteen players nearer the kick-off time.

It was a very hot, very sunny day as it so often is on the opening day of the football season.

Saturday, 19 August

At lunch Bally asked the trainer where the salt tablets were. Instead of fobbing him off with a wisecrack like, 'I've left a ton each in your bedroom,' Don Taylor said, 'they're at the ground.' 'That's no bloody good,' said Bally. 'It's here we want them.' One of the other players said, 'Put plenty of salt on your steak.' Don might have lost a little face to Bally, the old pro, in front of the other players but at least he'd remembered to bring salt tablets with him which was to his credit.

I didn't see Bondy before the start. We arrived at two o'clock and everything was changed round at the ground. The secretary's office was stuck away in the roof somewhere and I had to go on a route march to get some tickets. You never see much of Bondy before a game. Most managers meet in the referees' room at half past two to exchange team sheets, and then have five minutes' chat and a cup of tea. But Kenny Brown, Bond's assistant, takes the Norwich sheet in.

When he was at Bournemouth, I used to hear from John a lot but he hadn't called so much since he went to Carrow Road. It was me who advised him to take the Norwich job. He has a tremendous amount to offer the game and we have a lot to offer each other. Maybe he became less eager to ring because he was a bit jealous. I'd won things and he hadn't and I'd had more publicity. His was a bit forced. We all get pulled around by ego trips in this game.

He would be taking this match more seriously than one against, say, Manchester United because of MacDougall and Boyer, two players he had with him at Bournemouth and later at Norwich.

I met the referee before the start, John Homewood. He's a chirpy Cockney, a good lad. 'Dissent and ten yards at free kicks are the big things this season,' he said. The League had probably issued some more instructions. We wished each other good luck.

I spent a little time geeing up the lads in the dressing room, not too long. Lew Chatterley looked nervous. 'Don't forget your sponge,' I said and winked. Anne and the two younger children were in the directors' box but on match days I'll only nod to them, I won't say anything.

We didn't play well. We gave them too much room and lost 3–1. The score flattered them. MacDougall missed a couple of chances which he would normally have put away. One of them only needed a touch. As soon as he came into the dressing room he apologized, which is unlike him. I told him not to let it affect his confidence; good players still need to be told they're good. The keeper cost us a goal. He came and stopped for a cross. Jimmy Neighbour, the Norwich winger, turned Peachy inside out and Peachy was so frustrated that he was booked for a foul and after that lost his confidence completely. In defence, Mike Pickering looked out of his depth. The midfield we hadn't challenged as we should have done. Graham Baker and Bally aren't markers. Normally I don't go steaming in after matches and sound off but I did this time. 'Before you start making excuses, I think you let yourselves down badly,' I told them. 'You gave them far too much room.'

I didn't have much to say to the press lads, just that it was disappointing and we had a lot of hard work to do. As we were about to leave, Bondy asked me if Bally could play in Martin Peters' testimonial later in the season and I agreed provided it didn't clash with any of our games. He wished me all the best and we were off to catch the 5.42 train. I was more disappointed at losing to him than if it had been almost any other team in the First Division. In the coach Bally said, 'It could have been worse. We could have lost at home.'

For weeks, I'd been looking forward to the start of the season. Now I wished it hadn't started.

Monday, 21 August.

Sunday is the day managers are supposed to unwind but I hadn't been able to unwind yesterday after the team had been beaten. I had another problem: Golac. The previous Thursday I discussed with Mr Woodford how we could get him playing in the side. It was very frustrating having a good player on your staff and not being able to play him. I said to the chairman we should make him a non-contract player, the equivalent of the old amateur and we might not need a work permit.

Mr Woodford said, 'Let's do it openly.' I agreed with him. We contacted George Readle, the secretary at the Football League, and he said a footballer needed a work permit even if he was playing on a public park. I said, 'Where's the rule that says that?' Readle said the League would need to see Golac's immigration certificate.

In fact, he didn't have a certificate, only a stamp in his passport saying he could stay six months. We made arrangements to have it photocopied and taken to the League's subsidiary office in Cheapside, London.

The next hurdle was clearance from the Yugoslav FA and that soon came. But the Football League still weren't giving Golac permission to play in the home game against Bolton which was now a little over twenty-four hours away. To put added pressure on, Mr Woodford spoke to Bob Mitchell, MP for Itchen, and he said he would talk to the people at the Home Office. His reading of it was the same as ours, that if Golac was classed as a student – he was doing agricultural studies in Belgrade – he wouldn't need a work permit. He was a special case.

I had kept all this quiet but when a *Daily Mirror* reporter, Graham Baker, rang and asked for the team, I included Golac in the squad and he said, 'Golac? Can he play?' I said he was now on a non-contract basis. Some time later, the club had a call from the League saying that Golac couldn't play until he was cleared. It was obvious what had happened. Baker must have rung the League. When he came on again, I was furious. 'Have you rung the League about this?' I asked. He explained that his sports editor had told him to get a reaction from the League. 'You can get lost,' I said, slamming down the phone.

Tuesday, 22 August.

Mr Woodford rang Mr Hardaker, secretary of the Football League, and Hardaker said a decision would be given by seven o'clock. The kick-off was half-past seven. The Home Office had said they had no objection to Golac making his debut. Now only the permission of the League was needed. His papers had been cleared.

Poor Golac looked in a state of shock when he arrived for the team meeting. The call eventually came at ten past six. Readle, who made it, gave our secretary, Brian Truscott, a rollicking because he said he'd been trying for half an hour to get through and it was time he could be spending on his dinner. Readle said Golac could play against Bolton and he would call again tomorrow. Golac was overjoyed. He hugged me when I told him he was in.

Bolton, who came up with us from the Second Division last season, are old friends. Ian Greaves, their manager, wasn't with them.

He was away scouting and his assistant, George Mulhall, was in charge of the team.

As I walked along the line to the dug-out the crowd gave me a rousing reception and I blew them a kiss. I found it rather embarrassing. In my first year these same people, or some of them, jeered me. We should have won but I was satisfied with a 2–2 draw, our first point. We hustled much more than we did at Norwich and defended better.

Graham Baker, the nineteen-year-old footballer not the journalist, headed the first goal and we ought to have gone in one-up but we gave away a bad goal from Frank Worthington's free kick. If Peter Wells had stayed where he was, the ball would have hit him on the chest. In the dressing room, Bally went full pelt into Peachy. Peachy isn't a quiet lad but he's not a Ball or a MacDougall and he should stand up for himself more. Bally said Peachy should have got on the other side of the wall instead of being the spare man. He said what Peachy did was completely useless. I calmed them down and told the players that if they kept the pressure on, they'd win.

The free kick was given against Golac when one of their players fell over his outstretched leg. I told him he had to watch out for that in England. Opponents see a leg and they fall over it to get the free kick.

MacDougall put us ahead but we gave away another free kick which Worthington converted, this time from a bender. Bally was the last man out as a cross came over his head towards Neil Whatmore who was standing behind him; he jumped up and handled to prevent the ball reaching Whatmore. Bally sounded off at the other defenders, but, as I said afterwards, 'if you'd moved up a yard with the others, Whatmore would have been offside.'

This was his second game since he came back from America and he knew as well as I did that he hadn't played like the old Bally. He'd been playing in too much mediocre football in America. I debated whether to give him a couple of days off. He's never had a weight problem so he didn't need extra training. I told him, 'It will come, just persevere.'

Golac was a trifle down. 'Two free kicks, two goals, very bad,' he said. 'I can do better. His English was good enough to get by on. I let a couple of local reporters interview him and he spoke well, saying all the right things.

Wednesday, 23 August.

I had made up my mind to take a day off and take the family up to London to visit Harrods and maybe a show. But Alison was unwell and we abandoned the idea. I said to Anne, 'Why don't we go to the Spurs *v.* Aston Villa and see the home debut of the Argentinians, Osvaldo Ardiles and Ricardo Villa, as a busman's holiday?' She likes football so off we went with a carload of six, including Fred Scott and Lew Chatterley. Miraculously Tottenham were able to find us the tickets.

Anne likes to come to matches and, where I can do it, I like to involve her. Jimmy Bloomfield had his wife there and Alan Dicks was with his fiancée. The wives should form a union for they suffer as much as the menfolk. We are not the only people who are a bag of nerves on a Saturday afternoon.

It was a great night, full of atmosphere. Afterwards a reporter interviewed Sean, my son, and asked him what he thought of the two Argentinians. Sean gave a false name. We were the last car into the jam-packed car park at twenty-past seven so we had to get out early and shift it. I was manœuvring it when Ted Croker, the secretary of the FA came along. 'What's this, a German car?' he said. 'Now I've got a German car I've got no chance of the England job,' I said. I've always found him a very nice man.

Friday, 25 August.

Staff meeting at the ground. We were short on the coaching side and I had been tossing a few ideas around. One of them was to bring in someone from abroad to introduce a few ideas. The name that had been mentioned to me by a contact was that of Miljan Miljanic, the Yugoslav coach who had been with a number of leading Continental clubs. Miljanic was half interested but my contact said he was liable to make capital out of my approach and I didn't want that. The more I thought about it, the more I veered against it. It was my club, it had my stamp on it, and that could be upset if we had a big name coach coming in.

Instead, I decided to recruit another coach for the youngsters and move John McGrath up. The person I had in mind was Ian Branfoot and I rang Lincoln manager, Willie Bell, to ask permission to speak to him. Willie said he could release him, but only after a couple of weeks in which to find someone else.

I broke the news to John McGrath and George Horsfall. We would now have four trainers, which was more than many of the big clubs. That would enable us to divide the squad into four groups in the afternoons and the players could join whatever group they wanted. Each group would be doing something different. It was a good idea and the players liked it.

Saturday, 26 August.

Lunch with the players at the hotel before the home game against Middlesbrough. Some managers eat with the directors but I think my place is with the players. I have what they have. In the Fourth Division the players don't have a choice. They eat what the manager orders for them but at this level they can have what they like. Some have cornflakes, a poached egg maybe and others have a steak. I had a fillet steak, toast and tea.

Usually we watch the Saturday lunchtime football programme on television but now I have a room of my own with a set at the Dell I left to watch it there. We didn't have enough time, however, and I missed it.

I had a cup of tea and a chat with John Neal, the Middlesbrough manager. He's a nice fellow. We talked about Ardiles and Villa at Spurs and about his efforts to sign Rene Houseman, another Argentinian World Cup player. I said if I were him I'd back-pedal a bit on that one. There was a lot of money involved and I had heard of some disruptions behind the scenes at Spurs.

Middlesbrough are always a hard side to beat. We made a disastrous start, our inexperience showing at the back. They scored first and it was another terrible goal to give away. The fellow headed if from the far side of the box, almost on the by-line, and Peter Wells started to come, stopped and saw it go over his head into the net. The players' heads were down at half-time and I had to do a massive encouraging job.

Bill Ashcroft, the Middlesbrough centre-forward, was injured and should have come off early in the second half but he stayed on which I thought was unprofessional. We equalized through Chris Nicholl from a free kick after Peachy had been obstructed. Ashcroft was marking Chris and couldn't jump. There was a sense of relief right round the ground. Bally won it for us with a world-class chip-shot twelve minutes from time. He was being forced away from

goal when he turned and chipped over three of them. He was so
excited he nearly jumped over the stand. Afterwards I thought I'd
have my little go at him because he never scores as many as he
should. 'Was that one of your four for the season then?' I said.

Curran, whom I'd had in my office earlier in the week to reassure
him after being substituted against Bolton, had a great game on the
wing, constantly beating the full-back. Ted MacDougall always has
to have a moan and he was unhappy about the type of crosses he
had received. He was right in a way. Terry could have varied it
more and he needn't have beaten so many players. He could have
got it over quicker. In the end we had won well, hitting the wood-
work twice. It was a relief to get our first win. Three out of the
next four were away and that wouldn't be easy.

I made a note I would have to see Wells early in the week. He
asked for a meeting. I know what he's going to say, that the extra
work he's had to do has affected his performance and he's lost his
confidence.

Afterwards I sat and talked with David Coleman. He loves going
to games when he's not working. Lew Chatterley came home with
me and we watched 'Match of the Day' after supper. I asked him
to stay the night but he wanted to get back to his digs.

I'd changed our telephone number and now only people close
to me knew the right number. We jumped a mile in the air every
time the phone rang. I wondered whether I'd done the right thing.
At the ground I had been speaking to Ronald Allison, the BBC man
who became press officer to the Royal Family. He said his way of
getting round the problem of being continually rung up was to
switch over to an answer-phone when he came home at night and
ring back the people he wanted to speak to later in the evening.
Perhaps that would have been a better idea than going ex-directory
but it was too late now.

Monday, 28 August.

Bank Holiday but there's no holiday for footballers. We were in
for training as usual. When we finished, Bally said something which
pleased me: 'We were dead at half-time on Saturday,' he said. 'The
only way we were going to do it in the second half was out of affec-
tion for you.' I'd had to work hard at half-time, just as I had had
to in the Bolton game. I told him I was earning my corn at the

moment. The players lacked confidence but, now we were getting some results, it would return and they would be able to rely less on me.

We discussed with the aid of the tactics board how we would play at Birmingham in the League Cup the next night. I said I would be playing with a sweeper in some away matches as we had the previous season but for Birmingham I was going to change it and bring in another defender, Manny Andruszewski, for Graham Baker in midfield and use Manny exclusively to stop Trevor Francis. Francis was one of the top three forward players in the country and if you stopped him, I was sure our other ten players could match theirs. I told Manny to get between Francis and goal and prevent him making runs. It was a key job but I said I was certain he could do it right.

It didn't mean we weren't going to be positive. 'I want the front three to stay up,' I said. And, looking at Terry Curran, I said, 'I don't want you saying I'm like all the other managers who tell you to get back behind the ball. I want you up there getting in crosses. Crosses are what it's all about. That's why we've bought you.'

Tuesday, 29 August.

The team coach left early for lunch at Solihull before the Birmingham game but I stayed behind. The players go to bed after lunch and I always find that a boring time because I don't go to bed. It's a time for hanging about and I don't like hanging about. I'd rather go for a good walk. Some players sleep, others just rest and take it easy. I don't allow card schools, nor do I allow three or four players in one room. They have to keep to the arrangement of two to a room. Golac shares with Chris Nicholl and gets on well with him but I'm wondering what to do when Nick Holmes returns because Nick always shares with Nicholl and they play chess together. Chris eats like a horse and Golac isn't far behind him. Golac likes English food but prefers it to be more tasty. He smothers his plate with tomato sauce and French and English mustard.

Ted Bates and I drove up in the Mercedes to join the players for tea. I work my frustrations off on Ted and shout and bawl at him. He laughs it all off. We're good for each other: I bounce off him.

The game went better than I'd dared to hope. We won 5–2, an incredible result away from home. Manny did a tremendous job but Francis is such a great competitor that he kept going while all the others were dropping their heads and scored Birmingham's second goal. The reaction of the crowd was frighteningly hostile. I congratulated my players. 'You've shown you can do it,' I said. But always you remember the next one. 'Don't get cocky. You've got a tougher one up here on Saturday at Villa. You'll have 40,000 screaming at you.'

Golac made the first and fifth goals and I patted him on the back. He said he was having difficulty in sleeping because he was worried about where he was going to live. The professional in him was coming out. He wasn't saying it directly but it was a hint. He wanted to live in a furnished house and saw that it was a good time to make his point. I thought it was a nice time to tell me: while the sweat was still on his brow. I intended to stay up and watch Aston Villa the next night but changed my mind. 'We're driving straight back,' I said to Ted. 'I want to get round to the estate agents and find him a place.' We arrived back at one o'clock in the morning, a round trip of 280 miles. After a game no-one sleeps well, particularly managers who are dog tired.

Wednesday, 30 August.

Thanks to Norman Benson, an estate agent and a good supporter, we found a house for Golac, his wife Bratislava, a former law student, and children Andrijana and Ivana. It had four bedrooms and was well situated in Chandlers Ford, near my home. 'Don't get the wrong idea about living in England,' I told him. 'You've got a mansion there.' In Belgrade he has a flat.

Among the letters was a report on Aston Villa from Bert Johnson, a former coach who is not doing much these days. We pay him expenses only. It's something for him to do. His report confirmed what I knew from watching Villa at Tottenham.

After a day clearing up things in the office, I then did something silly: I said to Lew, 'Let's see the Oxford *v.* Plymouth match.' It wasn't necessary to see it but it's a kind of compulsion. If there is a game, managers will rush off and see it even though they'd be doing themselves more good having a night at home with the wife and kids.

We dropped in at home for a quick snack – Anne is expert at rustling up meals at short notice for any number of people I might have with me – and we arrived at Oxford just as they kicked off. It was good to see Malcolm Allison, who had taken over as Plymouth manager earlier in the year. There were two good-looking girls in the directors' box, as usual when Malcolm is around. One of them said hello and I thought she looked very personable. It was the girl he married a few days later.

Whichever club he is with, Malcolm always likes to indulge his fantasies. In this game, he had Plymouth playing a new system of two arcs of five players, with no centre-forward. To try anything like that it's preferable to have good players but Malcolm was experimenting with Third Division players. It showed his confidence. He was saying, 'I'm going to try it this way,' and it was a brave statement to make. You have to give him credit. He thinks about the game and he's not worried about getting the sack. The system means you have extra width all over the field but if a passing movement breaks down, you could be in trouble through lack of depth. Plymouth led 1–0 but were held to a draw. Bob Daniel, the Plymouth chairman, is one of the modern club chairmen and Malcolm knew he had a good man to work for.

Bob told me had been at a meeting of the Football League Management Committee and my name had come up. They weren't too happy about the Golac business and, now they'd discovered some irregularity over the signing of a schoolboy by Southampton, they were prepared to hammer us. It was Ted Bates's mistake, a small administrative error but as manager, I would have to take the blame.

Saturday, 2 September.

Because Villa play with two men wide and two centre-forwards, I decided on another tactical change which brought Manny Andruszewski back to take Brian Little and made Malcolm Waldron play sweeper. It meant we had five at the back but we still kept three forwards up. Alan Ball and Steve Williams would be the only midfield players but as Villa only have two in midfield at home, Mortimer and Cowans, it didn't matter. I tried to explain all this to the reporters afterwards but it didn't seem to get through. Most of them still called us both defensive and too aggressive. It was unfair. We worked hard for our point in a 1–1 draw and though we were a shade lucky, it was a good character performance.

Before the game I had a chat with Ron Saunders, the Villa manager who had just been given a new contract after half the board resigned. He told me about the background manœuvres and it made me realize the difference of managing a club like Southampton and managing a big city club like Villa where there were so many political things happening. Although Ron is a bad loser, he always shakes hands.

On the team sheet which we exchanged before the start, I noticed that the names of Andy Gray and Leighton Phillips, both of whom had been injured, were written down in a different coloured ink. Whether that meant they were late choices, or whether it was just a bluff, I don't know. At the press conference, I thought Ron made too much of his injuries. I was first in, and he raised a laugh when he walked in and said, 'I don't agree with anything you've said.' I stood and listened to him giving his version and suddenly all the lights went out and we were in pitch darkness. There are no windows in the Villa press box. 'Well Ron,' I said, 'what you've said couldn't be true because we've all been struck blind.'

This time I hadn't had to lift the players so much at half-time. They were doing it themselves, inspired by the atmosphere and the challenge of playing a good team. But it helps if, in the middle of what I am saying to the players to encourage them, I can throw in a tactical point to show them I have spotted something which they haven't seen. I said they were letting Cowans put in far too many dangerous corners. I pointed at Steve Williams: 'You should be standing on the by-line to make it more difficult for him to drive them in at the near post. If you're ten yards away, he'll have to lift them.' I couldn't resist saying to Bally; 'I thought you would have done something about that.' Bally said, 'You're right but I'm not the only one who can talk, am I?' I picked on Bally because I looked on him as an extension of me on the field. Bally was taking the near post. You don't really need men on the posts but they give the goalkeeper confidence to go out for the ball. You don't want defenders doing the job. You want your defenders to take opponents. Bally isn't a defender: he could be spared. Chris Nicholl should talk more – he is experienced enough.

On the way back, we stopped at a Swindon hotel for a meal and found ourselves in the middle of a wedding reception. The bride wanted to kiss me. We were all very happy. There is nothing like getting a result when you are not expected to.

Sunday, 3 September.

Ian Branfoot and his family came down to look at some houses I had arranged for them to visit. The price was the snag. Houses in Hampshire were much more expensive than where they came from in Lincoln. His wife was sceptical about moving south but she was soon sold on the idea. We had lunch at The Angry Trout in Stockbridge. The sun was shining and Hampshire was at its best. Jim McCalliog, one of my former players, was back from America and was taking Ian's job at Lincoln.

The Chatterleys were also house hunting. They had sold their boarding house in Torquay and I had advised his wife not to be frightened about going in for a bigger mortgage. Lew was in the big time now.

Tuesday, 5 September.

During Saturday's reserve game, Austin Hayes swung on the crossbar and the whole lot came down, forcing the game to be abandoned. I detailed Fred Scott to make the necessary repairs. The box which held the post in the ground had cracked. Just imagine what would have happened if that incident had occurred two minutes from the end of a First Division game against Manchester United!

At training we were without Bally and MacDougall, whom I had told to have a couple of days off because they'd worked so hard and deserved a break. Peachy soon exploited the situation. He said he couldn't do a certain exercise because his two partners weren't there to help him. He still did it but he had had his little dig. 'All right, you can have tomorrow off, if you feel as old as Bally.' I had made my point in a jocular way.

But there was an incident later which needed a more aggressive response from me. Trevor Hebberd, one of the reserve forwards who had played in the first team, started dribbling on the ball in a two-touch practice and I told him off. He muttered something and as he walked away made another comment. 'Here, what did you say?' I said. He said he hadn't said anything. 'I've had enough of you,' I said. 'Get off to the dressing rooms.' I'd noticed previously that he had been developing an unprofessional attitude. After lunch there was a knock at my door and Hebberd, looking very sheepish, poked his head in and asked if he could apologize for his behaviour. I had him in and gave him a fatherly chat. It wasn't the time to crush him. He'd done the right thing in making the first move to sort it out. But I was firm. 'If you don't knuckle down I'll loan you out and that goes for anyone else in the squad,' I said.

3. Colin Todd

With five points from the first four matches, Southampton had made a reasonable start to the season but were arguably conceding too many goals. In the Second Division the previous season their defensive record was outstanding, only thirty-nine goals given away in forty-two matches, less than one a game. Now it was one and a half.

Mike Pickering, the tall, Huddersfield-born defender who missed only one of the Second Division matches, the final one against Tottenham, was out of the side and unhappy about it. Malcolm Waldron, a local player from Emsworth, was doing his best but lacked experience. If the team needed strengthening it was at the back where a First Division-class defender was needed to partner the reliable Chris Nicholl.

McMenemy heard that Colin Todd, the twenty-nine-year-old Derby County defender, was available at £300,000 and decided he wanted him. If the deal went through it would have been a club record, surpassing the £265,000 Southampton paid Chelsea for Peter Osgood in March 1974.

Thursday, 7 September.

Board meeting at the ground. Mr Woodford, previously acting chairman, was confirmed as the new chairman. It's important for the manager to know who he has to deal with. That little bit of business was barely over before I gave Mr Woodford his first big headache. I told him I wanted to spend a lot of money on a player.

I explained that I read in the newspapers that Tommy Docherty was saying Charlie George would not be leaving Derby and

Docherty was looking for a striker to play alongside him. Between the lines, Tommy was saying he needed some money in. I knew he didn't have any. I thought about which players he might have available. Every player has his price. I told the directors I had rung Docherty on the off-chance and that he had said Everton had been in a couple of weeks ago for Colin Todd but their offer of £250,000 wasn't high enough. Derby wanted £300,000 clear and I needed a sweeper urgently.

Todd was twenty-nine and still a very good player. He would do us a lot of good. Mr Woodford thought £300,000 for a player of nearly thirty was a lot of money and I could see I would have to sell the idea.

I agreed it was an expensive deal but it was like selling your house! You were amazed at what a high price you could get but you needed the money for the next one. I then reminded the directors that it was down to me that we had got so much money for Mike Channon the previous year: they had been prepared to settle for a lower figure from Manchester City but I insisted on £300,000 and by holding out we had got it. A final payment on that deal was still due. It was good business because Channon was a forward aged thirty and forwards don't usually last as long as back-four players like Toddy. I also said that before the season started, we agreed that a fair sum should be available to strengthen the side. So far I had bought two players, Golac and Curran, for just £160,000 and both had proved good buys. Golac hadn't cost us anything yet but it wouldn't be much whatever happened. There was a lot more money in the kitty and I wanted to spend it on at least one very good, proven player who could do the job I wanted from him.

I knew some of the older directors hadn't been too keen on my previous big deal, the £265,000 we paid for Osgood, but I always maintained that we wouldn't have won the FA Cup without Ossie's experience. In my book, he hadn't been a bad signing. Some clubs go into the red to buy new players but Southampton never did. By spreading payments over a period to coincide with the time of the year when the proceeds from the sale of season tickets were coming in we usually stayed in the black. It was a question of having a regular cash flow and being able to meet payments. I knew we could afford Todd's fee. We had forty professionals in the staff which was too many and we could raise some cash by selling some of them. Mike Pickering had been in to see me, saying he would like a transfer. I told him the season had only just begun and it was early to be talking of going but if Toddy came we could let him go for about £60–70,000. Throw in a couple more reserves, and we could get £100,000 back and the amount we would be saving on their wages would cover Toddy's wages.

The board finally agreed I could negotiate with Derby over Todd but wanted the spread to be over as long a period as possible. I rang Docherty and he said he would give me permission to talk to Todd. On the money question he thought Derby would want it quickly. 'But I don't handle the details of that,' he said. 'Speak to Stuart Webb, our secretary.' That was the difference between Derby and Southampton: I handled everything. Webb told me George Hardy, the Derby chairman, wanted the money within a year, not two years as we proposed. There would have to be some haggling and the outcome would be affected by Everton's interest in the player. If Gordon Lee could meet Derby's requirements, and Todd's, I would have to improve our bid. At the moment we were ahead because Everton had only offered £250,000. It was stimulating to me to be in competition with one of the game's biggest-spending clubs.

My next call was to Todd. He seemed surprised that Derby were willing to let him go. 'I don't really want to leave,' he said. But he agreed to come down and see me on Sunday.

Friday, 8 September.

The next stage was to keep our side of it out of the newspapers. If there is a leak it can prejudice a deal. It's like letting the other player know what you have in your hand at cards. Nothing would come from our end and Docherty said he wouldn't announce anything either.

I knew what Todd could do but I didn't know much about what kind of person he was off the field. It is essential to know that. You don't want to pay out £300,000 and find the player you've bought is a big drinker, a womanizer or a heavy gambler. I rang one or two contacts who knew Todd intimately. One of them was Cloughie but he wasn't in and I spoke to Peter Taylor instead. Taylor told me, 'He's no worse a player now than he was when he won a championship medal with us in our Derby days.' He added that Todd was a very quiet lad who behaved himself and then said something which surprised me: 'He's not very ambitious.' I thought that was odd as he had already won two championship medals. Taylor's final point was reassuring, especially for those directors who might still be doubting the wisdom of the deal. 'He'll play until he's forty,' said Taylor.

I rang Docherty again and he said Everton had made a second offer, this time of £275,000, and they were willing to make a big cash down-payment. It still didn't match our offer. We were still ahead.

I'd taken Anne into hospital in the morning to sort out a minor problem and I collected her at half past six.

Saturday, 9 September.

After two good results at Birmingham and Villa, we were at home against one of the strugglers, Wolves. Yesterday Bally asked me if we were going to have a team talk and I said no. 'Everyone thinks it's going to be a stroll, there's no point,' I said. But at half past one I called the players together and gave them a thirty-minute lecture about not taking Wolves lightly. 'They're supposed to be a relegation team but we're only two points better off than they are,' I said.

We won 3–2 but not as convincingly as we should have done. We died fifteen minutes from the end. That wouldn't have happened at one of the hotbeds of football like Anfield; the crowd won't let it; they lift the team and the players respond. We haven't got that kind of crowd at the Dell. The players have got to do something first, then the crowd will chip in.

Afterwards I said to the players that they failed either because they weren't fit or their attitude was wrong and I was sure it wasn't down to their lack of fitness. David Peach even missed a penalty, his first in thirty-nine attempts. I thought he took too long a run. Bally said it was a good save by Paul Bradshaw, their keeper. 'If you hit it right, no goalkeeper stops a penalty,' I said; 'not without moving first.'

The two points took us to seventh position in the table. Not a bad start.

Sunday, 10 September.

Anne and I met Colin Todd, his wife Jennifer and two boys aged four and eight, at the Dell at quarter past eleven to show them round the area. It was the second Sunday in a row that Anne had done the wife's bit. I feel it is important to treat a prospective new signing as a family unit. If the player's wife is happy, the player will be happy.

Jennifer Todd said one of the children had to attend speech therapy classes and was amazed when I told her Southampton Football Club would fit a similar arrangement if Colin joined us. We all piled into the Mercedes, our children as well, and drove around the New Forest, stopping off at lunch at the same place I had taken the Branfoots the week before. The owner of the restaurant recognized Toddy but I hoped he wouldn't pass the information on. In the afternoon we all landed at Mr Askham's house. It was wrong to take so many people but I was fighting for a class player. Toddy's children ran all over the house and Mrs Askham kindly made tea.

Toddy said he was due a testimonial in two years time which he thought would earn him a good sum. He wanted that covered if he moved, and he was also due a large loyalty bonus. I said we would have to look into the situation and the possibility of using pension funds.

Both the Todds were impressed by the area and by what we had to offer. I thought we were well on the way.

Monday, 11 September.

The *Daily Express* had a story about the Todd situation written by one of their northern reporters. It couldn't be helped but I would have preferred to keep the news quiet until I had signed him. Tommy Docherty told me Everton had upped their bid to £300,000. I felt there must be some problem at Everton. Perhaps John Moores didn't feel Todd was worth that money. There seemed a reluctance about the way they were handling it.

I spoke to Jennifer Todd and she said she had enjoyed her day. Three-quarters of the way there! After dinner, I spoke to Todd and he said Gordon Lee wanted to see him on Wednesday. 'Why can't he see you right away?' I said. 'He's over in Ireland,' he said. 'He ought to hire a helicopter and come over to see you if he wanted you that badly,' I replied. Without saying it in as many words, I was implying that Everton weren't trying as hard as they might to get him. This goes on all the time in big money transfers involving more than one club. I was sure Gordon Lee would be telling Todd he would be better off joining a club like his, one that was more likely to win a major prize than Southampton which had only just got back into the First Division. The line I was putting across to Todd was that he would be happier with us because there wouldn't be the same pressure on him. Everton were expected to win every match and living near Liverpool, there was also the chiding Everton players can expect from Liverpool fans. He was a quiet lad and if he wanted the quiet life Southampton was the place.

Tuesday, 12 September.

Anne and I went to a Frank Sinatra concert at the Royal Festival Hall as the guest of a friend from Leeds, Geoffrey Port. I had met him on a train going to Carlisle two years earlier. He was a larger-than-life character, a man who made a lot of money and spent a lot of money. In our first meeting, he said he thought I was a better manager than the only other manager he'd met, Don Revie, and that we wouldn't lose another game that season. The next day we lost 1–0 at Carlisle but we did have an unbeaten run of seventeen games afterwards. You couldn't call Geoffrey a lifelong friend but I had no hesitation in accepting his hospitality. Being a football manager in the public eye puts you into contact with this kind of person. I enjoyed his company and I knew there would be times when I could repay him.

There was a reception at the Grosvenor House Hotel with a trio playing before we were driven in a Rolls Royce to the Festival Hall. Sinatra was brilliant and the atmosphere was something I had never experienced before. The warmth of the man came over, so different to his public image.

There were several other football people there that night, including Brian Clough, though I didn't see him, and Bob Wilson. Some more managers were going in a party later in the week. It was as though the top people in our profession were drawn towards the top man in the entertainment business.

Afterwards we went back to the Grosvenor in the Rolls for dinner. Anne, always the person to keep our feet on the ground, said as we were listening to a cassette of Sinatra's in the car, 'I would have enjoyed just listening to that and riding in the Rolls.'

Wednesday, 13 September.

Todd said he had been to Everton with his solicitor to see Gordon
Lee. Significantly, he hadn't taken his wife and family. He said it
was in the balance. I wheedled out of him what Everton was offering
and it wasn't much different from what I had offered except that
their contract was for two years whereas mine was for three. He
would have more security with us.

There is a lot of rubbish talked about what players make out of
transfers, under-the-counter payments and all that. I have never
paid a penny outside a contract to any player. Some clubs have been
said to give inducements to parents to sign but I never do. The
only time I did it was some years ago, completely innocently. I
went to see this couple and they laid on a spread for me which was
obviously much more than they could afford. As I was leaving, I
shoved a fiver into the woman's hand and said, 'Here, buy yourself
a drink.'

Todd said he was going to let Lee know on Thursday. I said I
wanted him to come down to Southampton on Thursday because
I felt we could settle it. Docherty had confused the issue by being
quoted as saying Todd would be staying at Derby because he wanted
to see his testimonial out and qualify for his loyalty bonus which
would together bring him in £30,000. I cursed Docherty. He was
putting pressure on us. He'd also rung Todd and said that if he
stayed at the Baseball Ground, he wouldn't get a testimonial, to
make Todd determined to leave. Docherty is a pal of mine but he's
a right Jekyll and Hyde. When he is nice, he is very nice, but when
his back is to the wall, he fights and spits. It's the Glaswegian in
him. There was no need to say that to Todd about his testimonial.

I tried to reach Docherty at the ground but they said he was
in London. I found out later he was there buying John Duncan
from Tottenham for £150,000. He would have to sell Todd now.
I spoke to Todd again and he agreed to come to the Dell the next
day with his solicitor to meet me and our financial director, Guy
Askham.

Thursday, 14 September.

Todd called from Derby at half past two and said he was on his
way by car. An hour later Stuart Webb rang and I said pointedly,

'I see you have been spending a few bob.' Webb said the Todd fee was now £290,000 because Gordon Lee had persuaded Docherty to accept £10,000 less and as Southampton had conducted their side of it so well, Derby wanted to be fair to both clubs. I didn't tell him that Todd was coming to see me.

I asked Todd to be sure not to tell anyone, not even his mates. Players have a habit of talking to other players and somehow the news leaks. Wives are the worst of the lot for gossiping. I was hoping we would get away with Todd's secret visit to the Dell but we didn't: it came out in the *Daily Mail*.

At ten past six Todd arrived with his solicitor, a young man named Roger Close. I didn't know why he brought a solicitor: we weren't going to do anything illegal. I advised him previously that an accountant, or a financial man, would be better. I outlined details of the pension scheme I had planned for him. I hadn't disclosed this earlier because I didn't want to show all my cards too soon. Everton might have copied the idea.

Under the pension scheme the money is only taxed when it is drawn out after the age of thirty-five. It is far easier to talk to a player of twenty-nine about pensions than it is to a younger player. Footballers pay so much in tax that any scheme to safeguard their income is bound to find favour with them.

Todd is a fellow Geordie and I was convinced we were getting on well. The situation about his family was more in our favour than Everton's. I said after an hour and twenty minutes of talking, 'No more mucking around. Let's have your answer.' He said, 'All right, give me two minutes.' He and his solicitor left my office. Guy Askham, who was still there, said; 'You've got him.' I felt the same way. I'd tried every persuasion. His hobby, apparently, was walking his dog and I said he could walk miles around the New Forest and not bump into a soul. Southampton was a club where he could spend four or five happy years without being under too much pressure and then settle into a little business somewhere. Bally had rung him over the weekend to tell him what a great club Southampton was, 'the best I've been at'.

There was a knock and Todd and his solicitor returned. The solicitor put out his hand and said, 'You've got yourself a player.' I shook hands with Todd and said, 'You're coming then?' 'Yes,' he replied. 'You'll not regret it,' I said. I suggested that he stay that night and come round in the morning to sign the contract but his solicitor said he had to get back. That was where I went wrong. My rule on transfer deals is never let the player out of the room until he's signed the contract but I missed out this time. Todd's brief chat with his wife while we were still in my office made me think it was all done bar the actual signing. 'I've joined them,' Todd told his wife. 'Thank Christ for that,' she said. I knew she said that because he repeated it to me.

We all shook hands again and at half past eight Todd and his solicitor set off to drive back to the Midlands. I felt pleased with myself. At home an hour and a half later, the phone went and the operator asked whether I would accept a transfer charge call from Oxford. I said I would ring the number back in case the operator was listening in. It was Roger Close with a query about the contract. Our offer appeared to him to be less than Everton's but I explained that as it was over a longer period, three years and not two, it was more beneficial to his client. Todd himself came on: 'I just wanted to check that,' and then he added, 'I'll ring you when I get home.' The first seeds of doubt had been planted. What did he want to ring me again for when we'd shaken hands?

Ten minutes later Jennifer Todd called. 'I suppose I'd better call you Mr McMenemy now, not Lawrie,' she said. She said she was pleased with the news and said the children were excited about coming to Southampton: 'Listen to the noise they're making.' I sat for a while watching television but there was no call from Todd as he had promised. I tried his number several times but it was constantly engaged. I was just about to go to bed at five minutes to one when the telephone rang again. 'I've got home,' said Todd, 'and it's turmoil.' 'What do you mean, turmoil?' I said. 'She says the phone hasn't stopped ringing,' he said. 'All her relatives from the North East are saying we've done the wrong thing.' I said, 'Relatives know a lot about our game, don't they? Let's be fair, it's what you want, not her relatives. Put Jennifer on, I'll talk to her.' 'She's down the garden with the dog,' he said. 'At this time of night?' I said. 'Hang on,' he said. He came back a little later and said, 'She doesn't want to speak about it.' 'All right, call me in the morning,' I said. 'My understanding of it is that we've shaken hands.' He said he would ring.

Friday, 15 September.

I got into the office early at nine o'clock but no call came. I tried his number several times and it was engaged. The third time it rang and rang. I called back and this time it was engaged. I rang Stewart Webb and asked what was happening. He said he didn't know but would contact Todd and get him to call me.

At midday, Todd telephoned and I said, 'Now then, what's happening?' 'I couldn't get her to change her mind,' he said. I said, 'Are you blaming her? You should stand up and be counted. Are you coming here or not? I know this is the right club for you.' 'I want to come. I'll go home, walk in, and say I'm going to Southampton, then see what her reaction is.' I replied, 'All right, do that and call me at home in half an hour.' Docherty called in the meantime and I told him it was the wife who was the trouble. 'I'm not surprised,' he said. 'She's the sort of wife who rings up at the training ground for him. I once gave the Derby players a lecture about domineering wives. "No successful footballer is at home every night of the week," I told them. He said he wasn't like that.' I said; 'We agreed at half past nine but by ten she'd turned turtle.'

A few minutes later, Todd rang. 'I've told her but I can't get her to change her mind,' he said in a doleful voice. In a way I was relieved. If he behaved like this, he wasn't the man for me. 'She thinks Everton would be best, but it's not all her,' he said. 'I think so too.' 'But what about us shaking hands on it?' I said. 'I'm sorry,' he replied, 'but it's a cruel game being a manager.' I remembered that Peter Taylor said he wasn't ambitious but his wife obviously was. I felt like saying he was saving my club £300,000. He said, 'No doubt you will be slagging me off in the papers now.' 'No, that's not my style,' I said. 'There's no need to, is there? I'd just like to wish you and your wife good luck. Good bye.' Surprisingly, there was no great feeling of regret. I may be proved wrong but I think the way it ended was best for Southampton. It was a high price. When a player goes to a club expecting to win things, as Todd clearly was, it didn't often work out that way. Mike Channon went to Manchester City for that reason and they didn't win anything.

I rang Docherty to tell him the outcome and after commiserating and joking about wives making tackles for you he said he was about to leave for London for the Sinatra concert. 'The only thing that's going to spoil it is that I'm in a group of football managers and their friends and one of them is a person I can't stand, Bondy.' I laughed. 'Tell him I went on Tuesday,' I said. 'He won't like that. He thinks I'm always upstaging him. In the summer he was saying he was about to go to Torremolinos on holiday and I spoilt it for him by saying I'd just come back from Portugal.' I don't mean to, of course. It's just coincidence that he usually does the same thing as me sooner or later.

Later, on the trip to Bristol for the game against City next day, it came over the coach radio that Todd had signed for Everton. None of the players said anything, not even Bally.

Saturday, 16 September.

We lost 3–1 after drawing 1–1 at half-time and appearing to have a point lined up. City's second and third goals were due to bad mistakes, one from Malcolm Waldron who would have lost his place had Todd signed in time. It was a disappointing end to a disappointing week. When we got back, I read that the reserves lost 3–0 at Crystal Palace. But the newspapers had it wrong: we had won 3–0 so it wasn't so bad. It brought a smile back.

4. A brick through the window in Dublin

After the first six matches, Southampton were in mid-table, comfortably placed. But the euphoria that follows promotion was fading and the hard slog of surviving in the world's most competitive First Division was about to begin.

Monday, 18 September.

An early start. A Catholic priest wanted to record an interview for his 'thought for the day' slot on Radio Solent. Though I am not fervently religious, I am not ashamed of showing my faith. One of the themes was cheating. I said I could never understand why some gifted footballers allowed themselves to cheat by not going full blast in matches.

This week is an international week with the 'home' countries (England, Scotland, Wales and Northern Ireland) taking part in European Championship matches. We had Steve Williams playing for the England Under 21 side in Copenhagen on Tuesday and Chris Nicholl playing for Northern Ireland against Eire in Dublin on Wednesday. I encourage my players to be picked for their countries but having them away certainly disrupts training. Manchester United and Arsenal, clubs who supply a large quota of international players, might as well close down for the week and go home. This is something I will talk to Ron Greenwood about. Williams left on Sunday and didn't return until late on Thursday. His match was on Tuesday. With the money they're making from internationals, the FA could afford to charter a plane and fly the players home right after the game, in this case on Wednesday night following the 4–3 victory of the senior side. Liverpool did it and so did we when we were in the European Cup Winners Cup. It means clubs can have their players for an extra day's training. Ted Mac-Dougall and Nick Holmes were injured so it meant we were without four players in training. To make up the numbers, I integrated the reserves and junior players into first-team training which is good for the younger players.

The FA announced that we had been fined £1,250 because our disciplinary record the previous season was so bad. It was the highest fine imposed. I didn't grumble at that because in the past five years our record of cautions and sendings off had been poor. When I took over, Southampton had an image of being a rough side and the directors stressed to me that this was one of the points they wanted changed. Bill Shankly used the phrase 'alehouse brawlers' about us and it stuck. Southampton had stayed up one season through kicking but you don't get consistent results playing that way and I was intent on altering our approach. As I told the FA Commission, I think I succeeded: most of our bookings the previous season were for dissent and minor fouls. In the past, we'd had a few players who could be nasty like Peter Osgood. But the player with the most disciplinary points last season was David Peach, the most inoffensive player anyone could meet. Nearly all his points were for mistimed tackles. He's not a great tackler.

A fine of £1,250 sounds a lot but it wasn't going to cost the club much because I collected £1,100 in fines from the players. We have a fining system, ranging up to £50 for the most serious offences, for players who are cautioned or sent off. It is automatically deducted out of their wages but they can appeal. I started it after speaking to the players themselves. They were in agreement. Now it was time for another meeting and I would arrange one. At our last chat, Ted MacDougall suggested that we have a bonus system to encourage good behaviour. At Norwich they got a bonus each time they went six games without any penalties. Maybe that was an idea we should try. Mr Woodford knew about the £1,100 we had in hand but I would make sure the other directors knew too.

Some of the bookings were for ridiculous things. Nick Holmes, who never opens his mouth from one week to another, was cautioned for dissent when he said to the referee at a throw, 'Away.' The referee thought he was saying, 'away with you!'

Tuesday, 19 September.

I had Peter Wells in to tell him I was leaving him out at Derby on Saturday. He expected it. He wanted a rest after the Middlesbrough match but I kept him in because we were winning. Now the results were going against us I had to give Terry Gennoe a chance. I signed Terry from Halifax for £35,000 at the end of the previous season. He's a giant of a lad, six feet two inches tall and a very nice boy. His eyes lit up when I told him he was in. It's hard for a manager to tell a player he is being dropped but it is balanced up when you give the new man the news that he's taking over.

I had an appointment at the Southampton Sports Centre with thirty-five taxi drivers who were giving up a day to take a hundred crippled and autistic children to Bournemouth on an outing. I was supposed to be seeing them off and the local press and television were due to cover it, but the press didn't show which made me very angry. It wasn't a big news story but it was worth covering for the locals. Being with these kids brings you down to earth. I've always tried to involve myself with activities of this sort, it helps you sort out your values in life.

I told the taxi drivers to bring the children down to the training ground before they set off so they could meet the players. The kids were delighted about that. Soon they were out on the field with the players. Bally was diving around in goal stopping penalties from them. Terry Curran was showing a kid how to kick a ball. Some other players were a bit shy. It's not easy for them. But I remember what Jimmy Savile once said to me, 'Treat them like you would any other kid.' I noticed that David Peach was looking a bit glassy eyed. One of his relatives had a crippled lad and he used to bring him down to the ground occasionally. Not long ago, the boy died.

Still incensed about the press's reluctance to come, I rang Peter East of the Southampton *Evening Echo* and told him what we were doing. 'Come on up with a photographer,' I said. He said he would try and get a cameraman.

There is a girl who still comes in. One of her relatives rang me and asked if she could come to the Dell to touch the FA Cup when we had it. Then the relatives explained, 'She's blind.' I said I would be only too pleased. We've been friends ever since. This is a side of the game you rarely see mentioned in the press which was why

I was so mad about the photocall going wrong. Football is not all louts and violence and bad things.

I called Peter East again and he said they couldn't raise a photographer. Then he said, 'Anything happening?' That really had me going. 'Yes, there's something happening but you lot can't be bothered to come up here,' I said.

Later, I watched the 'A' team playing. They are in the Hampshire League and I'm thinking of taking them out of it and applying to join the Southern Junior League. The Hampshire League is full of hard, senior players and it's bad for our teenagers to be learning the trade in this environment. It's no place to develop skills.

Wednesday, 20 September.

Over to Dublin to watch the first-ever match between Eire and Northern Ireland. Whether it was not having a proper meal or the tension of rushing about catching planes and taxis I don't know but I felt very queasy. The plane arrived an hour late which meant Ted Bates and I had very little time to get to the ground.

We were met by one of my friends over there, Tim Hutchinson, a nice old fellow. Typically Irish, our tickets were supposed to be waiting for us in a hotel in O'Connell Street but I told Tim we didn't have time to collect them. 'Let's go straight to the ground,' I said. Half an hour later some floodlights appeared as we turned a corner. 'You've done well Tim,' I said. There didn't seem to be many people about, just a couple of kids and an old drunk. I asked the drunk if this was the ground where they were playing the North and he said, 'You want Lansdowne Road, the rugby place. This is Dalymount Park.'

Tim was very embarrassed and I felt sorry for him. We raced off in the other direction, the police letting us through when they recognized me. I didn't need a ticket. 'We know who you are,' said the man on the main entrance, 'You're Mr McMenemy,' and they showed me into the directors' box. Most of the other managers were sitting in the row behind the box and Jock Stein was among them. 'Hey', he said. 'How did you get in there?' 'You should have a Mac in your name like me,' I said. 'A Jewish name doesn't do you any good over here.'

Also in the box was Roy Mason, the Secretary for Northern Ireland. Normally I don't approve of politicians filling up the best seats at football grounds, as often happens at Wembley at Cup Final time. But Mr Mason's presence was a good thing. It was giving the Government's blessing to a match which had immense political importance. In the end, it was a political result, o–o. Johnny Giles's team had the better of the first half and Danny Blanchflower's the better of the second half.

Giles had Eire playing like West Bromwich when he was there, a slow build up and keeping possession. I was disappointed to hear the crowd booing Giles. He made more bad passes than I'd ever seen him make but he'd done much for Irish football and didn't deserve such treatment. When I saw him later, he said, 'They've got short memories.'

Giles's players didn't change and shower at the ground like the Northern Irish but changed into tracksuits and were taken by a small bus to a hotel in the city centre. I couldn't see the point of that but Giles offered me and Ted Bates and Chris Nicholl a lift and we accepted. There were a couple of Northern Ireland players with us. It might have been their presence which caused it, but as we were driving away a brick was hurled through the back window, fortunately not injuring anyone. 'The daft buggers,' said one of the Eire players, 'they're our own supporters.'

At the hotel, we ordered a taxi to the airport and we shared it with Eddie Baily, who was there to make a report for Ron Greenwood. Eddie is one of the game's great characters and we ribbed him about his new-found importance in the game as one of Greenwood's right-hand men. 'I'm a power behind the throne,' he said. 'You're lucky to be given the chance to travel with me.'

Also on the plane was the Spurs manager, Keith Burkinshaw, and his assistant Pat Welton. I commiserated with Keith over the death of his mother. She hadn't been very old. It's a watershed in a man's life to lose his mother. I remember when it happened to me. I was told at half-time in a match at Grimsby.

Saturday, 23 September.

It was difficult to work out any tactics for the match at Derby because I don't think Tommy Docherty quite knew what he was going to do. There had been so many changes there since the start of the season, so many new faces. I thought he would play Gordon Hill, who had recovered from injury, and Roy McFarland but he threw me by playing neither and putting in two unknown Irish players he'd just signed. I tried the old bluff business by including Ted MacDougall in the squad and saying he was having a late test when I knew he had no chance. We played with only two up, Boyer and Curran. I joked to someone at the ground, 'Tom was halfway through his pre-match talk when he suddenly realized he was in the wrong dressing room.' Docherty is never short of a wisecrack and he'd said he was having the pre-season team picture retaken because he didn't recognize most of the players who were in it.

The papers were full of stories about how many players he'd bought and sold in his career. He was never out of the headlines. He's like a bottle of champagne, bubbling away, but sometimes you need to shove the cork back on. He could be a bit wearing, I would think, if you were working with him all the time. The publicity over his matrimonial troubles hadn't slowed him down. He was as bouncy as ever.

It was o–o at half-time but Derby got a lucky goal when a shot from Steve Carter hit Chris Nicholl and deflected past Gennoe. Boyer was through when he was pulled back but we didn't get the free kick. Derby came straight back up the field and Charlie George headed in the second goal at the far post. Peachy, who should have been covering, was still coming back from our attack.

Bally chased after the referee, Bert Newsome, complaining bitterly about the foul that wasn't given for the Boyer incident. The referee cautioned him for dissent and afterwards Bally said, 'He told me I was right, but was wrong to tell him so.' He added, 'They're cowards really because I kept giving him stick after that and he never said a word.' There are times when I have to agree with that. At Bristol, Norman Hunter jumped up and handled the ball after previously being cautioned. He should have gone off but the referee gestured with his backside and gave a free kick the other way for pushing by Curran. It was unbelievable. Everyone laughed. I have no wish to see any player sent off but that was a joke.

Boyer and Holmes were also booked by Newsome for dissent and Derby had three men cautioned too, including Charlie George. Charlie was sent off by Mr Newsome at Bolton a fortnight earlier and was just back after a one-match suspension. He kicked Bally in front of the press box and was booked. Then, nine minutes from time, he handled in the area to give Peachy a penalty. Deliberate hands after being previously cautioned is a sending-off offence but

Mr Newsome let him stay on. Other referees would have got the red card out. The inconsistency of referees is perplexing. It's the biggest complaint we managers have against them. You can't have eighty referees all acting and behaving the same way but you've got to have uniformity over simple issues like this.

On the way home in the coach, we stopped off at the home of one of our supporters in Newbury, Keith Cox. We were met by the butler at the door and served champagne and a buffet supper. I noticed Ivan Golac, who usually only drinks water, sipping champagne. 'Don't get the eye for a place like this,' I said. After living in Yugoslavia, it must have seemed a different world. Some people might have reservations about taking footballers into a situation like this but my players are the kind of people you could take anywhere.

Monday, 25 September.

I could sense the tension. Two away defeats meant we had to win the next game at home. Chris Nicholl asked if he could play in Keith Leonard's testimonial at Aston Villa and, though I'd told Ron Saunders, the Villa manager, that he could, I had reservations. Ted MacDougall hadn't played on Saturday. I didn't want to risk another injury.

Len Stansbridge, the groundsman, was putting in the new goalposts and I went to see how it was going. No-one ever notices goalposts until they collapse. These new ones were elliptical and they looked too pointed to me. I asked Fred Scott to check with the suppliers that they were the right ones. He came back and said that six other clubs had had them fitted recently and there were no problems. Len, a real old Hampshire Hog and a former Saints goalkeeper, said, 'They look too bloody dangerous to me. If you hit your head on that, you'd be for it.' I said, 'You must have hit your head a few times on posts, Len.' And he replied, 'Yes, and it had no effect at all!' He's one of the old type, thirty years on the staff and he still marks the pitch out with a paint brush by hand.

Tuesday, 26 September.

The reserves were playing at Plymouth and were supposed to be staying the night. I changed the itinerary so that they came straight back by coach, saving the club about £200. You had to show the younger players there was a difference between playing for the first team and the reserves. We were treating the reserves too well. I'd sent out a circular saying that we had some players for sale – we needed to clear the way for some of the younger ones to come through – and one, John Sharpe, who'd been on loan to Gillingham, had spurned the chance of going to Gillingham permanently. I could see why: we were too generous; no-one wanted to leave. Manny Andruszewski was another one who wanted to stay put.

Exeter wanted Steve Neville and I knew they'd just sold a player to Chester for £15,000 and had some cash so I quoted £20,000. Bobby Saxton, the Exeter manager, is a good type and I agreed they could have a generous spread. He said £20,000 would be a record for Exeter so we decided to keep that quiet. It would put pressure on the lad. The buying club always undervalues a transfer and I was amused to see the papers said it was £10,000. The selling club tends to overvalue it to give their supporters the idea they've done some good trading.

Gerry Summers, the Gillingham manager, another person I respect, came on on again about Sharpe and we agreed £25,000 clear. He said Sharpe was making what he thought were unreasonable financial demands and I had Sharpe in and told him, 'If you stay here, you'll be in the "A" team and I'll tell the papers you are making outrageous demands.' I said it was a good move for him; it would continue his soccer education under a good manager. He said he was soon to be married and was worried about a house. Later I heard he'd agreed to go. Perhaps I had been too hard on him but Gillingham had come up with a rented house and they'd been very fair. So as not to be too precise about fees, I told the local press that we'd got £50,000 for the pair of them. You're not supposed to reveal exact transfer fees, anyway, according to League regulations.

I arranged a practice match for the first team and popped out for a visit to Highfield Primary School, something I had promised to do. The children, particularly the girls, asked some brilliant questions. Kids really get to the heart of it but my stay was unduly prolonged because the headmaster asked me to sign autographs. Having signed one, I had to do the lot and there were 160 children. A ten-year-old had a violin and I surprised them by playing the scale. Coming from a musical family, I'd learned to play a violin when I was a child.

It was late when I got back to the Dell and I was incensed to learn that the practice match hadn't taken place because the ground-staff had only got one set of posts up. It's at times like these that you feel like sacking the groundsman on the spot. I gave instructions for the match to take place the next day. He wouldn't like that because it would give him less time to make the pitch look nice. Our match with Ipswich was on Southern Television and groundsmen like to see the pitch in good shape and the commentator say something about it.

The niggles were piling up. The *Express* had a story about us wanting Miljan Miljanic and they'd stretched it a bit. The *Echo* sent up a lad and I said I knew nothing about it. The *Express* had another story saying the FA were writing to Bally about an admission in his book that Don Revie paid him £300 when he was a Blackpool player. I didn't know anything about that either because we hadn't received a letter but the calls kept coming in. Sometimes the press think you are lying. It's hard to please all of them. Another reporter rang and said he'd had his backside kicked for missing the stories the *Express* had so I gave him a line that I was inviting occasional coaches like Tony Waiters down to do sessions with us. I mentioned Bobby Moore as a possibility. That came out that Bobby Moore and Bobby Charlton were going to coach at Southampton. I put my head in my hands. You try to help but it can rebound.

That night I went to Portsmouth *v.* Wigan at Fratton Park. There were 14,000 people there, an exceptional crowd for a Fourth Division game. The ground holds 40,000 and never gets full but I reflected that if we played there perhaps we might fill it occasion-ally. Portsmouth were doing well and I was pleased for their chair-man, John Deacon. He's ploughed a lot in and few people had re-ceived as much criticism as he'd had.

When I'd been to Portsmouth previously some of the players were coasting but against Wigan I didn't see a single cheat. I don't like cheats at any level. The play was terribly stereotyped as though three lines had been drawn across the pitch for the 4–3–3 formations both sides used. The pros in the box agreed there hadn't been a bad tackle all night yet six players were cautioned, bringing the total I'd seen booked in three games to almost twenty. It's a familiar story. The League sends out a directive about dissent and ten yards and the referees go jumping in.

Wednesday, 27 September.

I arranged for the youngsters to be mixed in with the seniors in the practice and it was a good, competitive game. John McGrath said it was a delight to see kids just out of school playing against the older players. They'd learned so much.

I hadn't been able to get through to Anfield to order tickets for the Liverpool *v.* Nottingham Forest European Cup tie because the lines, even the private ones, were permanently engaged, so I sent a telegram. This was the game we all wanted to see. You want to go because this is what you aspire to yourself. Just as I was leaving to catch the plane, Jock Stein rang and I said he could have one of my tickets.

We met at Manchester Airport and drove to Anfield. The atmosphere was music to a manager's ears. We were recognized right away and were bombarded with comments like, 'come to worship at the shrine then?' The guest room was full of other managers. I spotted Raymond Goethals, manager of Anderlecht, whom I had met when Southampton played his club in the Cup Winners Cup. He was smoking, as usual. Bill Shankly was holding court. You don't talk to him, you listen. I wondered what he was thinking. Since he quit, Liverpool had twice won the European Cup. Now they were out of it. How disappointed was he? It's a selfish game.

Pressmen were there from all over Europe and Cloughie upset them by not attending the customary after-match press conference which is compulsory under UEFA regulations. As we were leaving, Cloughie spotted us from the team bus. 'Hey, come on in, the pair of you!' he shouted. He had that wild-eyed look of a man who had just experienced a great triumph. Neither of us wanted to linger. We just poked our heads through the coach door and said, 'Well done, lads.' Cloughie had them going straight back home without any celebrations. It may have upset some people but he was thinking of Saturday's game. Jock and I drove out of the car park behind the coach, which was escorted by police.

I shared Jock's room at the Queen's Hotel in Leeds, a dreary, old-fashioned place, and we stayed up late talking football. Only at the end did he mention the Scotland job which had now become vacant following Ally MacLeod's resignation. He asked me what I thought and I said, 'Whatever you do at Leeds has been done before, but the Scottish team has never won World or European competitions.' His son and daughter liked Leeds and travelled down for all the games, but his wife wasn't so keen.

Thursday, 28 September.

The plane was held up and I didn't get back to Southampton until nearly four o'clock. I called Mr Woodford and he sounded subdued, 'You don't seem too happy,' I said. He said the other directors could be annoyed at hearing that Sharpe had been sold for £20,000. They didn't know about it in advance. I exploded, 'I rang your office two days ago and you were away. I told Mr Askham in Guernsey and Ted Bates, who is a director, knew all about it.' I shoved the phone at Ted, who was in my office. 'Hear, you talk to him,' I said. Ted seemed surprised. 'I wouldn't have paid £5,000 for him,' he said. I took the phone back and said, 'There are only three other directors: one is rarely at home; the other is in Mull; and the third one is at his castle in Anglesey or abroad. What am I expected to do?' Mr Woodford said, 'I'm sorry I didn't realize that. You have your job to do, but the directors do like to be kept informed.'

Friday, 29 September.

Chris Nicholl was out of the Ipswich match. He limped off in the practice match but the cynic in me wondered if he got it the night before in that testimonial. He's a good pro but even good pros cover up things like that. In the evening, we had a buffet get-together for the sixteen scouts from all over the country. I told them not to worry if we hadn't signed a single player they'd recommended. Now we were in the First Division our standards were higher. Quality before quantity.

At five minutes past midnight Jock rang. I could visualize him sitting in that hotel bedroom in Leeds, a man alone, anxious to talk to a friend in football. He was undecided about what to do if Scotland approached Leeds. He'd only been there forty days, less than Cloughie's forty-four days. 'There are still a few ghosts in the cupboards here,' he said.

Saturday, 30 September.

Nicholl's absence was crucial. We made a mistake in the middle in the fourth minute and Paul Mariner scored. We came back well in the second half but Ipswich won 2–1, our third defeat on the trot. We hit the posts twice. Was it the new shape? And Clive Thomas, a referee of great experience, failed to see that their goalkeeper, Paul Cooper, moved when Peachy's penalty was saved. He also disallowed a goal on a linesman's flag which looked good to me.

Bobby Robson, the Ipswich manager, is an old friend and was generous in his comments afterwards; he couldn't have been nicer. He is a man of extreme moods and a bad loser. At the time of the Leeds offer he wrote a considerate letter saying I had done the right thing. He'd been in the same position himself when Everton made him a similar offer. I hold Ipswich as an example of what a smaller club can achieve by sound management. If we can do what they've done in the next five years, I will be satisfied.

The family kept out of my way when I got home. They knew that I wouldn't be in the mood for chat after a home defeat. Television is always a good escape. I sat down and worked out my frustrations on John Bond, who was being interviewed in 'Match of the Day'. He spoke drivel and for some reason threw in Ted MacDougall's name. He was talking about the forwards knowing what each player was doing in the final third of the field and added, 'If Ted MacDougall is watching, he'll know what I mean.' Bondy has this bad habit of criticizing other clubs and extolling his own virtues. When your team is doing well, it's a time to shut up and let the team do your talking. He's never learned that.

Sunday, 1 October.

The family woke and waited for the first word from the master. But it wasn't going to be a gloomy day. We had been invited to the opening ceremony of a new Catholic church at Thatcham, near Newbury, by an old friend, Father Seamus Gilhoolley, a lovely Irish character whom I'd met before our FA Cup success in 1976. He had wheedled all this money out of his four hundred parishioners to pay for the building. It was a marvellous feat.

He persuaded me to let him have two Cup Final tickets which were to be raffled. It's illegal to raffle Cup Final tickets and he got round it by exchanging the ones I gave him for a couple which had been obtained by a local Canon. I promised him the tickets before we played Crystal Palace in the semi-final and the Sunday before the game took place, he asked the congregation to pray for a Southampton victory! After we won, he held a thanksgiving service which ended with him saying, 'The tickets are now on sale at the front of the church.'

We had a beautiful day, lasting right through dinner at night. Father Gilhoolley is a totally humble man and it was uplifting to be in his company with all his fellow priests, bishops and friends. We were late home. It had been a happy time and a welcome release from the pressures of football.

When we stay at home on Sunday, we are often disturbed by people driving up outside, stopping, and looking through the windows. This was one of the reasons why we were moving. It was a nice house but we wanted more privacy.

Thursday, 3 October.

League Cup third-round tie against Derby at the Dell. I felt we could beat them. At Norwich on the Saturday, they didn't have a forward on the field and were well beaten. But Charlie George was back and he'd make a difference.

I was surprised how hard Derby fought. They brought in a marker, Peter Daniel, to stick with Steve Williams and Daniel followed him everywhere. This was the first time I had seen Williams marked like this. Williams made the mistake of trying to lose him when he didn't have to do so. I told him at half-time to give the ball earlier and run. Daniel, an older player, wouldn't keep up with him. It was a cracking Cup tie. There could have been five or six goals but for some brilliant goalkeeping by Terry Gennoe and John Middleton. The only goal, scored by Phil Boyer, came in the fifty-third minute and it was a fine example of his opportunism.

I was very pleased with Gennoe. When I bought him I thought the £35,000 we paid was an inflated price. Southend, Watford and Crystal Palace were also interested and the night I went to see him, he let in five. But he seemed the right type. He was a teacher, newly married and when he wasn't in the side early on, he didn't put any pressure on me. He was prepared to wait for his chance. Now it had arrived, he'd taken it in style and that £35,000 was nothing. We had stepped up our goalkeeper training and he was benefiting. Mike Channon once told me how impressed he was by the amount of work Joe Corrigan did at Manchester City, even training on

Saturday mornings. Keepers worked harder these days. One of the first people into our dressing room afterwards was Tommy Docherty, which was rather strange. You don't expect to see the losing manager in there but the Doc is different. Mr Blagrave, our millionaire President, was also in to congratulate the players. 'I want them to have a drop of wine,' he said, which meant he had four or five bottles of champagne to give them. Docherty pointed to Mr Blagrave's hacking-type jacket, resplendent with leather pockets, and said, 'You shouldn't be a director, wearing a jacket like that.'

When Docherty and the President left, all the gaiety disappeared. The players were downcast, as though they had lost. I soon realized why: Ted MacDougall was in a foul mood, hurling his boots around and cursing. He'd played as well as I'd ever seen him play but was thwarted by a goalkeeper who stopped everything. He could have had a hat-trick, but that meant nothing. All he was thinking about was coming off empty-handed and he took his feelings out on Peachy who was substituted near the end because he had a 'dead' leg. MacDougall was quite venomous, particularly over one cross of Peach's which ended up by the far corner flag when MacDougall was unmarked in the middle. I waited until MacDougall went into the bath and told the others, 'That's his frustration coming out but don't let it take anything away from a good performance.' I would speak to MacDougall later in the week. There was no point doing it now when he was in this mood.

It was a much happier scene in the press room. Tom and I went in together and it was a real comedy act, different from the usual clichés which people soon get sick and tired of. The more experienced reporters don't ask too many questions because they know they will be giving away a good line to the others. You always get a daft question and the inevitable one came when I was asked, 'Are you disappointed with the 19,000 crowd?' That showed the reporter's lack of knowledge because 19,000 was a good crowd. In fact, it was the fourth highest of the round. 'Well, this is the South, you know,' I said, 'and we have got Gilbert and Sullivan appearing at the local Gaumont.' Tom was in like a flash with one of his one-liners: 'You should have told me earlier,' he said. 'I'd have nipped down there and signed them.'

The directors' tea room was full as it often is at midweek matches. Ken Shellito and Ron Suart were there from Chelsea, wrapped up in their suede coats. 'You're getting soft,' I said. 'It's not that cold.'

Three days later Shellito went to Belgrade to talk with Miljan Miljanic about becoming Chelsea's technical director but he didn't mention it.

One of the papers had a story saying that Chelsea were hoping to buy Ball and I had to deny it. Now Shellito and Suart were at the Dell and more questions would be asked; but they were only sizing Derby up before Chelsea's game at the Baseball Ground the following Saturday. Sometimes it is hard to convince people that you are telling the truth. Bally himself asked me about it and I wondered how much he doubted my denial.

John Benson, the Bournemouth manager, was also present with his coach, Fred Davies. John crept in as though he thought he shouldn't be there. I made a point of welcoming him. He'd earned his right to be in this company by the graft he put in at the lower levels of the game. He had more right to be there than most people, notably the hangers on who are found in directors' boxes. The England manager, Ron Greenwood, was also down and we had a long talk over a brandy. It was midnight before I left. The atmosphere had been relaxing: football people talking football over a drink.

Wednesday, 4 October.

Jock Stein rang to congratulate me on the Derby result. It was the day he was to be appointed Scotland's manager. The press was camped on his doorstep.

Soon after I arrived at the office, John Harris called from Sheffield Wednesday. John is a great example of a football man who has battled through everything and still survives. He was in the same mould as Stan Cullis and Bill Shankly in the fifties and sixties, and when Sheffield United got rid of him he went across the road to Wednesday and worked for them. He is the ideal man to work with Wednesday's manager Jack Charlton because Jack is more interested in coaching than administration. Once Jack finishes coaching, he's off shooting and fishing. He said to me once, 'The trouble with you is you're too dedicated.' John was inquiring about Mike Pickering. Pickering was from Barnsley, and Sheffield Wednesday would be just right for him.

Charlton came on the line and asked how much. '£60,000,' I said. 'You what?' said Jack. 'We're only a Third Division club you know and we haven't got any money.' I replied, 'That's why I quoted

£60,000. If it was a Second or First Division club it would be more. He's a good player.' 'I thought you were a friend of mine,' said Jack. But he quickly agreed terms because he wanted to sign Pickering within twenty-four hours so that he could play him against Rotherham on the Saturday. I said I would ring him back after I'd spoken to the lad.

Pickering is a cautious person who takes a week to make his mind up about anything. He talks a bit like Brian Rix and when I told him Jack Charlton wanted him, he said, 'It's a bit sudden, isn't it?' I reminded him that after he was left out he had said he wanted a move. Now he could have one and as a centre-half it would make him a better player working under Jack Charlton, a former centre-half himself. Reluctantly, he agreed to talk to Charlton. 'Have a shower and I'll see you after,' I said. I called Charlton back but he wasn't there and when I went to get Pickering he'd gone. In football language, he'd bottled it. In the summer, when he was trying to get a new contract, he waited hours to see me. Now there was a move in prospect, he had cleared off. I called his digs and the lady said he wasn't there but would be back at five for tea. At five o'clock I hadn't heard and by six he was still missing. I sent Lew Chatterley round and he called back at half past six to say Pickering had been driving round all afternoon, his mind in a turmoil. 'Tell him I've arranged for him to see Charlton at lunchtime tomorrow,' I said. I felt sorry for him. We were hustling him but it would work out for his benefit in the end.

Thursday, 5 October.

Charlton rang and we agreed a £50,000 fee and another £10,000 after Pickering played twenty-one games so we were making £20,000 profit. I remembered to tell Mr Woodford. This latest transaction had taken our income from transfers to £105,000 in a week and nearly £400 had been cut from the wage bill. We were building up some cash for new players.

I called John Harris to see if Pickering was signing. He said Jack had taken him to a pub for lunch. That was typical of Jack. There was a first-class restaurant at Hillsborough but if he went there his ear would be bent by silly people. Jack's people, straight people, were in the pub.

At training, I made a point of having a quiet word with certain players I felt needed talking to. I told Nick Holmes he had to be more aggressive and praised Gennoe for his work against Derby. 'That's all behind me now,' said Gennoe. I liked his attitude. It was professional. I told MacDougall that his attack on Peach was uncalled for even though I appreciated he was frustrated. Events like that would destroy us. I sensed it was partly a cry for help from MacDougall, and Bally too. They both felt we should be buying new players and that we'd only got a few results by running ourselves into the ground. When that burned out, they feared what would be left. I was tempted to tell them that I was making inquiries about a couple of internationals but couldn't reveal the names. You like to think you can trust people but these things have a way of coming out.

The League Cup draw paired us with the winners of the Reading *v.* Rotherham tie. I was pleased but caution soon creeps in: Watford had beaten Manchester United the night before. But I'd rather go to those clubs than Nottingham Forest or a big one.

Peachy was in the treatment room and, after the verbal beating he'd taken from MacDougall, didn't seem as though he was in the mood to play on Saturday. I asked him how he was and Dr Ramsey, the elderly club doctor who had retired from practice and should really be making way for the younger man I had in said, 'He won't be fit.' I replied testily, 'How do you know? I remember when Austin Hayes had a broken collar bone on a Wednesday and he played on the Saturday!' Doc Ramsey rarely spoke to me. It was time he left the club but he hung on. It was the worst thing a doctor could do, tell a player he wouldn't be ready for a match. Those conversations should be held out of earshot of the player. I said to Peach, 'Is it any better than yesterday?' and he answered, 'Yes.' 'You've got two more days,' I said, but I knew he wouldn't play.

In the evening I drove to Cheltenham to speak at a conference arranged by the Minnesota Mining Company. If I wished it, I could be out every night of the week but I had to be selective. This was something different and I enjoyed it. But it meant coming home in the early hours.

Friday, 6 October.

For the first time we were going to Everton by coach as an experiment. I told the players it would take the same time as the train but they were unhappy and seemed pleased when the bus shuddered in traffic. 'Are we going to make it?' they kept saying. I had to make a few cracks back.

We stayed at one of Liverpool's leading hotels and I had a suite which I used to entertain the directors and my trainers. The players usually go up and watch television after dinner but I was disturbed to hear that a couple of women we had seen in the dining room had been knocking at their doors.

The players had a laugh when they learned that Nick Holmes was one of the first to be asked, 'Would you be liking some company tonight?' He said politely, 'No thank you.' But it was no laughing matter. If any player had accepted, I would have come down heavily on him, imposing a hefty fine. I had never known this happen before in a provincial hotel. You hear of it happening all the time in London but not in Liverpool.

Saturday, 7 October.

Some of the Everton players drifted in to the hotel. One of them was Colin Todd and I made a point of speaking to him. He seemed surprised, almost sheepish. 'Nice to see you,' I said. Psychologically he was down because I took the initiative.

My team talk was as good as I've ever given. 'Let's give something extra today for Bally,' I said. Bally was back at his old club and it was a big occasion for him. The only tactical change I made was to bring in Manny Andruszewski at right-back to mark Dave Thomas, Everton's dangerous supplier, and push Ivan Golac, who wasn't such a good marker, into midfield on the right. I filled Peach's position at left-back by moving Nick Holmes out of midfield.

The Everton fans gave Bally a rousing reception. They're like that in Liverpool, and it affected Bally. Bill Shankly came in the dressing room before the start and I told him, 'I've got a fellow here who's like your idol Tom Finney.' And to gee Terry Curran up, I added, 'The trouble is he only does it for thirty minutes.' Shankly said, 'If he can do it for thirty minutes, he's some player.'

Fifteen minutes from kick-off, the professional in Shankly prompted him that it was time to go and as he left he said to Gennoe, 'Son, when you go out there, throw your cap and gloves into the net and make sure that's all that goes in!' Gennoe followed his advice, even saving a penalty from Andy King, and we drew 0–0 against the unbeaten second team in the League, an encouraging result. Shankly came in afterwards and said to me, 'You'll always have a job, but don't let them pee on you.' There was a trace of bitterness in his voice.

On the way back, we had to change buses when our luxury coach finally broke down. We stopped at the Europa Lodge, just off the MI for a meal and bumped into Ron Atkinson, whose team had lost 1–0 at home to Spurs. I said it was a terrible thing to lose at home and he tried to pretend it wasn't.

Tuesday, 10 October.

I called several managers to see what players might be available. As soon as you ask about their players, they ask you about yours. I might have to let someone go to get a couple in, even if I don't want to lose a good player.

We had a trialist over from Bruges, a sweeper by the name of Eddie Kraiger, and I arranged to play him in a practice match at the Dell, the first team against the reserves. He spoke bad English. That's going to be a problem with the foreigners. If they can't communicate, it's going to be difficult. Kraiger was good on the ball going forward, like many Continentals who play in that position, he linked well with Bally. He didn't look fit to me and I decided I would want to see a lot more of him before I came to any conclusions.

I had a speaking engagement at a dinner in Newcastle for the speedway rider Mike Watkin, whose career had been ended by a crash. I promised John Gibson, sports editor of the *Newcastle Chronicle*, that I would help the lad and I flew up from London Airport. Watkin is a very nice lad and so is Ole Olsen, the Dane who held the world speedway championship. But I was less impressed with the New Zealander, Ivan Mauger, who appeared a much more ruthless type of person. While Olsen was coming out with pleasantries, Mauger said something about how he was going to take his title off him, hardly a charitable thing to say at such an event.

Colin Milburn, the former England cricketer, was the other main speaker and in my speech I said it was ironical that two talented sportsmen, Watkin and Milburn, should both have their careers ruined at their peak by cruel accidents. Colin is good fun to be with: I like him. The 250 people who attended paid £10 a head and the organizers seemed happy.

Wednesday, 11 October.

The inevitable delay in flights and it was lunchtime before I arrived back at the Dell. It was a smashing day so I got changed and did ten laps on my own to get rid of the frustrations and tiredness. I felt much better afterwards. In the evening the coaching staff and I drove to Elm Park to see Reading beat Rotherham 1–0 in the League Cup. We were meeting the winners in the next round. It would be a big night for Reading, 30,000 people in and a First Division club there for the taking.

Thursday, 12 October.

After training, Brian Truscott reminded me that I was due to speak at a meeting of insurance men at the Polygon Hotel at teatime. I was late, as usual, and had to go in cold but I addressed about two hundred people for about thirty-five minutes and answered questions. There was the stock question about why do footballers cuddle and kiss and I joked that footballers are like wives, they need a cuddle and kiss sometimes. I led the fellow on a bit. I said, 'It's understandable sometimes when footballers react like that, especially when they can be on up to £100 a point. They don't think about money when they're out there but managers often mention it in the week to motivate them and make them realize what they are playing for. When Bobby Stokes scored that goal in the 1976 FA Cup Final I know how I felt; I could have kissed anyone near me, couldn't you?' The man said, 'Yes, I would that day.' I said that answered the question. Perhaps I had put him down a bit but it showed how intelligent people can fail to put themselves into the other person's shoes: when you are under great stress, you can be excused extravagant reactions. Footballers are no different to anyone else.

Saturday, 14 October.

Peachy was fit to return against QPR at the Dell but Andruszewski was out. Nicholl and Holmes were in after a touch of flu in the week. We were on 'Match of the Day' and players like to see themselves on the box. The club receives a facility fee from the BBC of £800 which isn't much. John Motson usually stays the night before but rang and said he couldn't make it this time because he was attending a farewell party for Desmond Lineham. Desmond, one of radio's best sports commentators, was transferring to television.

Alan Hart, the BBC Head of Sport, was supposed to be joining us for lunch but his wife called and said he had to stay in London. It was something to do with Frank Bough, I guessed. The week before Frank had a row with a producer in the 'Grandstand' programme and the newspapers were full of the story. Mrs Hart seemed to be having the same problem with her husband as Anne had with me. She told me, 'I'm starting a campaign to save Alan's life.' She was probably looking forward to a weekend in Hampshire.

At the hotel, we met some Rank Xerox people who are sponsoring a couple of matches at the Dell. I had the players go in and meet them. It's part of the game these days.

Steve Burtenshaw, the Rangers manager, came into my office before the kick off for a chat. He is a man I have time for, a good coach who has struggled at managerial level. It wasn't easy taking over at Rangers, there was so much to do, but he was pulling them round after a bad start.

Early on, Terry Curran was late tackling the Rangers left-back, Ian Gillard, and Gillard eventually went off to have stitches. We should have been three up in the first ten minutes but we only had a Ted MacDougall goal from a corner to show for all our pressure at the interval.

In the second half we were a shambles. Holmes was obviously affected by his illness and the way Steve Williams was playing it looked as though he had scarlet fever. It amazes me that players make mistakes in the First Division that they would never make in the Second. We lost a point when the substitute, unmarked at a corner, headed in at the far post. Bally, who had been booked, was almost shedding tears of rage in the bath afterwards.

One of the BBC team asked if it was all right to interview him. I was told it was for 'Football Focus' the following week and agreed. But when I saw it that night, I wasn't too happy because Bally had said we were struggling and weren't good enough. Right after a match is never the best time to be interviewed on television: you are not always rational; you can be too emotional; Bally also had a go at the referee, which wouldn't help his chances at the FA. I was interviewed myself and made some mild comments about refereeing generally, saying I was disappointed at how many players were being booked for dissent and not moving back ten yards. After that I would probably be unpopular with officialdom too but it needed saying.

Sunday, 15 October.

I saw refereeing that the professionals respect in ITV's 'Big Match' in the afternoon. Alf Grey, who was on the line when we played in the FA Cup Final, spoke to an offending player in the Spurs *v.* Birmingham match and you could see him smiling. While some referees see the humour of it, others swear as heartily as any player. But if the players swears back, he can be off. Consistency is the basic problem.

Jock Stein was on the phone and we talked about refereeing. 'I thought the standard up here left a bit to be desired but it's no better in England,' he said. He said he was delaying the announcing of his squad for his first match against Norway until the Tuesday, giving him an extra day to check the injured players. That showed his professionalism. He was intent on creating a family atmosphere among his players, as Alf Ramsey had done with England. Alf was looked on as a cold man but he was warm with his players. Jock said he would have them together on the first day and just talk. He would ask them how they wanted to play. It was as much their team as his team. I read him some comments from the English papers about Leeds and their defeat by WBA. He still had remorse about the way he'd left them.

5. Highbury

The next match was Arsenal away, followed by Nottingham Forest at home and Manchester United away, all hard ones. Southampton were already hovering just above the relegation zone. Fixtures like these wouldn't help them escape. The team needed a new player to lift it but half the clubs in the First Division, many far richer than Southampton, were also looking for players, including Arsenal who had £750,000 to spend, Nottingham Forest who had £1m available and Manchester United.

Monday, 16 October.

First thing on Monday morning, I started working on the tactics for Arsenal. The season before we'd done well at Highbury using a revolutionary system of three at the back and four marking in midfield with Manny Andruszewski on Liam Brady. Arsenal are pretty stereotyped and I was thinking of trying something similar. Someone would have to be dropped to let Manny in and the player I was thinking of was Terry Curran who had done well at home but not so well away. I knew MacDougall wouldn't like that but I had to think of what was best for the team.

One of the players I had inquired about and was hopeful of getting was the Scottish Under 21 player David Narey of Dundee United. Jock Stein swore by him and included him in his first Under 21 side as an over-age player at right-back. He can play either at the back or in midfield. Tommy Docherty tried hard to get him but upset Jim McLean, the United manager. McLean had a row with Frank Blunstone, Docherty's assistant, over alleged tapping at a

German airport on the way home from a European trip. McLean told me the directors had said they couldn't let anyone go at the moment. I thought that's because they are waiting for Narey to be given a full cap, which would increase the price.

At half past three I decided to go to Coventry to see the third League Cup match between Aston Villa and Crystal Palace and take another look at Leighton Phillips, an experienced defender who was available. Ted Bates and I got there late, as usual, and George Curtis, the Coventry commercial manager, had to park the car for us. We sat at the back of the stand with Dave Sexton, Jock Wallace, Ian McFarlane and Ken Shellito.

McFarlane, whom I had worked with at Sheffield Wednesday, was very cool. 'What's up?' I said. 'I'm not too happy about you,' he said. 'We'll talk later,' I said. The match was men against boys. Palace had all the write ups but their inexperience showed. Andy Gray and Brian Little pulled their defenders everywhere. Villa showed they had done their homework when they crowded John Burridge, who used to be on their staff, at a corner and Ken McNaught headed the ball down for Gray to score the first goal. Gray's second goal in Villa's 3–0 victory was a great goal. He pulled it across the defender and volleyed into the far corner. I saw Mac-Farlane outside in the rain. The fans must have wondered what was happening, these two big men going at each other. I was rather annoyed when he said it was about Jim Clunie. He was implying that I hadn't rung Jim since he went to St Mirren because I thought he had been tapped. I wouldn't have been bothered if he had been tapped; it goes on all the time. McFarlane was adamant. 'He's been very loyal to you,' he said. 'Aye, and I've been loyal to him,' I said. 'He had been made redundant by Rolls Royce when I gave him a job.' I said I hadn't rung him or a lot of other people. It didn't mean I was deliberately ignoring them. Jock Wallace, whom I was seeing for the first time since he came down to Leicester, was embarrassed by it. It was silly really.

I went back inside the guests' tea room to talk with Dave Sexton and one or two others. In a lull in conversation, Manny Cussins, the Leeds chairman, saw me and came over. I felt that everyone was looking at us. Manny made some joke that I could have had the Leeds job and named my own price. We all laughed. I said, 'Manny's doing his rounds.' Leeds were still no nearer finding a successor to Jock Stein. Ron Saunders said he had been offered a

£200,000 job in Kuwait and Terry Venables had apparently received a similar offer from the same people.

Tuesday, 17 October.

Bally was off to Norwich to play in Martin Peters' testimonial match. 'I'm going to the academy to learn something,' he said. It was a cynical comment. There was nothing more he needed to know about the game. The other players laughed. 'Bring back some knowledge,' one said.

Wednesday, 18 October.

I was spending every morning with the players. When things aren't going so well, that's the place to be. I could sense that one or two of them were having doubts about my plans for Arsenal. I asked Bally and he said he thought I was being too defeatist. 'Arsenal aren't that good a side these days,' he said. MacDougall agreed as I knew he would. I asked some of the quieter ones and Chris Nicholl said, 'We've started getting better at the back. We've only let in one goal in three matches.' I felt the senior players were agreeing with Bally.

That night we had the London schoolboys down to play a match at the Dell against our associated schoolboys. We had all the families down too and I went round to talk to them all. That is where football clubs get their talent and I never believe in ignoring what happens at the lowest level. It's the club's future.

Thursday, 19 October.

I did an about-face. Arsenal lost 2–1 in Split the night before and Terry Neill was quoted about all the injuries he had. It would be wrong to be too defensive. I told the players we would have a normal back four but would stick someone on Brady.

Curran must have suspected he was the one to be left out by the line-ups in training. In the old days I would have told him on the Monday but experience teaches you not to rush things. I went to talk to him after training and concentrated on bringing him down to earth a bit. He's only twenty-three but his attitude was 'give me the ball and I'll show you I'm a world beater'. I told him he still had a lot to learn about using space, checking out and things like that. In a few words, I bashed down his outward barrier and made him think about his game. A manager has to find a balance between being too critical and affecting a player's confidence, and letting him get too much of an ego which prevents him analysing himself in a way that benefits his performance. I felt the balance in Curran's case needed adjusting and I was happy that I had got it just about right. After my change of heart, he would play at Highbury and either Nick Holmes or David Peach would have to go.

After training, I drove to Rhondda in South Wales to speak at the presentation of a Rhondda Recognition Committee plaque to referee Clive Thomas. Frankie Vaughan made the presentation and it was a pleasant evening. Anne was with me, it was a nice change for her. Welsh mining people are like my folk from the North East: I get on well with them. Frankie Vaughan invited me to see his night-club act at a club afterwards but I wanted to get up early the next morning to get back at the Dell in time for training.

Friday, 20 October.

Terry Neill rang and asked if we could call off the reserve game between our clubs at the Dell because of his injuries. He was willing to pay the fine if one was imposed. 'What about your "A" team game, is that off too?' I asked rather pointedly, knowing that it wouldn't be. Arsenal were the big club. They should have enough players to field a reserve side. It would be a disappointment for our players who wouldn't get a game and also for the 1,500 fans we normally get for combination games.

Steve Curry of the *Daily Express* telephoned and said was it true that I'd spoken to Manny Cussins at the Coventry game. I said I couldn't deny it because I had but I didn't want to comment about it. At lunchtime I popped down to the docks to open a warehouse for a new company which had grown immensely in recent years. It was good business for us because the managing director said he would sponsor a game.

Saturday, 21 October.

The sun was shining and it was good to be going to a London ground. There is always an extra excitement about a London match.

Mike Murphy of the BBC called before we left about the back-page lead in the *Daily Express* which said Leeds had made me 'a name your own price' offer. I described it as a typical Saturday morning story, meaning that it had an element of truth but wasn't to be taken seriously. That comment was recorded for 'Football Focus', the pre-match programme.

We stopped for lunch at the Great Northern Hotel at the back of King's Cross Station and I introduced three young lads who were celebrating their birthday, sons of a friend, to the players and let them ride in the coach to the ground. I had to tell Peachy that he wouldn't be playing. He didn't like it but said, 'Fair enough.' On the coach he had to endure some ribbing from MacDougall who said Peachy wouldn't be asking for a move as some players would in these circumstances because he was too much of a Hampshire squire and didn't want to leave.

The match went well for us right up to the eighty-eighth minute. We were the better side and had all the chances. Brady hardly had a kick but near the end Frank Stapleton's shot came off Terry Gennoe and Brady scored. Bally complained to the referee, an ex-Royal Marine named Mike Taylor, that he should have given us a free kick at the other end when Steve Williams was knocked off the ball. Bally was right. It was a bad decision and cost us two points.

The players were fuming in the dressing room: it was such an unjust result. After the criticism Bally and I had received following our remarks about referees the previous week, I told the players not to comment to the press. I decided I wouldn't say anything either. I might get myself into trouble with the authorities.

I'd never seen so many press people in the hallway when I came out. There must have been forty. Some I recognized – Hugh McIlvanney, Jock Stein's friend, Alan Hoby of the *Sunday Express*, and one or two others – but many were fringe people and I never like saying too much to those I don't know. Things can be misconstrued so easily and built up into big headlines. 'I'll leave it up to you, gentlemen,' I said, and went up the stairs to the directors' lounge. David Barnes of the *Sunday People* followed me. 'I want to speak to you about something else,' he said. I realized they didn't want to talk about the game, but the Leeds affair. I was in no mood to talk about anything and walked away to the directors' room.

Neill, who can be smooth at the best of times, came up and said, 'Hard luck.' I felt like saying something about the reserve game being off but choked it back. Terry always has a smile on his face. He has had more luck than most managers. He wasn't doing too well at Hull when Tottenham came in for him and he wasn't doing brilliantly there either when Arsenal appointed him. He'd had a good season the previous season but had his battles with players. Bally was disparaging about him and I never liked that. I wouldn't want an ex-player of mine to criticize me in front of his new manager. I was disappointed to hear afterwards that Terry and Don Howe had been shouting from the bench that Bally had never been anything more than a Central League player. The only time I had ever come into conflict with Neill was two years earlier over the signing of Pat Howard from Newcastle. I had Howard lined up but Terry stepped in and got him first. I thought he went over the top on that one and I told Howard he was making a mistake; I was right because he was sold off to Birmingham not long afterwards.

Along the corridor, Anne and the children had met the American singer Johnny Mathis who was a guest of Arsenal. He came over to me later as though he knew me. 'Have you got it right?' he asked. I wished I had! Anne said she was put out by some of the comments about our players made by partisan visitors who were sitting behind her. That was the risk she ran attending away matches. She would hear a lot of critical remarks. The home team's guests would be particularly loyal and biased. At midweek games, the directors' box has a fair quota of experts, other managers and coaches. But on Saturdays it is full of privileged amateurs, people who don't know the game too well. Some do a lot of talking and others, like Denis Hill-Wood, the Arsenal chairman, usually restrict themselves to comments like 'jolly good game' which won't offend anyone.

I told Anne it was the price she had to pay for an enjoyable day out. It was a Saturday ritual for her, coming to matches. It was also our eighteenth wedding anniversay and when we got home, we celebrated it over dinner with Malcolm Price and his wife, who were celebrating their seventeenth wedding anniversary, and Harry and Doreen Allen, neighbours whose sixteenth anniversary was imminent. After some wine and some lively chat, I began to cheer up.

I never sleep soundly after matches, particularly frustrating results like this one; Christopher had recorded 'Match of the Day' for me and I stayed up until half past two watching it.

Sunday, 22 October.

Anne read out the reports in the Sunday newspapers as we lay in bed. There were several slightly barbed comments about me and I realized I had made a mistake in not talking to the press. They'd been niggled by my attitude. It was a mopey day: I scraped some leaves up in the garden and tried to keep busy.

Any negative thoughts about the Arsenal game evaporated as Alison, fearing her visit to the dentist the next morning, started playing up, even threatening to leave home. She hates going to the dentist! Ordinary family problems like these soon make you forget about where the team is in the table.

Monday, 23 October.

Ted MacDougall came to see me after training. He was a witness in a court case which was starting the next day at Winchester. Bournemouth, one of his earlier clubs, were suing Manchester United for £25,000 which they said was owed after he'd played twenty-five matches in the first team. United's defence was that he had only played eighteen League matches for them so the clause in the transfer agreement didn't apply.

MacDougall also said he was worried about his performances. He thought it was drifting away from him at this level and perhaps it was time to move. He was thirty-two and no longer as sharp as he used to be. He missed chances at Highbury which he would have buried a year or two previously. He said he thought he could be costing us points. I let him talk. The experienced manager will be suspicious of a moment like this. Was he being genuine? Or was there something else? He wasn't ever going to be a reserve player. He either had to be in the side or away. I paid £50,000 for him two years ago and his scoring record was forty-four in ninety games, or one every two games. Last season his fourteen League goals helped us earn promotion. We had had our money's worth from him. He'd been at seven clubs in his time and he was never going to settle. We both knew he would finish up at Bournemouth, where he first made his name. All his business interests were there. 'All right,' I said. 'Leave it for a day or two and I'll see you at the end of the week.'

Tuesday, 24 October.

London Airport to Edinburgh to watch the Under-21 match between Scotland and Norway at Easter Road. I could have gone to the senior match the next day, or to Dublin for England *v.* Eire but I wanted to look at young players, and Narey in particular. He was valued at £300,000 and I wanted to see if he was worth it.

Outside the ground I met Jim Clunie who said he was waiting for his tickets. I said I would see him inside but I never did. Along with Jock Stein, John Greig, Bertie Auld (Partick) and Billy McNeill (Celtic) I was in the directors' box. The lesser managers, Jim among them, were hidden away in the stand. That's typical of Scottish football. Class distinction!

Terry Neill and Wilf Dixon were up from Arsenal. Ian Greaves was there too, and Bobby Moncur of Carlisle. The match was a waste of time. Ally McLeod, an over-age player from Hibs, was the best player on the field and three years ago I was delighted when I sold him to Hibs for £25,000!

Wednesday, 25 October.

Jeffrey Archer had invited me to a lunch at his place on the Albert Embankment. It was being filmed for a television documentary about him and I was pleased to be able to go. I'd given the players a day off at the club.

There was an interesting cross-section of people there, reflecting his varied interests, including Jim Slater, the former financial expert and now children's story writer, Col. Colin Mitchell, 'Mad Mitch' of Aden fame, Peter Cook, the comedian, and Sir Michael Havers, Solicitor-General in the Ted Heath Government and a Shadow Cabinet spokesman in the House of Commons for Legal Affairs.

There was also someone Peter Cook kept calling 'Horace'. 'Horace, what is your attitude to massage parlours in London?' he said. It was then I realized it was Horace Cutler, chairman of the Greater London Council. 'We're trying to clean London up,' said Mr Cutler. 'We're cracking down on the more obvious things like the advertisements outside these places.' Peter Cook replied that he enjoyed massage parlours and thought they served a good purpose. I found him an engaging person. He was obviously a football fanatic. He said he stood on the terraces to watch us play

Spurs in the final match of the previous season. Spurs are his team.

Thursday, 26 October.

I had to choose between Tony Funnell and Trevor Hebberd to take over from MacDougall. Funnell was popular with the crowd. He was quick and scored goals. Hebberd was the better footballer but his goalscoring record wasn't as good so I chose Funnell.

Late in the afternoon Anne rang and said a Yugoslav woman friend of Mrs Golac had been on saying Mrs Golac wanted to see me. I was speaking at a local CID dinner in the evening and didn't want to keep the police waiting. I told Anne to ask them to come round to the house. It was clearly an important matter if she had got her friend to call Anne. It shows how a manager's wife is involved in his life. She is virtually a personal assistant as well as a wife. Mrs Golac was in a state and I sensed that she was ready to quit and go home to Yugoslavia. She wanted to know about the work permit. They didn't have a regular income and life was becoming very difficult.

I calmed her down and said I expected news from the Department of Employment within a week. She went away quite happy but it had taken so long that I was late for the dinner. I spoke and it went reasonably well. The police are vital to a football club and I was pleased to be able to attend. When they sent me the invitation, it was in the form of a summons! The cabaret was a couple of blokes in their forties, a drag act which I found very tame. I can never understand why the organizers of dinners have to hire these people and their blue jokes. I prefer a good comedian any time.

Saturday, 28 October.

Some games get you tingling from the moment you get up. This was one of them, home to Nottingham Forest, the current champions. Cloughie went to Majorca at the start of the week and there was some talk that he wouldn't be back in time but he was. I saw him briefly in the Forest dressing room before the game and said, 'Coming upstairs for a drink?' Managers often pop into my office for a cup of tea before the kick off. Cloughie declined the offer. He was going to shave, he said. A little while later, there was a tap at our dressing room door and a young lad poked his head in and said, 'Mr Clough said could he have two whiskies?' I don't approve of anyone, even Cloughie, drinking in the dressing room and I said, 'You tell Mr Clough if he wants a drink he can go to my office and get one. Now bugger off!' The lad must have got the drinks from the board room because I saw him coming back with two glasses later. The other drink must have been for Cloughie's mate, Peter Taylor. Taylor and Cloughie eventually came up to my office and we had a good chat for ten minutes about the game in general. Cloughie was as relaxed as I have ever seen him.

Cloughie upstaged me because I thought he was on the bench when I walked out. Someone said all the Forest lot had left the dressing room but he overlooked Cloughie. I got a cheer when I emerged and two minutes before kick off there were a few boos which turned into a crescendo of cheers as Cloughie strode along the running track. It was a great welcome but I felt I could have topped it if I had come out after him.

I noticed later that he was quoted in the newspaper as saying that Forest hadn't played well in the 0–0 draw which annoyed me a bit because we had something to do with that. When a smaller club does creditably against a bigger one, it's always said that the big club hasn't played well. But for Peter Shilton we might have snatched it. We had more chances than Forest. All the same it was a good result and put me in good spirits for the mini-break in Spain.

Anne didn't believe we would go until we were actually on our way. I think she felt that if we had a bad result against Forest I would cancel the arrangements. Originally Tommy Lawrence aimed to take us to Nice but we ended up at a smashing hotel in Marbella. The plane was seventy-five minutes late leaving Heathrow which meant we missed our connection in Madrid and we didn't arrive in Marbella until half past five. As we stayed in bed until midday, it meant that half a day was lost but we didn't let that spoil a relaxing two days in the sun.

6. A tug at the heart strings

Almost a third of the season had passed and Southampton's position, though not precarious, wasn't improving. Too many home points were being dropped and when he returned from his brief holiday, McMenemy had to find an experienced striker to replace Ted MacDougall. The snag was that most other clubs were also looking for an experienced striker. It's a cliché of the game: 'If I can just get someone to pop the ball into the net we'll be all right,' says your average football manager. Sometimes it comes off, like when Bob Latchford was signed by Everton. On other occasions, it is not the panacea to cure the club's ills, like when Manchester United paid £500,000 for Joe Jordan.

Southampton didn't have that kind of money and McMenemy had to consider exchanging a player. David Peach, his first signing in 1973, seemed a viable alternative to going into debt and negotiations were opened with Ipswich who had an experienced forward, Trevor Whymark, available. Norwich also wanted Whymark.

A new distraction was looming: Sunderland, the Second Division club, wanted McMenemy as their manager. Jimmy Adamson, their previous manager, joined Leeds and left Roker Park with few regrets on either side. He hadn't moved house from Burnley and the intensely partisan local press hadn't liked that.

Brian Clough was the first choice of both fans and press but, unpredictable as Clough is, there was no prospect of his leaving Nottingham Forest while they were in Europe. The next choice was McMenemy, another Geordie.

Tuesday, 23 October.

When Anne and I arrived back at Heathrow, Fred Scott was supposed to be there to collect us but there was no sign of him. 'Perhaps he went to Terminal 2,' said Anne. But he wasn't there either. Ian Branfoot had brought us up in the Mercedes and I let him go home to Lincoln for the weekend in it, returning to Southampton on Monday. I went to a telephone and rang the Dell. Lew Chatterley said Fred Scott hadn't left. 'He thought you might be staying on another day,' he said. I went barmy. 'You lot couldn't organize a cat's confinement,' I said. Lew said Fred would leave straight away but I replied, 'That's no use. We're not hanging around here all day.'

Furious, I turned to go back to Anne and the luggage when a little, oldish man stopped me and said, 'I'll run you home.' He was a pick-up man, a private-car owner making money from selected clients. 'How much?' I said. 'Sixty quid,' he said. I said I wasn't paying that. 'All right, seeing it's you,' he said, 'make it £40.' I accepted his offer and we went off in his Mercedes. He was good company and it was a pleasant ride down the M3 until a police patrol car stopped us. The man went white. We had been travelling over eighty miles per hour and he was breaking the law in another respect by carrying fare-paying passengers. The policeman was a serious looking type but he recognized me at once. 'It's all right,' I said. 'It's all my fault. He's doing me a favour.' The policeman's attitude changed. 'Seeing as you did such a good job beating Manchester United in the Cup Final you can drive on,' he said with a smile. It was one occasion when I was relieved to be recognized.

A women's international, England *v.* Belgium, was being staged at the Dell in the evening and I promised to attend. Ron Greenwood was also there. The attendance was 6,000, excellent really, and I was surprised by the quality of the play. The match fell away in the second half. Women only play eighty minutes but even that is too long I feel.

Wednesday, 1 November.

Ivan Golac's work permit still hadn't arrived and I contacted the Department of Employment man again. He had more queries.

What were the wages of the players in the first team pool? And could I check the appearances of our younger defenders? I lost my temper. This matter had been dragging on and on. I said I wasn't going to tell him how much my players earned. If he wanted that, he would have to apply to the Football League which has copies of every player's contract. Mr Woodford came in and suggested a compromise. He would tell the Department the wages without revealing which player earned what. That seemed sensible.

David Coleman called with an invitation to visit the BBC box at Ascot that afternoon. It was short notice but I was going to Arsenal *v.* Hajduk Split in the evening and it was on the way. Anne and I arrived in time for the second-to-last race. Some managers, and a good few players, are racing men but I am not. Ascot was impressive and someone else's hospitality box is the ideal way to watch racing.

At Highbury, I commented on the match, a UEFA Cup second round tie, for BBC radio. Arsenal qualified but were lucky, I thought. The Yugoslavs were technically the better players but were beaten by a lob from Arsenal's Willie Young, the last person you would expect to chip the goalkeeper. Willie looks as though he is made of spare parts. He makes countless mistakes, but is very enthusiastic. The 40,000 fans probably went home talking about him whereas they should have been talking about the superior techniques of the Yugoslavs.

This was the match where Liam Brady was sent off. He had been impeded all night and finally he took a swing at his marker. I sympathized with him but you can't do that, especially in European matches. He was later banned for three matches, reduced to two on appeal.

Thursday, 2 November.

For the Manchester United game on Saturday, I decided to play Trevor Hebberd in place of MacDougall because he was better at holding the ball than Funnell. Away from home you don't want to give the ball away. Hebberd is a twenty year old from Alresford, where John Arlott lives. He is a Hampshire lad and the type who makes you think that if you don't keep on at him he would be just as happy playing for the village team.

The board meeting in the afternoon was about the proposed new stadium which was being discussed with the local Council. Land was available near the station for a 40,000 capacity stadium and no firm decision had yet been taken.

In the evening, I watched the Youth team play Redhill in a Youth Cup match at the Dell, a good opportunity to see the younger players. In the dressing room, Ian Branfoot had his players warming up doing bench steps, stepping on and off benches for twenty minutes. It was an idea he picked up from Graham Taylor, Watford's manager, when they were together at Lincoln. It warms the players up but it wouldn't work with a roomful of Osgoods and Balls. You can get away with it with your own players but once you start buying stars problems arise. Star players won't conform to patterns and that is where they become all-powerful in clubs. Keeping the balance is one of the most delicate parts of a manager's job.

Our lads had the right attitude and swamped Redhill. Chris, our eldest son, scored a hat-trick, two from penalties and it was the best match I had seen him play. He still has another season as a youth player and I was pleased with his progress. He could eventually make it as a professional. Having your father as manager is a distinct handicap. There is resentment because you are keeping another player out. Kevin Bond, John Bond's son, made it at Norwich and I admire his father for riding over all the problems and turning his son, not the most naturally gifted of footballers, into a First Division performer. You have to be thickskinned to do it.

Friday, 3 November.

By train to Manchester: we had learned from our experiences on the coach to Everton! At the Post House at Northenden I told Hebberd not to eat too many pork pies because he was in the team. Most footballers would express some excitement about playing at a ground like Old Trafford but Hebberd said, 'I'm starving. I can't wait to eat.'

MacDougall, with his transfer to Bournemouth nearing its completion, was not with the party although I included his name in the squad. I wanted to help him as much as I could and he had sold a story to the *Sunday Mirror*. If too much leaked out in advance, it would ruin the impact of the series.

I was warned that a reporter from a rival newspaper *The Sunday People*, was in the hotel looking for MacDougall. After dinner, I met the reporter in the lobby and I told him off for trying to speak to the players without permission.

Saturday, 4 November.

I didn't give the team talk until we arrived at the ground. Old Trafford is such a splendidly imposing football arena that I felt just being there was enough to stimulate most of the players. One player who wanted to do well was Curran, who was always saying he was a better player than Steve Coppell, the Manchester United winger who was in the England side. I told him, 'Here's your chance to prove your point.'

We played some of our best football of the season and should have led 3–0 at half-time. The referee, Roger Kirkpatrick, said it was his last game at Old Trafford as he was retiring at the end of the season, but he earned no sympathy from me when he allowed Jimmy Greenhoff to score from what I thought was an offside position.

We continued playing well in the second half with one-touch and two-touch football, the way I like to see the game played. Bally missed a chance from six yards and started to pull his jersey off as if to say, 'if I'm not good enough to convert that I'll get off'. The crowd loved it. They responded to our football, applauding our moves. But they were critical of their own side. We equalized and got a point but we deserved to win.

Bally, watched by his father, Alan Ball senior, earned the praise in the press but he was generous. 'When Steve Williams plays like he did today, it's a doddle for me,' he said. Ball senior shook my hand. 'I've never seen your team play better,' he said. I like him. He has the qualities of a successful manager but blew it in this country by trying to ape people like Malcolm Allison. He had been critical of his son for going to Southampton instead of to a bigger club but that is his style. He is abrasive, like his son.

Listening to United being booed off made me realize the pressures on Dave Sexton, United's manager. Before the match his team were sixth in the table but the crowd were dissatisfied. He said he was concerned about some of the things Lou Macari had been saying in his column in *The Sun*. When Macari arrived later,

he called him over. I doubted the wisdom of that. Right after a
match, especially one like this, wasn't the best time to discuss such
matters. Lou Macari was a senior player, an influential player. But
that is something you have to admire about Dave Sexton: his single
mindedness and his strength of character. He is strong both physic-
ally and mentally and wouldn't be deterred by a player's reputation.
If he was sufficiently roused, you could see him being almost brutal.
His father was a boxer who had bottle and Dave has a similar tem-
perament.

Tommy Docherty's libel case against Willie Morgan and
Granada was about to start in the High Court and a lot of bad publicity about the club would dominate the news pages. It was a bad
time for Sexton but he was standing up to it well.

Louis Edwards, the United Chairman, was filling everyone's glass
up with champagne. United are that kind of club, the Ritz of football
clubs. As we prepared to leave, Les Olive, United's secretary, asked
if we could give a friend a lift back. It was a little man with a big
cigar. On the coach I discovered he was Cyril Lord, the former car-
pet king who now lives in Barbados. He was entertaining company,
a big name-dropper.

Monday, 6 November.

With the League Cup tie at Reading on Wednesday, it was going
to be a hard week but it started with a change of routine: a lecture
on management at the police college at Hartley Wintney. The college was a bit formal and stuffy but my speech went over reasonably
well. I knew the fee would only be nominal and told the inspector
who asked me about my expenses to stick the money in the kitty
and buy everyone a drink. 'Can't do that,' he said. 'It's Home Office
regulations.'

I made another speech at night at the South East Counties League
dinner in London. Some of the earlier speeches had dragged on and
I could see John Cobbold, the former Ipswich chairman and present
director, getting agitated. He prefers drinking to listening to
speeches. Alec Stock spoke and admitted afterwards that he hadn't
done too well. I had one or two serious points which I intended
to make but edited them out in favour of a more light-hearted
approach. One was about managers who criticize other managers
but noticing John Bond, sitting on a Norwich table, I thought it

might be too pointed. He seemed to be ignoring me anyway, turning his back as I spoke. I had a dig at the press coverage of the Mac-Dougall affair, relating how one newspaper said MacDougall went because he had a row with me over not marking Liam Brady at Arsenal. 'Ted can't even mark a race card,' I said.

MacDougall's transfer went through earlier in the day and I was disappointed that the only comment from John Benson, the Bournemouth manager, was 'I can't understand why Southampton let him go on a free but I'm not complaining.' I thought he might have thanked me. He was getting a good player for nothing.

Tuesday, 7 November.

Mr Woodford said, 'Could you help me? Some of the more senior directors think they are not being informed of what is happening at the club.' I knew what had upset them. At the last meeting the only item on the agenda was the new stadium and when I was asked about the team, I replied, 'There's nothing to report,' and walked out. They may have felt that was a snub. I told the chairman I would make a report at Thursday's meeting to satisfy them.

The reserves played Arsenal reserves at night, the game that had been cancelled. It was no contest. We won easily. About 2,000 people, above average, turned out probably because Arsenal had one or two name players in their side, including Malcolm Macdonald who was recovering from a third cartilage operation.

Tony Funnell, our centre-forward, was bouncing about, full of cockiness, but Macdonald, who had done it all in his career, hadn't time to be cocky. He was limping and should have come off in the second half but the substitute was already on. I went to see him in the dressing room afterwards. His knee was swollen and I felt very sorry for him. Comments like 'keep smiling' seemed totally inappropriate. He told me the shape of his leg – his leg is much more bowed than most footballers' – wasn't helping his recovery.

Wednesday, 8 November.

Reading in the League Cup. It was their Wembley and we knew it would be a test of character. All the hotels in the area were full and we couldn't book in for our normal lie in. We had tea and toast at the Post House and wouldn't have made it to the ground in time but for a police escort. The teams have to be handed in thirty minutes before kick off otherwise the League imposes a fine.

The game went as I predicted, not much football, few incidents, and ended goalless. We never looked like winning, nor did we look like losing. I had a go at some of the players afterwards, particularly the front three. I told them, 'You were as limp as lettuces.' That upset Phil Boyer and he came back rather aggressively at me which was unusual for him. 'You ought to be looking for someone else then,' he said and I replied, 'Don't think it hasn't crossed my mind!' Everyone is very touchy straight after a game.

Thursday, 9 November.

The fifth round draw paired the winners against Manchester City at home. If we won the replay it would mean that Mike Channon, the costliest player Southampton ever sold, would be back at the Dell.

In the afternoon the club's annual meeting took place and about fifteen shareholders turned up. You never get big meetings. With promotion, it had been a good, profitable year, and I was thanked for my loyalty in turning down the Leeds job. I knew all that business about going or staying would soon be back because the North East newspapers were full of speculation about the Sunderland job. Cloughie had been put up but, after a week of headlines, he said he was remaining at Nottingham Forest.

Friday, 10 November.

The first unofficial approach from someone at Sunderland, not the club. What could I say? For a Geordie it was a job that tugged at the heart strings. It was unsettling being connected with all these jobs. This one, however, was different. It had to be given serious consideration. Sunderland had all the things Southampton lacked: a big stand, all the trappings and a passionate crowd. There was only one way Sunderland could go and that was upwards.

Saturday, 11 November.

We threw away another point as we let Norwich make it 2-2 near the end. It was a drab game and a thoroughly miserable day. The crowd hadn't got involved and I didn't enjoy it.

Sunday, 12 November.

Mr Woodford called at the house. Sunderland had made an official approach. He was wanting me to say I wasn't interested but I couldn't say that. He said that if I was adamant about seeing their directors he could call a board meeting to discuss the situation properly.

The depression of yesterday was relieved somewhat when we went to the Vaudeville Golf Society at the Park Lane Hotel in London. The first year I spoke at the Society I was petrified with the thought of speaking in front of professionals. But this time I enjoyed it. Their business is much the same as ours. We were late home at half past three in the morning.

Monday, 13 November.

Mr Woodford called again. I hummed and hahed. I said I was heartily sick of the whole affair but wanted to see what Sunderland had to offer. My original contract, which still had five years to run, had two and a half years remaining and though the amounts had been changed, the original contract was the same. Perhaps I needed a new one.

At the ground the players didn't say anything. I was hoping Bally would just have a bath and go home. He looked weary on Saturday and needed a rest. But he was one of the first players changed and was soon out training.

I called Bobby Robson to ask about players. I detected he might be clearing a few out after reading some of his comments in the papers: 'If this continues, either they'll go or I go,' he had said. He told me Norwich were interested in Trevor Whymark and Whymark, who was valued at £150,000, was also wanted by Vancouver Whitecaps, the Canadian club managed by Tony Waiters which Robson used to coach.

Tuesday, 14 November.

Tim Neale, the new head of Radio Solent, came up with his sports reporter, Ian Henderson, to talk about radio coverage. I told them I thought there should be more personalized interviews with players. He agreed.

We went to the social club next to the ground for a sandwich at lunchtime, a place I rarely visit because I don't normally eat much at lunchtime. I'm too busy. I have tea and a piece of toast for breakfast and a big meal when I get home at night. Anne loves cooking and baking and I probably eat too much at the wrong time of day. When I first came to Southampton I used to have a training routine which I did with Ted Bates, running and jogging and kicking a ball about in the gym but, with so many other things to do, I never seemed to have time for it now. I had to watch my weight. I was about half a stone over.

There was a new steward in the social club and his wife told me a man had rung with a message, 'Tell Lawrie whatever Sunderland are offering him, I'll make up the difference.' She asked whether it was true that Whymark might be coming and that Peach might be going. All the members were talking about it. I was amazed. I'd told hardly anybody and it made me wonder whether anyone standing under my new office could hear me talking on the phone. The office was built above a turnstile and I could hear the turnstile clicking on match days. Perhaps they could also hear me.

Though it was a match day, I promised the man in charge of an old folks home at Bitterne that I would come along to talk to the residents. It had started some months earlier when an old lady wrote in saying she wanted to meet me. Sadly, she had died but they still wanted me to visit them. It was one of the first homes of its kind, catering for old people who get depressed and need company. There is one rule: no television. They can watch that at home. The idea is to get them talking together. These old ladies were wearing their red and white rosettes and they'd made a big cake with 'Welcome Lawrie' on it. I was late but was glad I was able to make it.

Most of them were in their eighties. One old fellow was very smartly dressed; I was told he had been in the Diplomatic Service and had been everywhere. I said I had just come back from Spain. 'I was there too,' he said. I named a few cities. 'Seville?' 'No, not Seville.' 'Madrid?' 'No, not Madrid.' Then he suddenly remembered: 'It was Singapore.' I tried to have a word with all of them but there was one woman who never said a word. 'What about you, love?' I said. She screwed her face up and put her tongue out!

I missed the pre-match meal with the players and went straight

to the ground for the replay against Reading. Maurice Evans, the
Reading manager, was in a dilemma because there was no mention
of bonuses in the players' contracts for replays and he wanted my
advice. Bonuses should be set out before a season starts otherwise
the more important a game, the more money a club could offer.
In some countries it's possible for bonuses to be agreed for indivi-
dual games but not in England. The League are very strict on
bonuses, and rightly so.

We beat Reading 2–0 and it was pleasing to be in the last eight
but we were rather a shambles in the second half. In the press room,
the reporters were more interested in hearing my views about Sunderland's offer than any comments on the match and I gave them
a long statement explaining my feelings. 'I'll be making a decision
in the next two days because it's not fair to keep them waiting about,'
I said.

Wednesday, 15 November.

A wet, miserable day, one of the first bad days of the autumn.
Reporters were phoning early about Sunderland but I couldn't say
anything. A board meeting had been called for two o'clock at a Winchester hotel and though Winchester, a lovely old town, is only four
miles up the road I didn't know the location of the hotel. I finished
up going along a one-way road and as I turned round, I saw Ted
Bates at the other end of the street. He started to run towards me
as though he thought I was changing my mind about coming. I
stopped for him and he guided me into the old stagecoach yard next
to the very old hotel. It was the most important meeting of my five
years at the club but all he could say was, 'That bloody goalkeeper's
timing has got to be suspect, hasn't it?' I said, 'Ted, you are unbelievable.' The meeting was about whether I was going to stay and
all he could talk about was Terry Gennoe.

All the directors were present, even Lt Col. Sir George Meyrick
(Bart), MC, TD who is sometimes absent. I explained that there was
a lot for me to think about. I knew the Sunderland directors and
knew what they wanted to do. It was my kind of club and I had
to think of security for my family. I reminded them that when we
were promoted I got better terms but the length of the contract
remained unchanged. One of the directors had said at the time, 'For
that sort of money we should keep it at the same period.' In other

words, he was saying they didn't want to pay me up a large sum if I was sacked. It was a negative thought.

Mr Bowyer, a gentleman type of director – well, they all are at the Dell – said, 'My grandfather used to have a saying "contentment before riches".' I said, 'That's very nice but your grandfather was never booed by 25,000 people, was he?'

We talked about how the club was going. I said I felt we were in the top twelve, the younger players would get better and, if the new stadium went ahead, there was tremendous scope for us all. I looked round. I was surrounded by friendly, intelligent faces who were swaying me their way. But I also knew that if I had been sitting in the Sunderland boardroom at this moment, the pull would be just as strong, or even stronger.

The meeting broke up without a decision but I suspected they would be coming back to me with an offer. I went home at five o'clock and at six Mr Woodford and Guy Askham knocked on the door. 'We would like you to stay and if you do, we would like you to sign a long-term contract,' said Mr Woodford. 'How long?' I asked. 'Eight years,' said Mr Woodford. It shook me. That would take me up to the age of fifty. I said, 'I don't know if I'll live long enough to see fifty.'

After they left, I rang Keith Collings, the Sunderland chairman, to tell him I wouldn't be coming to Roker Park. It was difficult to persuade him. He wanted me to fly up and talk and I knew if I did that it would re-open all the doubts. He was very convincing but I wouldn't alter my decision. 'They've been good to me in good times and bad,' I said. 'I've got to be fair with them. They've been fair to me.' I would be sticking it out with Southampton. No more offers! John Bond had just signed a nine-year contract with Norwich, taking him up to fifty-five, pensionable age with the Association. I thought about releasing the news about my new contract and then decided not to.

Thursday, 16 November.

Bally was in Fred Scott's office in his best suit. His eyes were red ringed and it looked as though he'd been up all night. I had him in my adjoining office and he started moaning and groaning about things. 'They're not playing with me any more,' he said. 'I'm presenting myself for the ball and Nick Holmes and Steve Williams aren't giving it to me. I was so bad on Saturday that I've banned my wife from coming.'

At Reading Bally had a go at Trevor Hebberd and Hebberd told him to f. off and I knew that had upset him. I was beginning to think I was making a big mistake promoting Hebberd. The arrogance was coming out in him and here he was after a handful of games insulting the club's most experienced player.

By now Bally was crying. 'That Nick Holmes, I can't understand him,' he said. 'I've always sat next to him in the dressing room and bossed him around. He's never said a word. But, now I'm older and mellowed a bit, he isn't taking any notice of me. He must think he's good enough now and doesn't need me.' Bally needs people a lot more at times than they need him. The worst thing that could happen to him would be to be left on his own. This is probably why he is such a good family man. 'You're carrying a knock,' I said. 'You're not doing yourself justice.' The phone rang. It was Bill Shankly, a long-time admirer of Bally. We chatted briefly about Sunderland and then I said, 'Here, talk to this fella,' and handed the phone to Bally.

Bally's eyes sparkled. I went out and left him to it. Shankly was the best medicine the little man could have. There was another reason for Ball's mood. He had received a letter from the FA asking him to give his views on allegations in his book that he had taken money offered by Don Revie when Revie was manager of Leeds and Ball was a player with Blackpool. When I came back, Shankly had rung off and we talked about a request Bally had received from Alan Mullery for a statement saying when Bally played in Mullery's testimonial match he hadn't been paid a fee but to give some indication of what it would have been. Mullery was appealing to the tax commissioners and it would be vital evidence. Bally said he wanted to help an old friend but I suggested he see one of the directors with knowledge of tax because this was a dicey area. Ball had troubles of his own with the taxman.

It was a day for sorting out the problems of the players. Holmes was the next one in my office. He said he wanted to apologize for shouting at me on the bench the night before. I'd shouted something and he had said, 'Shut your mouth.' At the time I thought he was talking to someone else on the bench. 'It was sheer frustration,' he said. I told him what Ball had said and he promised to go and see

Bally and sort it out. 'Use him,' I said. 'He's still a great player who can help you.'

Boyer was the third player in the queue. He came to remind me about the £100 which was owed him on his contract and we agreed it would be kept in reserve to cover his fines. We spoke about the ruck after the Reading match and he didn't take the opportunity to apologize. The incident showed me what made him tick. He was a lad with a smile on his face but you would never put your arm round him as you would Ball. The warmth you had for him didn't go that deep. Downstairs, Bally had put his arm round Peach and Peach said, 'What's come over him?' I said, 'He's downhearted, that's all.'

I was supposed to see the press at half past eleven to give the locals my reasons for turning down Sunderland but these inter-ruptions, plus several attempts to reach Bobby Robson, made me an hour late and I had to apologize.

Ian Henderson said something about the lads missing their deadlines, which upset me. 'I have a job to do,' I said. He said there were plenty of quotes in the national papers but the locals couldn't get my number. 'And you're not getting it,' I said. 'Your lot have rung me up at six in the morning and I'm not having that.'

When I eventually got hold of Robson, he said Whymark was dithering about Vancouver. Robson wasn't interested in Peach. I thought he might fancy a swap, maybe Mick Mills. When there is trouble in the camp, it's often a good thing to move a few out and try new people.

Foolishly, I had agreed to speak at Durham Technical College on the Friday before our game at Middlesborough, and Anne and I were driven to London Airport to catch a half-past-five flight. 'Foolishly' because I had let myself in for a hectic time in the very area where I had been in the headlines all the week, the North East. Eddie Doole, the treasurer of Bishop Auckland, fixed it all up and he'd arranged a whistle-stop tour including a visit to his factory, Smart and Brown. He even had a television camera crew at his house. After a meal we went to the local for a drink and normally that would be a pleasure but now everyone wanted to talk and shake my hand. I felt shattered.

Friday, 17 November.

The Technical College lecture had been given the year before by
Chay Blyth, the yachtsman, and Chay had turned down the chance
to tour the factory. Sensible fellow! It was most exhausting. Everyone wanted to talk about Sunderland and I must have signed
hundreds of autographs. Football is the religion up there and they
never stop talking about it.

Over lunch with the executives, my head was pounded about football and one particular man, very high up, got me going when he
said he didn't rate England's right-back. I knew he'd never seen
Phil Neal play except on television. 'All right,' I said, 'who would
you have, the Arsenal right-back?' 'Yes, I'd have him in front of
Neal,' he said. 'Well, he's an Irishman, Pat Rice.' 'Oh, in that case
I'd have yours.' 'He's a Yugoslav,' I replied. After lunch, there was
another tour, more handshakes, more photographs, more interviews. When we eventually got back to Eddie's house, Anne said,
'You look grey.' I felt it. I dropped off to sleep. Not for long, however, because Eddie's daughter wanted to see me before we went
off to the College. I wanted to arrive as late as possible but Eddie
had us programmed to arrive at half past six to meet everyone. By
now I was appreciating what pressures there were on the Queen
when she went on tours.

The audience of five hundred had some familiar faces and after
my address a man came up to me and said, 'Thanks for what you
said about my brother, Bobby Robson.' Robson is a Geordie, so
are Brian Clough and Bob Paisley.

I was asked about the Tommy Docherty case. Docherty withdrew
from his libel case in the High Court the day before after admitting
he had told 'a pack of lies'. I felt sympathy for Docherty. He may
have slipped up in some areas but in the world of football that is
easy to do. His quick repartee and damning remarks about people
weren't challenged in football but in the High Court he was laying
himself open to penetrating interrogation from some of the finest
minds in the country. Football managers aren't educated people.
We aren't trained for management, for making speeches, for being
businessmen. We pick it up. We are hoisted into a situation where
we have to compete with people who gained their education at the
right end of their lives. Docherty was ill-advised to go to court.
There were a lot of people waiting to attack him, like Pat Crerand,

his former assistant at Manchester United. I told the audience that the Doc was the kind of manager who would do well at Roker Park. Sunderland was like Manchester United. The passion of the crowd hurled the team forward. Docherty understands that passion. He fuelled it.

We had dinner with more executives at the County Hotel in Durham – a fine meal because they had an award-winning chef – before we joined the team at their hotel. I fell asleep in the car.

Saturday, 18 November.

Anne stayed in our room. She was apprehensive about being with the team but I told her not to worry. The match against Middlesborough was disappointing, a small crowd and two bad goals in our 2–0 defeat. During a lull in play Micky Burns, who scored one of the goals, shouted at me, 'We've read nothing else in the papers about what's happening with you this week.'

We went by coach to Darlington where we picked up the train to London. Brighton were on board and I asked Alan Mullery about Peter Ward, his young striker who was out of the side. 'I've just kicked his backside,' he said. 'He'll be back soon. We won't be selling him.'

7. Charlie George

December is often a bad month for football managers: the players are getting mentally tired; pitches are heavier; spectator interest dies as Christmas approaches. But for Lawrie McMenemy, December 1978 was one of the best months of his career. December usually is a good month for him but this one was special. His team knocked out Manchester City in the quarter finals of the League Cup to reach the last four for the first time in the club's history and the confidence that gave the team lifted them to the middle of the table.

And after a long-drawn-out transfer, twenty-two days in all, he signed his star player, twenty-eight-year-old Charlie George. Charlie is a latter-day Peter Osgood, immensely skilled, one of the best strikers of the ball in the game and a personality who invites a love-hate relationship from fans. But for all his ability, Charlie had played only seventy-seven minutes football at international level. The impression held by many people was that he hadn't done his talents justice.

He was controversial in his behaviour and some managers were wary of handling him. That made him McMenemy's type of player: someone who with the right prompting and help could at last fulfil himself. As a schoolboy, Charlie had been a rebel, ultimately being expelled from school, but marriage and parenthood had matured him. His career was ready for a good manager to exploit.

Monday, 20 November.

Another meeting with Council officials at the Guildhall about the proposed new stadium. The councillors, including the vice-chairman, John Deacon, who was also chairman of Portsmouth FC, seemed keen to go ahead. In the evening I had arranged a meeting with local school teachers who were concerned with schools football and about a hundred turned up at the Social Club, a good response. I told them that too many boys were picked on size and strength and that many who might have skill were lost because they were considered too small and frail. Boys' football had become far too competitive too early. I said when my own boys were playing in Sunday morning leagues I discovered that it was a shouting contest between the rival sets of parents, urging their sons on. There should be less competition and more emphasis on skill as there is on the Continent, with small-sided games to give everyone a kick. Abroad, boys are attached to professional clubs much earlier than they are in England where the signing age is fourteen and this is an idea we could copy. Often boys had developed bad habits by the time they were fourteen. With professional clubs, lads could receive expert advice far earlier. I would be willing to take groups myself.

The reaction from the teachers was encouraging but there is always someone who wants to knock your arguments down and a Northerner who disagreed with me interrupted and said, 'That's all right but what about the useless ones? There are plenty of those in a class.' I related my experiences gained while coaching spastic children to prove that it was possible to coach any boy, whatever his ability or state of fitness.

Tuesday, 21 November.

I had all the first team squad in the dressing room at half past six, an hour before the kick-off against Aston Villa and really laid into them. I said we had gone down without a fight at Middlesborough but I exempted the senior players, Ball, Boyer and Nicholl. Everyone knew that I was trying to buy players. I was kidding myself if I was holding out for class players who weren't available anyway. What I needed now was ordinary players and there were plenty of those about. I hardly mentioned Villa, except to say they were a good away side. I got up and left and didn't return until ten minutes before the start to remind them of one or two tactical points.

We murdered Villa. The score was 2–0 but it could have been far more. Bally missed a penalty. He nipped in ahead of Peachy, the usual penalty taker, and the referee held him up because he said

some players were encroaching. Bally picked the ball up and put
it down again to occupy himself but it was a long delay and Jimmy
Rimmer, who was a team mate of his at Arsenal and knew him well,
dived to make a fine save. I blamed the referee. The ref. shouldn't
have delayed it. If someone was encroaching, he had the power to
make Bally take it again if he failed to score. By taking so long he
had penalized us unfairly.

Wednesday, 22 November.

Jim Mossop of the *Sunday Express*, who was down for the match,
stayed on to do an interview. I never mind doing it but as Lew Chatterley reminded me, whenever anyone has written a favourable piece
on a Sunday we usually get a bad result.

On the way to the ground I called in at a garage in Chandlers
Ford to do a deal with my father-in-law's car, trading it in for a
four-year-old Marina. He is an ex-mechanic, now retired, and he
and his wife have done Anne and me many favours in the past like
looking after the children when we were away and I wanted to repay
him by paying the difference. He was overjoyed. I like giving but
I don't like the slushy bit afterwards.

The BBC and Southern Television were each paying a third of
the cost of a new television gantry at the ground and there was a
meeting with STV executives to finalize it. They were pleased that
ITV had won an exclusive three-year contract for televising League
football at the BBC's expense but I told them the way the deal had
been negotiated smelt a bit. In my view, BBC were streets ahead
of them in presentation. They said it would benefit Southern
because they would be able to increase their coverage of our
matches. Up to this stage of the season, they had televised only three
matches in the area.

We entered a team selected by the players in the *Daily Express*
five-a-side championships at Wembley but I didn't go because I
remembered that Watneys were making a presentation of a thousand cans of beer for the backroom people at the Dell who had
helped with the promotion effort the season before. I told the Wat-
ney managing director, 'I'll have to sign up a few of our 1976 Cup
Final team to help us get through it all.' The packed audience in
the Social Club understood the joke.

Thursday, 23 November.

I had Nick Holmes in to my office for a talk. I said I wasn't happy at the way he ran back to the centre circle shaking his fist after scoring against Villa. He hadn't been playing well and now he was doing extravagant things like that. He said it hadn't meant anything. 'I was just frustrated,' he said.

I asked, 'After a while the manager can't say anything new to his players because they've heard it all before. Is it that? Is the magic wearing off?' 'No,' he said, 'it isn't that. You're still the boss.' David Peach was next in for a chat. I told him I thought he was far too casual in his training and he was amazed. I said he was still a nice fellow but he wasn't putting enough into his work. He said, 'I'll go away and consider it and, if I agree, I'll start working harder.'

The club doctors arrived and we discussed the re-organization of the medical side which meant the younger one, Dr Lawrence, working more closely with me. If a player had been given tablets I wanted to know because it could affect him in training.

The talk with the doctors made me late for a board meeting but the directors understood. I reported that I had made no progress towards getting new players. The only chance of getting a player was to make an offer the other club couldn't refuse. I said Trevor Whymark had signed for Vancouver Whitecaps but I lost interest anyway after I heard that he had a bad knee.

That night I spoke to parents at the King Edward Grammar School. It was my fourth successive night out.

Friday, 24 November.

My secretary made out a list of people I had to see on the trip to Leeds for the game at Elland Road: Yorkshire cricketer Geoff Cope, Bobby Kennedy, the former Bradford City manager, Stafford Heginbotham, the former chairman of Bradford City, Geoffrey Port; the list seemed endless. It was coincidence that last week I was in the North East after my rejection of the Sunderland offer and now I would be at Leeds, the other job I turned down.

Before I left, Arthur Cox, the manager of Chesterfield, asked me if I could mention his name at Sunderland. People in football are always asking you to put their names up for jobs. It's nice to be in a position to help.

Saturday, 25 November.

The Leeds players were very friendly. Trevor Cherry, Paul Hart and David Harvey all came up to shake hands and it went through my mind that they had been well brought up. They wouldn't have been hard to manage.

Ray Illingworth, the former England cricket captain, was there and he said, 'I was hoping you'd be coming up here to join us.' I had to find a few extra tickets for the people I had invited but that wasn't the problem. Often players didn't need their quota. One of my guests was Edward Reaveley, a man of seventy-five who was a director at Gateshead when I was there. We had kept in touch all these years.

As he comes from Yorkshire, Terry Curran wanted more tickets than the rest of the team put together and we were able to scrape enough together for him. He asked permission to drive up the night before to stay with his folks and I granted it. When he joined the team he was wearing his John Travolta outfit. He was only the substitute but he was looking more flash than anyone else and the lads were laughing at him.

I was becoming more and more disenchanted with Curran. He was a cheap buy but he wasn't doing anything for us. He's not nasty but his attitude annoyed me. He made a point of mixing more with the Balls and MacDougalls and called the other players 'son' though he wasn't much older than they were.

I decided to put him on when we were losing 4–0 – we had been totally outclassed, humiliated almost – and he went through a showy warm up as if to say, 'Look out, here comes a star.' When he went on he got the ball in a corner and, with Frankie Gray backing off, proceeded to put his knee on the ball. I put my head in my hands. If we had been winning 4–0 it might have been a good thing to do but not when we were losing 4–0! When he next came near the dug-out I gave him a right volley but it had no effect. I made my mind up that he would be away from the club by Christmas. That kind of fannying about was no use to us in our position. I was still ranting and raving about it in the dressing room afterwards and I asked him why he'd done it. 'To show control,' he said. Peter Osgood was in the dressing room at the time, just recovering from an ankle injury. I pointed in his direction: 'That fellow could play better than you on one leg,' I said.

Our players were scared stiff of Leeds and hadn't competed. Tony Currie was brilliant, scoring the best goal against us all season when he got the ball about thirty yards out on the left, took it past a defender and, with another defender in front of him, directed a viciously bending right foot shot past Terry Gennoe. Currie led the applause himself which was excusable but I hadn't liked the way he tried to take the mick out of one of our defenders earlier after being fouled.

Great players like Bobby Charlton and Franz Beckenbauer get up and walk away disdainfully but there are players of a certain type, such as Osgood and Stan Bowles, who make uncalled-for gestures. Professionals are all in it together and no-one likes to have this done to him.

The response from the Leeds directors afterwards was as friendly as that of the players and supporters. Manny Cussins, the chairman, pinched my cheek affectionately. He appears to be a nice, harmless old man though Brian Clough said otherwise! I envied the facilities, the training ground at the back, the superb organization.

Jimmy Adamson spoke about the pressure he felt at Sunderland and told a story to illustrate it. Dave Merrington, his assistant, took his children to be introduced to their new school and the Head-master suddenly said, 'I wasn't too happy about the way the team played on Saturday.' He meant it too.

I didn't join the team for a meal on the train back. I sat alone for most of the time. A defeat of this nature was a new low in the season. I thought back to what Lew Chatterley had said about giving interviews to Sunday newspapermen.

Monday, 27 November.

The first of the new twice-weekly doctor's surgeries was held and Steve Williams soon proved its worth. He hadn't been sleeping well because of sinus trouble which was causing him to cough in the night. Arrangements were made for him to have a minor operation, cauterizing the inside of his nose.

Alan Ball came to my office. He was anxious to see that I wasn't too downhearted about Saturday's result. He said he was talking to Trevor Cherry afterwards and Trevor was impressed with the way we'd stuck at it. 'The last team we beat 4–0, Derby, packed it in after half-time,' he said. I told Ball, 'Packing it in is the least of our problems.' After he'd gone, I reflected that it was a thoughtful gesture on his part. Usually it is the other way round: the manager has to cheer the players up. A local travel company had come up with a good offer of a trip to Marbella and I decided to accept for sixteen people, fourteen players and two staff. It would be a reward for all the hard work the players had put in.

The immediate priority, though, was buying a forward. There were four players I thought might be available: John Deehan of Aston Villa, who had been mentioned in transfer talk most of the season; Mike Ferguson of Coventry; Charlie George of Derby; and Peter Kitchen of Orient. I'd known Kitchen at Doncaster. He was on the transfer list but wasn't the type I wanted. He was too much like Phil Boyer, a forward who played off the centre-forward. Ferguson was more the type. He had scored seventeen goals in thirty League matches for Coventry the previous season but was out of the side. I rang Gordon Milne, the Coventry manager, and asked what the position was about Ferguson. In the past, Coventry had to let players go to balance the books. Gordon, one of the game's solid, dependable types, said, 'We're not desperate for money.' Jimmy Hill is a much maligned figure but, as Coventry's managing director, he's done a good job at Highfield Road. Coventry are a well-run club. Milne said if they did let Ferguson go, it would be for a huge amount, in the £400,000 region. Ferguson wasn't too unhappy at the moment. 'If he gets upset and you have to sell, let me know,' I said.

Tuesday, 28 November.

The reserve game against QPR had been called off so we played a practice match of first team against the reserves. I didn't give the players a lecture about Saturday. I said, 'Let's go out and have a good game and work it out of your systems.' The first team played well, creating a lot of chances all but one of which they missed, proving again that we needed a class striker.

Chris Nicholl, who had probably had his worst game of the season at Leeds, was away with Northern Ireland in Bulgaria. It wasn't a good time for him to be away. After training, there was a queue of players to see me. Manny Andruszewski was first. I guessed what he was going to say. Before the last board meeting he handed me a letter which I hadn't opened. I knew it was a transfer request.

'I know how frustrating it is for you but I can't let you go,' I told him. He's an honest lad. He said, 'I don't want to go really. This is my only club and I like it here. I want to stay.' He meant 'stay and be in the first team' which wasn't so simple.

David Peach was the next to knock. 'I've been thinking about what you said, and you're dead right,' he said. 'I'd be a fool to leave.' He had four years remaining on his contract and, with a further year added on, he would qualify for a testimonial. He said he wanted it in the papers that he was staying. 'But no-one has said you're leaving,' I said. The only paper that hinted that he might be transferred was the *Echo* so I said I would ask Peter East to put a line in.

The next player in was Terry Curran, as I expected. He was very sensible, accepting that it hadn't worked out for him. 'I fancy going to America,' he said. 'Any chance of a loan in the summer?' I said loans were out but added, 'I'll put the word around that you want a club over there.' We should be able to get our money back.

Ivan Golac's housing problem was still with us. I was getting sick and tired of it. He expected us to provide a house for him on a permanent basis. I had to tell him that he had to take out a mortgage himself but we would give him the necessary advice. It wasn't him so much; his wife, who didn't speak a word of English, was on at him.

Wednesday, 29 November.

England were playing Czechoslovakia in a friendly at Wembley. I was going anyway, but the BBC asked me to assist with comments on radio which I always enjoy doing. I took Lew Chatterley and Ian Branfoot with me and had to apply to the FA for tickets for them. They sent us back £8 tickets behind a goal. When Don Revie was England manager, the FA used to give complimentaries to managers. Perhaps it was overdone then but things had swung back too far the other way. A First Division club shouldn't have its representatives stuck behind a goal.

Before and after the match, I attended a function at the Wembley Conference Centre arranged by Ranjit Anand. His functions used to be looked on as places where any self-respecting football person ought not to be seen. People like Stan Flashman, the ticket tout, would go but attitudes seem to have changed; the England manager and his players attend and so do most League managers: it's become legitimate. Members of the public pay a fair sum to mingle with the celebrities and it is a successful formula. I sat next to Jimmy Tarbuck, whom I rate the funniest funny man of the lot.

I forgot that I was due to speak on the quarter to seven sports news on Radio two and had to rush upstairs at the stadium, just getting to the radio point as Peter Jones was in the middle of his piece. Peter introduced me as 'an out-of-breath Lawrie McMenemy'.' As a car-radio listener, I hear Peter Jones, Alan Parry and Bryon Butler a lot. They are all distinctive voices and good professionals. Your respect for them increases when you are actually working with them and experiencing the same pressures. Whereas the television people are served a cold buffet and drinks, the radio men only get a plastic cup of coffee. They have to keep talking even when there is nothing to talk about. The danger, as I found, is that you can be too flippant, too critical. You try to be as honest as you can but there is a need to be guarded.

England won 1–0 but the Czechs played all the football. In the reception area where the managers and officials meet afterwards I saw Ron Greenwood and he wasn't kidding himself about the game. England had been lucky to win. 'The Czechs played the way they were facing,' he said.

On a frozen pitch that was the only way to play. Kevin Keegan, England's captain, looked completely washed out. As I talked with him later (about babies because his wife Jean had just had their first child) I wondered whether he was doing too much. He was rushing around doing commercial things and it must have taken it out of him.

I chatted with Phil Woosnam, the Commissioner of the North American Soccer League, about our experiences together on an FA coaching course in the early sixties. He said now was the time for managers to go to America. 'If you wait too long it will be too late,' he said. I didn't necessarily agree with him.

Ray Clemence, who had lost his place to Peter Shilton, was with Phil Neal. They are two players who impress me in their manner and their appearance. The Liverpool players are all good ambassadors for their club and these two are about the best. I made some remark about Shilton having a fine game and then wished I hadn't.

Ron Atkinson, looking more subdued than usual, talked about his trip to Germany to look at artificial pitches. I brought up the subject of Willie Johnston who wanted a transfer and wasn't in the team. I knew that Ron was keen to get Charlie George and that Ally Brown was mentioned in a part-exchange. We boxed around the subject.

Thursday, 30 November.

A good morning's work-out. We didn't have enough players to make changes and I named the same squad for Saturday's game against Birmingham. At lunchtime I opened a show house for Laing Properties at Netley, autographed some balls, posed for pictures and drove back to the Dell to meet Mr Woodford. I said the need for a new player was urgent and he agreed wholeheartedly. Somehow the money would be found.

Friday, 1 December.

I rang Tommy Docherty at home at half past eight in the morning about Charlie George. Mary Brown, whom he lived with, said he was still asleep. 'Is it urgent?' she asked. She said he had been at a function the night before. Like Brian Clough, Tommy Doc speaks at a lot of dinners in the North. 'Hang on,' said Mrs Brown; 'he's just woken.' I told him that I was interested in Charlie George and he said that WBA had been talking about an exchange deal but nothing really had happened. 'It's up to the boy,' he said. 'If he wants to go, then that's that.' We arranged to talk later in the day.

At the ground, what had started off as a good idea on Monday, the trip to Spain, was now becoming less attractive. Golac, immersed with his house problem, asked to be excused and I agreed. Then Phil Boyer said his wife didn't like to be on her own and could he stay too. It was pointless to upset him so I agreed. It wasn't that kind of trip. I just wanted the players to have four days rest in good weather before the League Cup quarter-final against Manchester City. It was a perk not an obligation. John McGrath's wife came on to say his cold was worse and he wouldn't be able to make it. I needed a rest more than anyone but decided to stay to try and sign Charlie George. I asked Ted Bates to go in my place and he started to make excuses. I thought, how ironical: when it's a free trip to Barbados they're queueing to get on the plane but they're not so keen on a brief visit to a less glamorous place. Then Don Taylor joined the absentees, saying his wife had to to see a specialist. There would be a few vacant places.

I had to chase Docherty in the evening by phone. He wasn't at the Dragonara Hotel in Bristol where Derby were staying and I caught up with him in Harvey's Restaurant. He readily agreed to me talking to George but as Ron Atkinson was in from the start, he had arranged for him to see the player first. We also agreed terms. Once again there was no messing on money. He wanted £330,000 clear and mentioned something about a house loan of £18,000 which had to be paid back. I said we would talk about that later. By the time we paid the ten per cent levy, half of which goes to the Football League's Provident Fund and the other half to the player, plus VAT which we get back at the end of the trading year, the total would rise to about £390,000. He said that Charlie wanted to play in America the following summer and I didn't think that would be a problem, not for one year at least. The American club pays his wages and that can be a considerable saving. At this money, Charlie was still cheaper than Deehan and Ferguson, the other players I had been talking about. And he was more experienced.

Later, I confirmed with Mr Woodford that we were making progress and said the directors ought to know that some big money might have to be spent very soon. He had raised no objection to Ferguson but when I mentioned Charlie George, he said, 'What about his disciplinary record?' 'David Peach has a worse record than he has and you know he's not a bad lad,' I said. 'Charlie is a bit flamboyant but he's not a bad character. Anyway, that's my strength, handling players like him. If we signed him, he'd put a few thousand on the gate. Ferguson wouldn't.'

I called George at his home. He sounded a reasonable person. He said he had to see Ron Atkinson first. 'That's all right,' I said. 'Get a plane and come down here afterwards.' He said he had a daughter at school. 'Bring your wife and family as well,' I said.

Saturday, 2 December.

I could see the chairman wasn't too happy about convincing his colleagues on the board that George was a desirable acquisition so I went into the directors' room with him to help him sell the idea and he was grateful. After a short discussion, the board gave me the go-ahead.

Before the match, I had a long chat with Jim Smith, the Birmingham City manager. Some years ago I offered him a job as a trainer at Grimsby when he was manager of Boston. He is a good, honest sort, one of the game's workers. We compared notes on our foreign players and agreed that having overseas players had its problems. Alberto Tarantini, his Argentinian international, was a wealthy man apparently. He was taking time to settle in. He couldn't speak much English and today would be a test of his resolution because the weather was freezing cold and the pitch was very hard. The Pools Panel was in operation for the first time as more than thirty matches were postponed.

Tarantini had a slight pull in training and was feeling his leg as the teams lined up. Bally noticed it, clapped his hands and said to the others, 'Come on, these buggers don't want to play today.' After fifteen minutes, Tarantini went off. A Phil Boyer goal won it for us but it was a dour, uninteresting game. It was one we had to win.

Sunday, 3 December.

There it was in the *Sunday People*: 'WBA and Southampton want Charlie George'. It was a typical Tommy Doc situation: the story comes out in the papers and no-one knows how it got there. But it is no use complaining.

When I called Charlie George at home he was at the ground training and his wife Sue answered. 'I've been trying to get him but they don't answer the phone down there on Sundays, Mondays and Wednesdays,' she said. Reporters from the nationals started calling and I had to be diplomatic. It was Colin Todd all over again. When I eventually spoke to Charlie, he said he was committed to seeing Ron Atkinson first. I said that was fine, provided he kept his word to come and see me. He said he would.

There was a further complication with the Spanish trip. Nick Holmes, a bright lad, turned up without his passport and had to chase over to the Isle of Wight after his wife who had it. It meant him missing the flight and having to go out by himself later. We normally insist on retaining the players' passports at the club. I think we'll have to revert to that.

Monday, 4 December.

I fixed with Charlie to meet him at the Kensington Hilton, the hotel the BBC World Cup panel stayed at in the summer. As it was late evening, there wouldn't be time for much else except to drive him back home and start talking after breakfast. I was impressed with his football knowledge. He talked sense, like most players who have been in the game some time. He appeared more mature than I expected.

Tuesday, 5 December.

Guy Askham came round to the house after breakfast to discuss a contract. I always like to have him present at big signings. At this salary level it is vital to have expert advice on such matters as income tax and pensions. I asked Charlie how the talks had gone with Ron Atkinson and he said Ron had agreed to everything. I asked, 'Did he have a director or the secretary with him?' Charlie said, 'No. He was on his own.' It was Ron's biggest deal and Albion weren't a club with a tradition of making big money signings. Their record fee paid out up to then was the £138,000 they paid Glasgow Rangers in 1972 for Willie Johnston. Willie was about the only high flier on their staff.

I said to Charlie, 'You're twenty-eight, an international player and it seems to me that you haven't got a lot to show for it.' He had to admit that was true. I said Southampton believed in offering a new player a package which would help him after he retired. He was happy with my offer and when I put him on the Waterloo train at Eastleigh he promised to ring back later with a decision. I was satisfied we had matched WBA's terms.

The newspapers, which were full of stories that he would go to Albion because there was more chance of glory there than with us, hinted that Nottingham Forest might come in and I knew that if that happened we would stand little chance. Any player with pride would want to go to Forest. Clough had waited quietly in the background and when I was interviewed by Jeff Powell of the *Daily Mail* I said I was quite confident of signing George 'unless he was waylaid by a highwayman'. Powell wrote a fine piece, outlining the selling points I had presented to George: if he had been a Southampton player since leaving Arsenal, Charlie would have won another FA

Brian Clough in a
Napoleonic pose. We're
speaking at a televised
debate at the Neon
Club in Jarrow. I've
never seen Cloughie
looking so posh – pin
stripe suit, waistcoat
and tie. Usually he's in
a track suit and floppy
plimsolls having just
come off the squash
court or about to go on
one.

Every time I see Ron
Greenwood he looks
younger. Brian Clough
and those other
managers who are in
line for his job will have
to wait a few years. Ron
is fifty-eight and seems
determined to carry on
as England manager for
a few years yet.

The final whistle in the League Cup semi-final against Leeds. It was going through my mind 'That's three visits to Wembley in three years, can't be bad.' I wear two coats at matches usually – this reddish brown leather one (the hand marks wash off easily) and a heavier suede coat. In moments of victory the manager is mobbed. But there are times when he is molested. That's when you need the heavier coat as protection!

The Leeds semi-final. Lew Chatterley, my trainer, embraces me. Lew, who was trainer-coach at Torquay, ran a small boarding house and he obviously finds this more exciting than serving up egg and bacon every morning. Next to me is Manny Andruszewski, who had marked Tony Currie so well, and the physio Don Taylor. The dug-out at Southampton only seats five, or six at a squeeze. It's not like Wembley.

Right right arm . . . Alan Ball, the club captain. It's amazing to think that thirteen years previously he gained a World Cup winners' medal. He played every match for us and was an inspiration to all the players. We've shed a few tears together. This was one of the happy moments. Notice my tie. Later in the year I was voted one of the top ten Tie men in the country. Someone said I was pictured in this tie on thirty occasions!

Emlyn Hughes's testimonial dinner. Max Boyce, the Welsh rugby comedian, is on the left. You will see that we've all got empty glasses and Emlyn and I haven't eaten our bread rolls. Three lads with similar backgrounds. And now we're all fairly prosperous.

That's the secret of Jimmy Tarbuck's success: his wife. She is a smashing lady. We're at a Super Sports function organized by Ranjit Anand. Jimmy is in my view the best ad libber in the business. He's a football fanatic, a Liverpool fan. They're all fanatics, Liverpool fans.

Talking to the comedy duo Eddie Little and Sid Large. Notice this time I've got the heavy coat, not that I'm expecting any trouble. Eddie looks serious because he's talking about his favourite club, Manchester City. He's trying to explain what went wrong. We knocked them out of the League Cup.

Signing four new apprentices at the Dell, always a happy moment for a manager. These four have interesting backgrounds, Joe Blochell comes from London, Rueben Agaboola from Trinidad, Johnny Pang is son of a Chinese restaurant proprietor and Steve Baker comes from Walker-on-Tyne, Newcastle. The only other player of Chinese extraction who made a name for himself in English football was Frank Soo. Johnny Pang could be the next.

Being a football manager doesn't mean you just talk to footballers. You have to address all kinds of people at all kinds of functions. Here I am at a Boys Brigade do at a church hall in Northern Ireland. I was invited by a man named McMenemy. It's an Irish name originally though half my ancestors went to live in Scotland and the other half in England.

Touring the Thorn Electric factory at Spennymoor. I had just turned down Sunderland's offer to become their new manager. The ladies were very persuasive. 'If we'd got you a day or two earlier, you wouldn't have turned it down,' they said. And perhaps they were right!

Having a job like mine helps you appreciate your family all the more. *From left to right:* Chris, Alison, Anne and Sean.

We started the season with this squad. *Left to right* (*at back*): Ivan Golac, Mike Pickering (sold to Sheffield Wednesday for £60,000), Malcolm Waldron, Peter Wells, Terry Gennoe, Chris Nicholl, Trevor Hebberd, Manny Andruszewski. (*Front*): Graham Baker, David Peach, Phil Boyer, Alan Ball, Ted MacDougall (free transfer to Bournemouth), Steve Williams, Nick Holmes, Terry Curran (sold to Sheffield Wednesday for £100,000).

If Madame Smith had predicted that we would reach Wembley, I would have had a bet on it. But as the notice says, she was closed for the day.

Riding in the town coach to open Newcastle's Summer Exhibition. If only my mother and father could have seen me! They are both dead. My father died of cancer and my mother died six months later of a broken heart. But most of my family were there. I have two sisters and five brothers.

I'll have to show Clive Thomas (*right*) the yellow card. He told me it was a dinner jacket affair! Clive was being presented with a plaque by the Rhondda Recognition Society and handing it over is Frankie Vaughan.

Bell's local man Bob James presents me with the First Division Manager of the Month award, my sixth Bell's award. It's a heavy coat day I notice and I've also got that number one tie on again! I asked the players to autograph the bottle and we raised £500 from a raffle at the local Ford works. The proceeds actually came to £520 because some supporters whose coach broke down on the way to Wembley chipped in the money they received back from the coach company. The money went to provide a guide dog named Saint.

A big event for the 'Big Man' – Jock Stein, manager of Scotland. The City of Glasgow laid on a dinner for him as part of his testimonial and here we are in the Lord Provost's room. Billy McNeil, manager of Celtic is on the left and the Lord Provost is standing next to me.

My costliest signing, Charlie George from Derby County for £315,000. You have to pay 8 per cent VAT on top of that. It's silly really because at the end of the year you get the money back! I called him my frozen asset because he had a knee injury and couldn't play many games. If he'd been fit we would have gained at least ten more points and probably got into Europe.

Presenting the supporters' Player of the Year award to Malcolm
Waldron. If we had been successful in signing Colin Todd earlier in the
season, Malcolm might not have played so many matches. He
thoroughly deserved the award. He's a quiet lad and he improved so
much that he was our most consistent defender. There were some
10,000 votes cast, nearly half our average home attendance. On the left is
Alan Woodford, the chairman of the board of directors.

Cup Final medal; played in eight European matches; and he would also be in the last eight of the League Cup. I didn't mention Albion but everyone knew they couldn't match that. Albion's average attendance was no better than ours. We had the potential to develop into a big club when the new stadium was built but they would always be overshadowed by Aston Villa and Birmingham.

One or two directors still had reservations about Charlie. They thought he might upset things at the club. But I told them, 'When I came here this club had so many gangsters that Al Capone would have struggled to get a game but I sorted it out. We need someone with a bit of flair and excitement otherwise we'll be known as the Saints convent team.'

Wednesday, 6 December.

I was confident we had done all we could but would have been happier if we could have taken Charlie with us to Spain. At half past twelve I rang Mrs George who said he was at the ground. 'I'll say some prayers,' I said. 'You don't need to pray,' she replied. I felt excited.

An hour later Docherty called and I thought he was going to say it's us. 'Brian Clough has been on and I'm telling you and Ron Atkinson that I've given him permission to see the boy at three o'clock,' he said. 'Hang on,' I said. 'Bloody hell, he's had long enough to come in. I suppose we'll now read all about his magnificent methods of buying players.' It made me wonder whether Derby had kept him informed all the way through. 'Here,' said Docherty. 'My chairman is next to me. Have a word with him.' George Hardy took the phone and said, 'He's going to see Clough but there is no way we'll let him go to Forest, so sit tight. He wants to go South.' Docherty also said Clough wouldn't let him go to America and that was another reason why he wouldn't sign for him. I wasn't so sure. Cloughie was the type who would blockbuster it through. His club were in the European Cup and, given a choice, any player would prefer that to joining a club that was in the lower half of the table.

George telephoned at six and said all three clubs had made similar offers and he was sleeping on it. He would let me know in the morning. For someone who was supposed to be unreliable, he had been on time as promised with every call he had made and that impressed me. That night I watched WBA beat Valencia in the UEFA Cup on television.

Thursday, 7 December.

George rang at a quarter to nine, fifteen minutes earlier than he promised. 'Look, I'm sorry,' he said, 'but I've decided to go to Forest.' He apologized for his wife making me think with her remark about praying that he was coming to Southampton. 'What happens if the Forest thing breaks down?' I asked. 'I've made my mind up to come to you,' he said.

Anne had made a couple of appointments to see people in connection with the house. The first one was at the ground. As we drove into the car park I saw Phil Rood of the '*Echo*' and, not wanting to say anything to the press at this stage, I drove straight out again. Anne said, 'You realize that the fellow we're supposed to be seeing is back there at the club!' I asked her to get him over to the garage across the road so we could meet there.

At a quarter to one Guy Askham and I had a meeting with officials of the Trojans club about their ground which we were hiring for four years and paying for in advance so that they could build an all-weather pitch.

Back in my office, there was still no call from Derby. I heard on the radio that the Forest deal had been vetoed because it would take season-ticket holders away from Derby. At three I went to a showing of a Rank Xerox film I helped make. It was about management and was to be shown at firms all over the country; good publicity for me and the club.

At four o'clock I met the players back from Spain and they had a good sweat session in the gym. 'They were no trouble at all,' said Lew Chatterley. I gave Bally a lift home and we talked about how important the month of December was to a club. He said the atmosphere was good in Marbella and the players had even spoken about having a swear box. He asked about George and I told him we were still hoping. I said Charlie was a better class of player than those we had and Bally interrupted, 'A Division better.' He doesn't say too much at times but what he was saying was 'I hope you get him.' He's a little gold nugget is Bally.

Friday, 8 December.

Before leaving for Manchester for the game against City I had the players in for a talk. I spoke about our bad away record. 'Is it due to our approach? We don't skimp. You can eat what you like, four or five courses, have the run of the sweet trolley. It's much more than you eat at home. Afterwards, you don't go for a walk, you go to your rooms. I wonder whether you're being too greedy. I'm not saying you are. I'm just throwing it at you. It's a good club with good relationships but could we be a bit more professional? I'm asking you to think about it.'

I also spoke about bad language. It was becoming more prevalent and I was disturbed by it. In an aggressive sport you were bound to get swearing but I was hearing younger players like Steve Williams swearing for the sake of it and I didn't like it. It showed a lack of respect. 'We've got a happy environment here but don't mistake it for softness,' I said. 'I'll come down hard on anyone who steps out of line.' I had had one young lad into my office to tell him off about swearing, an eighteen-year-old trialist named Martin McGrath. He was the son of a bank manager and had a good background yet Ian Branfoot told me in one 'A' team match he gave a right mouthful of abuse to a player he accused of making a bad pass to him.

Saturday, 9 December.

A brilliantly sunny day. A nice hotel, Mottram Hall at Wilmslow, and I was feeling in good spirits when Lew Chatterley knocked at my door before breakfast. 'You all right?' he said. 'You won't be when you read this.' He handed me the *Sun* which had an article by John Sadler saying Southampton weren't a big enough club for someone like Charlie George. 'It's like Nureyev playing the lead at the Christmas concert at my village hall,' he wrote. 'If we get to Wembley I'll invite him to the concert,' I said. In my younger days as a manager I got very angry with criticism like that. There was a time when I would be on the phone to the journalist but you learn to live with it, however hurtful the tone of the article.

Peter Swales, the Manchester City chairman, is usually cool to-wards me, probably the aftermath of my insisting on getting £300,000 for Mike Channon when the directors were happy with less. At my England interview at the FA he was the only person on the panel who didn't ask me a question. But after the game he held out his hand and said, 'Well done, you were the better team.' We had won 2–1, our first away win of the season, and had played exceptionally well. Manchester has that effect on us.

Tony Book, City's manager, was very upset. It was their fourth game they'd lost in a row in the League. Granada, who televised the match, wanted to interview him but he wasn't ready. He was in the bath. Though they don't do anything active, managers often have a bath after a match. If it's been a bad result, it means they can take longer to come out and there won't be so many pressmen around. The television interviewer asked Booky a silly question about why he didn't change the team after the 3–0 win against AC Milan in the UEFA Cup. You couldn't change it after a result like that.

Bill Taylor, the City coach, came in with a message from British Rail that there would be no hot meal on the train. We were too high to mind. Curran, who had played well, said it was the best trip he had ever been on, cold food or not. I told the players that the pressure would be on us now on Tuesday night when Manchester City came to our ground in the League Cup. 'You've stirred them right up,' I said. Anne had recorded 'Match of the Day' and I stayed up until two in the morning. I needed a long time to wind down.

Sunday, 10 December.

A happy day. We bought a couple of Christmas trees and spent most of the day dressing them. I took Christopher in to the ground for some treatment in the morning and when Mr Woodford (who hadn't been to Manchester) rang to congratulate me on the result, Anne said, 'He's down at the ground.' Mr Woodford said, 'What a man he is!' In fact, that was the first time I had been at the ground on a Sunday for some time! I am a regular churchgoer and I go to the local Catholic church, St Edwards. Today we all went to the seven o'clock service. The priest, Father Scantlebury, had just been promoted a Monsignor by the Bishop of Portsmouth and he thanked me for my telegram of congratulations. It was reciprocating the one he sent me when we won the FA Cup in 1976.

The phone rang on and off all day. One call at night was from a journalist who was tapping me about Chelsea. Miljan Miljanic wasn't going there, was I interested? I said I wasn't. I didn't want to comment.

Jock Stein rang and asked if I was going to the BBC 'Sportsman of the Year' awards on Wednesday. As members of the World Cup panel, he thought we ought to but I said we hadn't done anything to warrant being on the top table. I said I probably wouldn't go. I asked about Frank McGarvey, a St Mirren forward who was available. Terry Neill had inquired about him. McGarvey was a little lad, quite skilful, but I understood they were talking in telephone numbers. He was too much like Phil Boyer for my liking. I wanted a player to complement Boyer, not duplicate what he could do.

Monday, 11 December.

Gordon Banks, who had been playing for Fort Lauderdale in America, arrived at my invitation to spend a few days working with our goalkeepers. He wanted to add to his coaching experience and I suggested he should visit a few top clubs and offer to train their goalkeepers. He was one of the best keepers of all time and would be an asset to us on a short-term basis.

It had been bucketing down with rain over the weekend and I was getting anxious about tomorrow's League Cup quarter-final. The Dell is a good draining pitch, especially since we had it sand injected, but there is a limit to the amount of water any pitch can take.

Tuesday, 11 December.

I took a couple of hours off in the morning to go Christmas shopping with Anne. She likes me to come along when she is choosing clothes. We went to a dress shop near the ground and a woman who turned out to be Swiss recognized me, thrust an envelope out and asked for my autograph for her son. The woman who owned the shop, a French lady, told her off for disturbing me! I didn't mind. It was pleasant to be able to relax even though dress shops aren't my scene.

Soon the tension was building up: would the match be played or not? While we were having our pre-match meal at the Royal Hotel, Brian Truscott rang with the news that Clive Thomas, the referee, wasn't too happy about the pitch. I said I would be round in a few minutes. The traffic was bad, and it took more than twenty minutes to do the journey of under a mile. There were huge queues outside the ground. Normally we would open the gates at this time, six o'clock, but it was unwise to do so yet until we knew whether the game was on.

Clive said he wasn't able to bounce a ball in some places because there was surface water. He's his own man and wouldn't be influenced by anyone else. Referees have the sole power to call games off but some allow themselves to be persuaded by managers who might not want to play. You couldn't do that with Clive. The week before he over-ruled a linesman on offside. He's that kind of referee. While he went out for a further inspection at a quarter to seven, Tony Book and I stood by the side of the pitch. Obviously Southampton wanted it on. The whole town was ready for it. But after being beaten at home, Booky wouldn't be so keen though he didn't say so.

If we opened the gates and the game didn't start, we would have to give the fans pass-out checks to allow them to come again. But the pass-out checks were locked up in the safe and bad organization wasted a long time getting them to the turnstiles. It was nearly seven o'clock before Clive said we could go ahead and when the match started thousands of fans were still outside. To make it worse, one of the turnstiles was out of action. We hadn't done too well really.

Footballers don't like uncertainty but I gave my players the right stimulation by saying City were a bit afraid of us after Saturday. Booky had changed his formation. He was now trying a 4–4–2 line-up and was packing the midfield. There weren't any cards I could play but Booky's reaction indicated to me that he wasn't too confident about the outcome. He was relying on the experience of the Pole, Kazi Deyna, and Colin Bell in midfield and had left out Peter Barnes. Barnes is a frustrating player who often doesn't do his talents justice but on this pitch, where defenders would struggle to turn, he might have been a match winner.

Fifteen minutes before kick-off I was called to the phone. Charlie George was on the line. 'I'm coming down there tomorrow,' he said. 'I've packed in the idea of going to Forest.' I was delighted. All we had to do now was beat City again.

It was one of the best Cup ties in my experience. We outplayed them. The result was 2–1 but it should have been 4–0. Chris Nicholl scored an own goal near the end and gave us some anxious moments before we were sure of being in the last four of the competition for the first time.

Afterwards we had a session in my office which went on until one o'clock in the morning. Mick Channon, who was staying down while the City party flew back to Manchester, popped in for a beer and chat with Malcolm Allison and Ellis Stuttart, his scout but didn't stay too long. He was sick at losing. Allison revelled in the football talk. Earlier in the season I told him I had one or two reserves that might interest him and he came to watch Hebberd. But Hebberd, who scored the second goal, had just had his finest game for us and even if George signed, I would still need him for the Cups. Charlie was Cup-tied for the League Cup. 'I'd take the fella back with me now,' said Allison.

Wednesday, 13 December.

The train drivers on the Waterloo–Southampton line were on an unofficial one-day strike so Fred Scott drove up to St Pancras to collect Charlie. I arranged for Dr Lawrence to come in to conduct the medical and Don Taylor fixed the X-rays at a local hospital for both knees and ankles.

Charlie had an open envelope with him containing his medical record and the details of the transfer and how we were to pay the money. I was slightly surprised that Derby should let him see the financial side but there wasn't anything I could do about it.

The press and local television people were hanging about and I asked them to come back at half past three for a press conference. Charlie looked a bit tired and showed the indifference of the old football pro when questioned later by people who didn't know the game too well. One TV man asked, 'Do you intend setting up in business here?' Charlie replied, 'No, I'm here to play football.' Inevitably, he was asked if £350,000 wasn't too much. His eyes sparkled: 'Not for me it isn't!'

The medical part was cleared but we still had to finalize the question of the house loan with Derby. I tried to call Stuart Webb, the Derby secretary, but couldn't reach him. Charlie didn't want to stay the night and I had him driven back to St Pancras.

Thursday, 14 December.

The pre-Christmas drink with the directors and players. Mr Woodford, Bally and I all made little speeches. I thanked the directors for their support and for sanctioning the short break in Spain which I felt had been beneficial.

The draw for the semi-finals of the League Cup came through, away in the first leg to Leeds, the best side we'd met so far. But I preferred them to Forest. I could never see a way round Peter Shilton every time we played them.

Later in the day Malcolm Folley of the *Daily Express* rang. I thought it was about the Cup draw but he said he had a story which presented Southampton in a good light after signing Charlie George: we were supposed to have turned down a big bid from Arsenal for Steve Williams, and this showed we were an ambitious club which could hold on to its good players. I was very angry. 'I don't want anything like that written,' I said. 'To start with, it's not true. We haven't had a big offer for him. If that gets in, all the other papers will follow it up and it will rock the boat.' He said I had favourite reporters and he wasn't one of them. 'Well, you're not if you write things like that,' I said. I remembered he had upset me before with stories about Peter Osgood and Ted MacDougall.

Friday, 15 December.

Williams came in, almost as I expected. He said someone from the *Express* rang him at four o'clock and he wanted to know what it was all about. That was two hours before Folley called me which meant he was ringing the player first, something I will never tolerate, especially when it is a naïve twenty-year-old like Steve Williams. This is where a manager's mean streak comes in. He has to turn a bit nasty to make sure he doesn't have a disaffected player on his hands. Williams was one of the outstanding young midfield players in the country, worth at least £400,000. When I had been discussing possible deals with other managers, some had asked, 'What about Williams? Will you let me have him in part-exchange?' That was as far as it had got. No manager had put a firm bid in because he knew Williams was unavailable. I wasn't having a young reporter causing trouble at my club so I rang his boss, Ken Lawrence. When I eventually contacted him, Lawrence said he had to speak to Folley on another matter and asked me to leave it with him.

I had to open a Ladbroke's betting shop at Fareham, which is close to Portsmouth. When a football team does well it enlivens the whole area and I could sense the mood as I arrived. There was a big crowd, clapping and shouting and I posed for pictures. Ray Crawford, now manager of Fareham Town, was there and the manager of the shop was Kevin Hart, a nice lad who used to be an apprentice at the Dell. Steve Mills, whose career at Southampton was ended by a car crash, was manager of another Ladbroke's betting shop.

Betting seems to attract footballers. I look on it as a mug's game but I've had plenty of gamblers on my staff: Channon, who is more closely involved with horses than most, Bally and Peter Osgood among them. Footballers have so much time to kill that racing is a convenient way of doing it. I can never understand those players who sit at home and watch on telly and bet. Bally, Osgood and Channon go to meetings because they like the social side of it as much as the betting. That's more understandable.

Back at the ground, Mr Woodford and Guy Askham arrived to talk about the George transfer. I was still trying to speak to Webb, who was at the Royal Lancaster Hotel in London. I suggested to Mr Woodford it was now a matter for the two chairmen to sort out. The press would be sniffing about. I had said a small formality was holding the deal up but I couldn't keep saying that. I arranged for Charlie to come down to watch our game with Coventry.

Saturday, 16 December.

Charlie made it in time for lunch despite going down the A3 instead of the M3. There was a good crowd in, more than 20,000 which is excellent for the last home game before Christmas, and they gave him a fine ovation as he walked with me to the bench before the kick-off. He looked nervous but I made him laugh when I said, 'I hope you don't think that's for you. It's for me!'

We played well again, winning 4–0. Coventry played with three at the back, which is a risk even when your side is playing well, which they weren't. Charlie asked if he could leave at half-time to avoid the crowd and I agreed since he might be asked some embarrassing questions by the press afterwards. I had to leave right at the end myself because I had to be in London with Anne at eight o'clock to attend a dinner at the Hyde Park Hotel with Don and Elsie Revie, Jock and Jean Stein, Elton John and one or two other football people.

Monday, 18 December.

This was the day Don Revie appeared at the FA offices in Lancaster Gate to answer a charge of bringing the game into disrepute. Alan Ball had made some allegations in his autobiography that Revie paid him £300 twelve years ago while he was a player at Blackpool. Leeds wanted to sign Ball, who had refused to sign a contract, and Revie was alleged to have said he would make Ball's wages up.

For the first time the FA were allowing legal representation. Bally had his solicitor, Tony Wilson, with him and Revie was represented by a QC, Gilbert Gray.

There was some fog at Basingstoke and I arrived five minutes late. Bally pleaded guilty. His solicitor said he was a young, impressionable player at the time and I was called to give a character reference. I said Ball was now a much more mature person who helped me enormously by giving good advice to the younger players. 'It's a pity he didn't have someone like that to give him advice twelve years ago,' I said. It was fascinating to listen to the cut and thrust between Sir Harold Thompson, the FA chairman who presided over the Commission, and Mr Gray. Tony Wilson made the good point that Bally had turned down a sizeable offer from the *Daily Mirror* to co-operate on their series about Don Revie which was the subject of a libel writ. Sir Harold ruled that the charge against Revie could be heard. The case was not *sub judice* and we were told the FA would communicate their decision in writing. I hoped it wouldn't be a ban for Bally. He was playing well and was vital to the team.

As we left, Tony Wilson made a short statement to the big gathering of press, radio and television men. But Revie refused to say anything and was given a rough ride before he found a taxi.

Tuesday, 19 December.

After another hard training session, Charlie George said, 'What's happening?' I told him we were still talking with Derby. They were putting the pressure on. Stuart Webb said his directors wanted us to make two payments, the fee plus money for the house loan. We weren't able to agree. It had to be one figure. When we first started talking, the loan figure was mentioned. Now it had crept up. There had been a similar hitch over Terry Curran's transfer. The item in dispute then was the money Derby had loaned him for a car. Mr Hardy wanted to split that down the middle but we had refused. Derby had ordered £500 worth of tickets when we played them in the League Cup at the Dell and hadn't paid for them. We had assumed they had written that off against the Curran car money. No matter; when Derby played at the Dell again we would deduct it from their share of the gate receipts. How petty!

Wednesday, 20 December.

I was neglecting the team because of the Charlie George transfer. A meeting of the directors decided we couldn't change our position and Stuart Webb was informed. I had a feeling that this was the end of the affair. Derby had lost two matches and weren't scoring goals. They could use the house loan as an excuse to hold on to Charlie. We had worked so hard to get him to the club, and Charlie showed he was very keen to come. It was such an unusual way of doing business. None of us had known anything like it before.

Anne reminded me that we were supposed to be moving out of our house on 2 January and we still hadn't obtained a rented house to use until our new home was completed. I had promised also to attend Alison's school nativity play. She had a big part but, though I wanted to go, I knew it would be impossible to get there. These events were often embarrassing anyway: my presence took the spotlight away from the children for the parents were more interested in me than the performers.

Late in the evening Guy Askham called to say he had spoken to Webb again about making a final effort to resolve the problem. To his surprise Webb called back to say his chairman was willing to compromise.

Thursday, 21 December.

Charlie was involving himself in the dressing-room chat and was happy with the latest news. Brian Truscott arranged to catch the ten past twelve train to Waterloo to hand the cheque over to Webb in London. But just before he left the ground, Webb was on the line again with a different story. A board meeting was in session at the Baseball Ground and because one director had objected to the way the money was to be paid George Hardy had retracted. We were back where we were. Derby were giving us until two o'clock to agree to their formula. Mr Woodford didn't want to make concessions. It was off.

I told Charlie the news in the middle of the afternoon after his second training session of the day. I wished I had a camera to record his expression. Neither of us said much, we were too upset. We didn't even shake hands as he left to catch the next train to London.

I thought to myself he was the second top-class player I had failed to bring to the club. First Todd and now George and both from the same club, Derby. It could affect my whole future at Southampton. We made a breakthrough with Osgood when we paid Chelsea £265,000 for him and several other good quality players followed him to the Dell. Ossie had perhaps been past his best but Charlie was in his prime. Other good judges, like Brian Clough, wanted him. He was a demand. Fred Scott ferried Charlie to the station and when he came back, he said, 'Charlie's very upset. From what he was saying, I fear for the safety of those people up there who are stopping him coming.'

I sat at home in the evening, thoroughly miserable, looking at television and the newspapers without taking anything in. It was like losing in the third round of the FA Cup to a non-League club. There was just one hope: that Charlie himself might make the move to break the deadlock.

He called at ten o'clock. 'It's not over yet,' he said. 'I was going to sell my house to a bank manager but Gordon Hill hasn't got a place yet. If he buys it, that would solve the problem.'

Friday, 22 December.

The chairman came in on his way to work to console me. I was never convinced he really wanted Charlie. You get cynical about it. He was surprised when I said the deal was now likely to go through.

At half past ten Brian Truscott reported that Webb had rung saying everything was clear and he or his assistant would bring the necessary forms down to be altered. A meeting was arranged at St

Pancras. Charlie's signature was needed, so I rang him and asked him to come as well. We were getting him for a fee of £315,000, exclusive of the ten per cent levy and VAT. Brian took with him our cheque for the first payment. It totalled £215,000. The remainder would be paid off after a year. We had enough money on deposit to cover the outlay without going into debt and still had some left to buy another player if I wanted one, though not as pricey as Charlie. The signing ceremony took place in a refreshment room at St Pancras Station.

I felt a great sense of relief. In the afternoon, I joined the office staff at the Christmas party and it was the best little do we'd had at the club in my time. I had a couple of glasses of wine and when I was interviewed on Southern Television later the interviewer, David Bobin, tried to be serious but I couldn't help being light-hearted.

It was an anti-climax when I heard that the night match at WBA had been cancelled because of snow and ice. It suited us to have it off.

Saturday, 23 December.

Another transfer deal was completed when I signed Michael O'Donoghue, a twenty-two-year-old clerk who plays for Wembley Town FC. The Wembley chairman was on the phone at nine o'clock in the morning to say his club wanted £5,000 and not a penny less. I had to smile but I had been in non-League football myself and knew that that money was just as important to them as the £315,000 was to Derby County.

O'Donoghue was the fourth child of a family of ten and, coming from a large family myself, that appealed to me. He was from Holloway, Charlie's birthplace. We weren't short of forwards but the London scout recommended him and if you fail to act on advice like that and another club signs the player, you regret it later. He might be another Cyrille Regis.

Before having a quick lunch and setting off to watch Chelsea's 0–0 draw against Bristol City, I did a brisk hour's shopping. Lew Chatterley who was with me was amazed I did it so quickly, straight out of the car into the shop and out again. But I had to cut it short when I tried to cross the road to a newsagents and was stopped by autograph hunters. I didn't have the time for that.

It was Danny Blanchflower's second match in charge at Chelsea and he clearly had a lot to do. BBC radio wanted me to comment but I declined. We were playing Chelsea on Boxing Day and it wouldn't be timely for me to criticize them in public.

Eddie Baily was in the tea room. 'They tell me you've signed a player,' he said. 'Yes, you've seen him,' I said; 'can he play?' 'I wouldn't want him in my team,' he said. 'I didn't ask you that,' I said. 'Can he play?' 'You've got to make him play,' he replied. 'That's good enough for me,' I said. 'If someone of your brilliance and knowledge thinks he can do it, then I'm in business.' We always have that kind of wind-up conversation.

Sunday, 24 December.

Earlier in the week I advised Bally to say nothing in the press about his £3,000 fine. Today there was an item in one of the papers saying he wasn't going to appeal. There was no point. He didn't have much money and I knew he would struggle to find it. I told him, 'You are a great asset to this club and we won't see you suffer. If you want a loan, we'll look on it sympathetically.' League regulations allow clubs to loan players money but it has to be done legally at the current rate of interest.

Four days previously an insurance man came to the Dell with a suggestion that we have a collection at the next home game for Bally. I said I couldn't get involved in that but put him on to Peter East at the *Echo*. On Friday night there was a big piece in the newspaper about an appeal fund. This morning the insurance man came round to training. 'Offers are pouring in,' he said. 'I had £35 stuffed through my letter box last night. How about you?' he added. 'Have you got your wallet on you?' I thought he had a cheek. 'You come back when you're near the £3,000 and we'll see about it then,' I said.

Bally and I talked about the previous night's 'Match of the Day'. Manchester City drew 0–0 with Forest. 'They've got the players at Maine Road but they're not helping each other,' he said. 'They've lost what we've found.'

I had to rush off to see a house which an agent had lined up for me to rent at Romsey. In the excitement of the Charlie George transfer, I was overlooking that we only had a few days left in our present house. Anne had to bear the brunt of the packing and all the other arrangements.

8. Leeds in the semi-final

The semi-final of any competition is not the favourite match of the football manager. If his team loses the depression that follows usually has a bad effect on League performances. If it wins, the players start thinking about being fit for Wembley, and League form suffers.

The sides that are often able to overcome this are ones that are also challenging for the title, like Nottingham Forest, the 1978 League Cup winners. In their semi-final Forest beat Third Division Watford 3–1 on aggregate to reach the Final for a second successive year.

McMenemy knew that if Southampton beat Leeds – a result which not one critic forecast – it might lead to problems in the First Division. Unless he got a grip on it, his team could start sliding. Leeds, eight places higher in the table when the semi-final matches took place, reached the last four by defeating WBA, Sheffield United, QPR and Luton Town.

Monday, 25 December.

It may be Christmas but it is still a part working day for football people. Before going off for training at six, I was determined to have a normal family Christmas. The children are older, Sean will be fifteen on 4 January, Christopher eighteen in August and Alison is ten, but they still put their stockings out.

We spent the day by ourselves. My mother and father are dead and our relatives are a long way away in the North East. In football, you move about the country so much that you don't stay in one place long enough to make close friendships, the friendships that lead to sharing the Christmas dinner. I rang a few relatives to wish them well. Then I thought it would be a good idea to ring John Bond. His wife had been ill and it had been on my conscience that we'd grown apart. Inevitably we started talking football. Anne said, 'You only rang to wish him a happy Christmas and you've been on the phone half an hour.'

After the Christmas dinner, we watched *Sound of Music* and my eye was constantly on the clock. I took a couple of bottles of wine in for the players to drink after training. Only Bally and Peachy had any. Times have changed at the club. We spent the evening watching television in our rooms at the hotel. It's not the same as being at home.

Tuesday, 26 December.

The game against Chelsea was an eleven o'clock kick-off and there was a danger of it being called off because of the rain. The referee, Mr Bates of Bristol, was indecisive. 'I've been out there with a ball and it's not good,' he said. 'With respect ref., you're wearing wellies, not football boots,' I said. We wanted it on for obvious reasons and Ron Suart, Chelsea's general manager who was with me, was willing to go ahead. The crowd was piling up outside and we didn't want a repetition of what happened before the Manchester City game. 'All right, we'll play,' said the ref.

It was unsatisfactory. Conditions became farcical in the second half and we couldn't break Chelsea down. It ended 0–0 and Danny Blanchflower summed it up well when he said, 'That will do us some good and you no harm.' I saw the ref. afterwards and as I suspected, he had worn rubber studs. In those conditions, I told him, he should have had ordinary studs. He made some feeble excuse about not being able to carry so many pairs of boots around with him and I said, 'Well, you are a professional, aren't you?' I don't look on referees as amateurs. They get paid, even if it's not a lot, and they receive expenses.

That niggled me. And I was also upset that none of the directors had gone into the dressing room to speak to the players who had slogged through the mud for ninety minutes. On another occasion, after a victory, some directors would probably be in. I know how players view that. 'They only come in when we've won,' some will be thinking. I told Mr Woodford about it and he said he thought two of his colleagues had called in.

Ronnie Corbett was in the guest room, surrounded by a group of fawning people. I sympathized with him. He would probably have preferred to speak to the players. John Mortimore was also there. He was suffering from a detached retina and was going to hospital. He was still manager of Benfica and we discussed the possibility of him joining us in some capacity. He is a good organizer and a good type. He wanted to come home soon because his fifteen-year-old daughter had developed anorexia nervosa and was down to six or seven stone in weight. It was a worrying time for him in Lisbon while his wife coped with the problem at their Farnham home.

Friday, 29 December.

Training in the gym was becoming a bore for the players. They couldn't go outside because of the soaked pitches and it was a test of my ingenuity to think up different training routines for them. At a quarter to two the referee for tomorrow's game against Liverpool, Brian Stephens of Gloucester, arrived and soon called it off. It was frustrating for all of us but unavoidable.

None of the projected houses were suitable for us to rent and Anne and I went to see Mr Corbett, one of the directors, at his hotel, the Royal, at Winchester. He offered to put us up until a house became available. It is a nice, old world place but if it had been the Hilton it wouldn't have made any difference. I don't like hotel life.

I spoke to Gordon Lee, the Everton manager, about our goalkeeper, Ian Turner. Gordon wanted goalkeeping cover and I recommended him to have a look at Turner. Turner is a sound type, a grafter, and I wanted to help him. He was on loan to Lincoln and they were dithering.

Saturday, 30 December.

Went to London to see Leeds, our semi-final opponents, outclass QPR 4–1. I felt sorry for Steve Burtenshaw, the QPR manager. Some of his players showed such lack of character that if he had to rely on them he would be in trouble.

Sir Stanley Rous, former President of FIFA and the Rangers President, appeared in remarkable shape for a man in his eighties. I told him that Mrs Reader, wife of our former chairman, had died. He was a good friend of Mr Reader.

I also noticed Merlyn Rees, the Home Secretary, in the directors' box. 'Are you on holiday as well?' I said. He looked at me over his glasses as if to say I ought to know better. He was handling the petrol crisis which had cropped up over the holiday with the deliverymen wanting more money. He said the future prospects weren't too good either because of the Iranian situation.

That night I looked at the League tables and was pleased to see most of the clubs below Southampton had failed to win so we were still tucked in around halfway. It had been a satisfactory first half of the season, except for the weather. No-one can predict when the weather is going to be bad but I favour a short break in early January for us all to recharge our batteries.

Sunday, 31 December.

The rain had turned to snow and at half past eleven Bill Nicholson rang to say our game at Spurs on New Year's Day was off. I was relieved he called early. It meant I could tell the players they could have a day off and see the New Year in at home. Three of our last four matches had now been postponed, and just when we were striking some form.

Monday, 1 January.

John McGrath and George Horsfall weren't in for training which disappointed me. They'd had plenty of time off. Sometimes you need to talk to your staff to remind them that they have a good job. This year I made sure that five of the coaching staff received a £100 bonus from the commercial pool, money from players posing for pictures and the like.

Only the two new coaches, Lew Chatterley and Ian Branfoot, mentioned it. The others said nothing but they would soon have complained if their wages had been £100 short. After training it was discovered there was no hot water because there was no oil left. It was very annoying: I would have to kick a few backsides. The petrol drivers' unofficial strike was on at the time and I could only get round it by contacting the managing director of the company direct. He ensured that we had six hundred gallons.

There had been another example of inefficiency when it was found that two of the drains around the pitch were blocked up. Someone had shoved rubbish down them. It wasn't good enough.

Tuesday, 20 January.

Snow and ice everywhere and we were moving house. Anne had done much of the removal men's work for them. The neighbours were keeping some of our furniture in a spare room, the rest went in a container until the new house was ready and our day-to-day essentials went into suitcases for the stay at the Royal Hotel.

One of the removers, a big fellow, had moved us five years before. 'Got any more spare jackets?' he asked. 'I've just used the last one you gave me to lag a pipe this morning.' Football people move house a lot. The wives get used to it but this particular move was worse than most.

The hotel depressed me as soon as we arrived. It was like a library, quiet and sombre with high ceilings, and the children were almost frightened to say a word. The dinner menu at £3.50 was reasonably priced but it meant that it was going to cost us £20 a meal. We were on a very favourable rate, £150 a week for three rooms, but the cost and the effect it was having on morale decided me that it would be as short a stay as possible.

Wednesday, 3 January.

I thought 'what the hell am I doing here?' I spend much of my life organizing everyone else but I hadn't been able to organize my own life. I felt desperately sorry for Anne; I'd let her down. I contacted an agent and arranged to inspect some more houses.

We cheered up somewhat when we went to the club dinner at the New Forest Lodge and I was pleased to be able to tell two apprentices, Martin McGrath and David Puckett, that I was offering them full contracts. Their eyes lit up.

Thursday, 4 January.

I gave the players a day off as it was impossible to find a playable grass pitch. Peter Corbett, son of Mr Corbett, arranged for us to see Ashley Manor at Kings Somborne, a house rented by Ronnie Corbett, who was appearing locally in a show. It was owned by Mr Bromley of Russell and Bromley and was ideal for a family. He specialized in breeding ducks and inside the house was like a museum. It was a fascinating insight into how rich people live but as he wasn't sure about whether he wanted to let it out again, nothing came of it.

On the way back we bought some fish and chips and smuggled them into our rooms which weren't particularly warm despite the extra electric fires we had been given.

Friday, 5 January.

I was half hoping the FA Cup Third Round tie at Wimbledon would be off and it was. We weren't ready for it. You are always worried about playing lower opposition and this tie was more worrying than many I had encountered because of our enforced inactivity.

I had to speak about 'Motivation' at a conference of insurance agents at Slough. Malcolm Musgrove, the former football manager, works for them and so does Brian Usher who used to play for Sheffield Wednesday. They were shouting 'yippee, yippee!' and when one of them started singing 'Zippety do-dah' they all joined in. I was supposed to be talking about motivation and here they were showing me that they didn't need it. As I started my speech, I said, 'I thought I was in the Blyth Spartans' dressing room just now.' Blyth's manager had his players shouting and stamping before matches to get them in the right aggressive mood.

Saturday, 6 January.

We came down for breakfast at twenty-eight minutes past nine and a young waitress said it was too late though the closing time was half past. I told her she was wrong and said could she please serve us. We could hear her shouting in the kitchen. Anne was upset so I said, 'All right, we'll have tea and toast in the room.' The housekeeper apologized and, when she saw that we were packing to leave, she was perturbed but I assured her that we weren't leaving because of the breakfast incident. We had seen another house at Colden Common, Twyford, which hadn't appealed before because the heating was off but now it seemed like a palace. We couldn't get in quickly enough. The upheaval of the week had affected Anne and she wasn't too well.

It was an odd Saturday: no football and I wasn't home in time for 'Match of the Day' because I appeared on a BBC panel in the evening.

Monday, 7 January.

Charlie George twisted his knee in the gym and, as Dr Lawrence wasn't available, Dr Ramsey, my old adversary, fixed an appointment to see a specialist, Dr Fitzgerald. He said he feared a cartilage operation might be necessary although he added, 'I won't try and influence the specialist's decision.'

I suspected that he had probably told Charlie that it was a cartilage. Dr Fitzgerald had more X-rays taken and the knee was injected with a special fluid which shows up cartilage damage. It would be a blow if Charlie needed an operation.

Tuesday, 8 January.

Don Taylor came up to say the X-ray showed there was no internal damage. Charlie didn't need an operation. I was very relieved.

The thaw set in, we were able to train on grass and the players were in the right mood for the tie at Wimbledon. They'd had so little football that they were eager to get out there and our 2–0 victory was a very professional performance. Phil Boyer got both goals and the second, a volley on the turn direct from Terry Gennoe's kick, would have made headlines if Cyrille Regis or Kenny Dalglish had scored it. As an unfashionable club, we had to reconcile ourselves to a down-page mention.

Curran, the clown, reached the by-line twenty times in the first half but only one cross reached a colleague. I think he was expecting a rollicking but at half-time I congratulated him. 'Not many players can get to the line as often as that in a season, let alone forty-five minutes,' I said. 'Just keep going.' His expression showed that this mild piece of psychology had got home. Early in the second half a lucky clearance from Steve Williams sent him away and, though his eventual cross was late, it reached Boyer and we got the vital first goal.

Thursday, 11 January.

Before the routine board meeting, I saw Dr Ramsey about the medical side and he said, 'You've been gunning for me a long time, I am resigning.' I said, 'You've got nothing to resign from. You officially retired twelve months ago. Someone else has already been appointed. But I want you to relinquish your contact with the players and hand over the entire responsibility to Dr Lawrence.' I said he would continue to have his two tickets for the directors' box. After forty years we weren't kicking him out. It was a nasty business but I had to be firm. I'm a professional and can't afford mistakes.

When I arrived at the rented house, Father Gilhoolley was there. 'How did you find us?' I said. 'I knocked at a few doors,' he said. That meant the whole neighbourhood would know we were there. There would be no more privacy. He had come to ask a favour. He wanted me to bring the team over for one of his fund-raising dances. I said I would see about it.

Friday, 12 January.

Most games were already off in the Midlands because the snow and ice had returned, but John Barnwell was keen to play our match at Wolverhampton. Alex Hamill, a local referee, inspected the Molineux pitch at half past one and said it was still playable so we travelled overnight.

Frank Sibley, newly appointed manager of Walsall, had rung previously about Ian Turner and we completed a £15,000 deal.

Saturday, 13 January.

At a quarter past nine the referee said there was no chance of us playing so we went back to Southampton. It was irksome and costly. The decision could probably have been made the day before. I was back in time to see the reserves beat Luton 3–1 at the Dell. O'Donoghue, the new signing, scored as fine a goal as I had seen all season and, though that was very satisfying, it added to my problems because I would now have another player pressing for the striker's role.

Sunday, 14 January.

As we were due to play the first leg of the semi-final of the League Cup against Leeds on the Wednesday, I agreed to speak at a Variety Club Sportsman's Night at the Queen's Hotel, Leeds. The post-ponements in the FA Cup meant that the game was put off a week but I decided to attend even though it meant a 230-mile drive each way.

It was an evening dress function attended by about six hundred people paying £20 a ticket. The celebrities were asked to take a bow by the Chief Barker, Harry Swales, Kevin Keegan's agent, and John Charles, who is very popular still in Leeds, received the warmest reception along with, surprisingly I felt because Leeds isn't a rugby-union stronghold, Gareth Edwards.

When I arrived, I saw this magnificent horse being led in and was told it was Red Rum. Ginger McCain, his trainer, was there and Greville Starkey, the jockey, came first in the voting for the Yorkshire Sporting Personality of the Year with Gareth Edwards second and Alan Minter third. As always with these big dinners the food wasn't good. The main course was steak. In my speech, I congratulated Ginger on getting Red Rum in such fine shape and said, 'He tasted beautiful. A bit underdone though.'

After the wit of the impressionist, Aidan J. Crawley, who took off Brian Clough, John Rickman and Muhammed Ali brilliantly, the Home Secretary, Merlyn Rees, was formal and there were some objections when he said that hooliganism wasn't just for the police to handle, but that the clubs had a responsibility too. Turning to Gareth Edwards, he said, 'In your sport, the problem is not off the pitch, but on it.' He was greeted with boos and cries of 'rubbish' but he handled the barracking well.

A silver bust of Red Rum was sold for £8,000 and the proceeds from the auction came to £33,000, an incredible amount I thought. The money went towards the building of a new children's home. There were some footballing friends there, Ron Greenwood, George Mulhall of Bradford City, Francis Lee and Mick Buxton of Huddersfield. I had intended to go on to the Preston *v.* Derby Cup tie the next night but it was postponed.

Tuesday, 16 January.

The weather eased so we went ahead with a Football Combination game against Crystal Palace. We played 4–2–4 against their 4–3–3 and lost 1–0. Palace had some experienced players like George Graham, Tony Hazell and Phil Holder in their team and, though we had most of the play, our youngsters couldn't adapt tactically. Mick Buxton and his assistant John Hazelden, who used to be a player with me at Doncaster Rovers, were down to look over some of our players, Tony Sealy and Austin Hayes in particular. I had them in for a drink afterwards. It was a long way for them to come and I remembered my own days as a Fourth Division manager. I dropped them off at their hotel on the way home.

Chris, who had played in the Youth side that beat Chelsea 1–0 at Stamford Bridge, had just arrived home. He was very pale with exhaustion and tension. I shook him by the hand and we had a talk about the game. Anne was there and it was good that she should hear me praise him. Often she became anxious that I was putting too much pressure on him but that was part of his education.

Wednesday, 17 January.

The Wolves game was on again and we set off. Near Gloucester there was four inches of snow so I asked the driver to stop for me to check again with Molineux. The game was still on. In my pre-match talk I told the players this one would be a big test because Wolves would be expecting to win.

The first half proved that my fears were right. Wolves led 2–0 and I strode in at half-time and tore into the players. 'You've really let me down badly,' I said. 'They're ahead because they've battled and you haven't.' In the second half Wolves hardly saw the ball but it ended 2–0 and as we walked off John Barnwell said, 'You played us off the park in the second half.' That was little consolation. I told the players, 'Let that be a kick up the backside for you. At this level, you've got to go flat out the whole ninety minutes.' Chris Nicholl, normally so reliable, had his worst game for a long time and Malcolm Waldron was poor too. We would need them to be much more effective than that at Leeds.

As I sat dozing on the bus, I was worried about the possibility of an accident because it was icy and foggy. We have a different

driver every time and you never get to know the man who has your
life in his hands. We got home at half past two in the morning and
Anne was waiting up, as she always is.

Thursday, 18 January.

Yet another moving day. The Golac house was going to become
available at the end of January when they were moving into a
£25,000 house in Chandlers Ford. But Ivan's wife had to go back
home with an elderly relative and he was alone so we booked him
into a hotel and took over his rented house ourselves. He wouldn't
want to look after himself for a few weeks and it suited all of us.
With most of our furniture in storage, it was a quicker move than
the last. I couldn't stay. I had to attend an IBM function at Good-
wood House, near the racecourse in Sussex. Anne and two of her
friends had to work hard cleaning up. They spent four hours just
on the cooker, which was in a filthy state. It was very unusual for
a manager to go into a house which has been used by a player.

Southampton still own a few houses near the Dell but these days
players would never live in such properties. They want £40,000–
50,000 places in nice areas. We were having these houses pulled
down and the land used to extend the club facilities.

Friday, 19 January.

The snow was falling again which was surprising.

I thought we'd had our quota for the year. I warned Alan Dicks,
Bristol City's manager, that tomorrow's match might be off but he
decided to travel.

I had the reserves in for a gee-up talk. I asked them for their
views about our failure against Palace and detected from their
answers that my suspicions were accurate. There was an air of cockiness and willingness to pass responsibility on to others and I warned
them that this would have to change. I said I still loved them but
I wouldn't put up with it.

After they went, I spoke to the coaching staff about their own
standards. I said I felt they were taking things for granted too much
and cited the case of the £100 bonus. John McGrath jumped in
and said, 'I never look what's in my wage packet.' 'That's all right,'
I said, 'I'll deduct £100 next time and see if you notice that.' In

the past five years, I reminded them, their working conditions had improved a hundred per cent but they hadn't improved with them. I said, 'Some of those young players are getting away with it, answering back when they shouldn't be. If they show a lack of respect, nail them.'

To end a day of reprimands, I lectured Fred Scott about deficiencies in his department. When he worked as a scout from his home in Nottingham, he did a sound job. He was a good judge of a player and he'd got us Peter Wells and Peter Rodrigues. But now he was working from the club, he was getting too close to the players. He was living with Curran and I think it's a bad idea for members of the staff to be living with players.

Ted Bates came in when they had all left and said he had arranged to go to Spurs *v.* Leeds tomorrow. I said that was taking the easy option. Preston, our FA Cup opponents, should be the priority, not Leeds. We know enough about Leeds. Ted altered his plans and we ended the afternoon doing some laps together on the pitch. It helped clear the cobwebs.

Saturday, 20 January.

John Homewood, one of our best referees, called the match off. It was sad that someone with his ability had to quit at the end of the season. He was fit enough to continue. Alan Dicks stayed on for a chat. He complained about some transfer business with Derby coming out in the newspapers, a familiar story. He said he had a bad knee and might have cartilage trouble. That is what comes of being too well entrenched at a club: you put on weight. Lew Chatterley rang the players to tell them the match was off and said he was making plans to hire a coach to take them to Spurs *v.* Leeds. Most of them seemed keen but by the end of the morning, they had lost interest. It was too much trouble. Bally had heard Kempton Races were on.

In the car to London, I amplified my views to Lew about how I felt the club should be going. He said he thought I might be aiming too high and I replied that if the staff couldn't compete at that level some might have to go. Leeds showed the depth of their squad by being able to rest Paul Madeley, Trevor Cherry and Eddie Gray and still win 2–1. Manny Cussins reminded me again that I could have been enjoying their success if I'd accepted his offer. It made me think of what one of the punters had said at the dinner in Leeds, 'Do you know what they call Jimmy Adamson at Elland Road? Howard Hughes: because they never see him.' Leeds had only lost once in seventeen matches since he took over so Jimmy's way must be right. Perhaps he, Brian Clough and Jack Charlton, who don't spend too much time with their players, have the right idea.

I felt sorry for Keith Burkinshaw, the Spurs manager. I noticed that he was talking his way through the game. That's allowable on the bench but it's a bad sign when you are in the director's box. The crowd had a bit of a go at him.

Sunday, 21 January.

The Dell was firmer so we had a hard session, including a sixty minutes' match against the reserves which the first team won 4–1. We were hardening up again, and getting ready for Leeds. The players seemed to think I would bring Manny Andruszewski in to do a marking job on Tony Currie but I hadn't made my mind up. Brian Flynn and Eddie Gray could be just as dangerous as Currie. If Manny did come in, I wouldn't leave Curran out. I was determined to play my winger.

I was worried about Steve Williams. He hadn't been playing so well. At times, he was undisciplined. Opposing teams rated him highly but they didn't see his warts and pimples. I resolved to have a talk with him to test him out. I knew that if I said to Bally I was planning to leave him out in the interests of the team he would accept it, but if I said that to Williams, I might lose him and never get him back. He was young and proud.

Monday, 22 January.

I intended to have Williams in for fifteen minutes but it developed into an hour. I said he was giving the impression that he knew it all and had nothing more to learn. 'You're not working hard enough off the ball,' I said. 'You only want to play when you've got it. You're not as aggressive as you were and you're not scoring any goals. 'If I took a vote among the other players, they'd prefer to have Manny in the side rather than you, the way you're playing.' As I thought, he objected but not in the way I feared. He'd taken it all in. He would be a better player for it.

I saw Lew to remind him about one or two tactical ideas I wanted the players to practice. One was to attack the far post, not because Leeds were weak there but because they were so strong at the near post.

John Benson, Bournemouth's manager, had resigned. Pressure on his wife and children he said. Kids were making remarks to his children at school. We were discussing that at home when Sean walked in and said, 'I've had that all my life.' Anne was quite shocked and it made me realize again what it meant to have a football manager for a father. Some wives might glory in the situation but Anne never did. That day someone recognized her in a chemist's shop and said to the other customers 'That's Lawrie McMenemy's wife.' She was very embarrassed.

John Benson's going reminded me of a conversation I had had with Alec Stock at QPR earlier in the season. He said he was a little tired of pouring the gin and tonics as a director at QPR and fancied going back into management. Did I know a club on the South Coast that might want an elder statesman? I knew Harold Walker, Bournemouth's chairman, and liked him. My conscience was clear. Benson had left and there was a vacancy so I rang Mr Walker and said Alec Stock was interested. Alec was a person of stature in the game, an honest man and a reviver of lost causes. Earlier in the month Lew Chatterley asked me to put a word in at Exeter for a friend of his, Brian Godfrey, and I spoke to the Exeter chairman. Bobby Saxton had left to take Malcolm Allison's job at Plymouth and Godfrey was appointed in his place. Managers do this recommending all the time. Directors often advertise jobs but nine out of ten posts are filled through personal contact. When I was first approached by Southampton, the chairman rang Don Revie and asked him what he thought of me.

Tuesday, 23 January.

Cars were slithering about all over the roads in the icy conditions and it was no surprise when the London coach firm who were contracted to take us to Leeds rang and said the coach wouldn't be at the Dell until three o'clock instead of the scheduled one o'clock. I said, 'Don't waste time coming down here. We'll hire another coach and meet you halfway.' The man suggested Richmond. I said Oxford was better and we met by a roundabout outside Oxford in mid-afternoon. The driver didn't impress me. He was cocky and when I suggested a route said he knew a better one. The heating was blowing out cold air and the coffee machine which we hired at great expense only produced cold coffee. There is nothing worse for footballers on the way to a big match than irritations like these that they can moan about.

The hotel was in Bradford and as we came into the city it was obvious the driver didn't know where it was. That infuriated me because he should have looked it up on a map. I resolved never to use that particular company again.

Wednesday, 24 January.

Stafford Heginbotham, an old friend, came in his Rolls to take me to Elland Road for the pitch inspection. They have under-soil heating at Elland Road and Alf Grey, the referee, passed the pitch as fit. I knew Alf from the 1976 FA Cup Final when he was on the line.

The players trained under Lew at a local ground in the snow and when I arrived they were frolicking around in the snow like kids. That was a good sign. They hadn't let the journey depress them.

At the hotel Mick Buxton came to talk about buying Tony Sealy but Sealy didn't want to go North. Mick's presence was a distraction because I wanted to concentrate totally on the Leeds match but I had lunch with him nevertheless. He'd made the effort to come and was a fellow manager after all.

Ted Bates was keen on a swim in the hotel pool while the players went to their rooms in the afternoon for a rest but I wanted to be alone to think about the game and jot down a few points for my talk. I'd decided to keep an unchanged side leaving Williams in and putting Manny on the bench.

The talk went exceedingly well. I thought I got it just right, gee-ing-up the players to play above themselves. Leeds liked to play the ball around and slow it down and I said, 'You've got to quicken it up and stop them playing it their way.' I spoke for thirty minutes and it was one of the key talks of my career. The theme was that my players were up against better players on the day but, if they went about it the right way, they could cancel out the superior ability of Jimmy Adamson's team. I had a slightly different role for Bally, which he accepted, and I asked Phil Boyer and Trevor Hebberd to pressurize Paul Madeley in particular.

The favourable mood which I had created was almost ruined by another disaster on the coach taking us to the ground. The driver found himself on the wrong part of the MI and had to reverse a hundred yards down the motorway to get on to the right road. That meant we were caught up in the traffic going to the game and it was five to seven when we finally arrived.

There was a crowd of 33,415 in the ground and the atmosphere was tremendous. There weren't many fans from Southampton but that wasn't surprising. The ones that came didn't arrive home until five in the morning.

Tony Currie beat the offside trap to score in the twenty-fifth minute and Boyer was booked for a tackle from behind on Brian Flynn after the ball had gone. I had no complaints about that but I didn't agree with the critics the next day who wrote we had been too physical. When a team is determined to raise its pace and hustle and challenge for every ball, there is bound to be physical contact. I was faintly amused that it should be Leeds who were complaining. They pioneered the business of intimidating opponents and it was said that in their heyday the manager used to sit on the bench wearing shinpads. The two worst fouls weren't mentioned in the press: an over-the-top by Arthur Graham on Alan Ball and a whack across the nose by Ray Hankin's elbow on Bally which drew blood.

At half-time Golac complained about his shoulder. Don Taylor, the physio, had been left behind at the Dell to look after Charlie George and Lew Chatterley was the spongeman. Lew said, 'I'll go and get the doctor.' I'd finished my tactical discussion and came over to see if Golac was fit to continue. I lifted his arm aloft and then brought it down slowly. I am no medical expert but I could tell from the movement he had that there was no break. When the doctor arrived, he said it was bruising, nothing serious, so Golac went out again.

Three minutes after half-time we misjudged a free kick and Hankin crashed the second goal past Terry Gennoe. Golac started to walk towards the bench. He was packing it in. I said to Manny, 'Get warmed up.' Lew drew out the number two substitution card but before the linesman could attract the referee's attention to make the substitution, Gennoe's long kick put Terry Curran away down the right and Curran's deep cross was headed in at the far post by Nick Holmes. It was the move we had been practising and if I had been a young manager, I would have boasted to the press afterwards about how it had worked. Golac seemed to have changed his mind now we were back in the game. Bally spotted it at once and had a go at him. He'd bottled it. Staying on was a mortal sin because it meant that he hadn't been too badly injured. I was livid. Perhaps this was a weakness of the overseas players. You judge people in football by imagining who would leave the room first when the fire bell goes. In my list Golac would now be near the top. I vowed I would bring this up in the next team meeting. I would be quite ruthless about exposing him in front of the others.

The best goal of the night was the volley which Steve Williams put away in the sixty-fourth minute to enable us to take a 2–2 score back to the Dell for the second leg. Things couldn't have worked out better. Unfortunately some of the joy was taken out of it nine minutes from time when Boyer was sent off for ungentlemanly conduct.

Boyer had chased after Currie and fouled him and Currie picked up the ball and, as he threw it at Boyer hitting him in the testicles, he said, 'Here you are little boy.' Currie is like that. He can be arrogant and bait opponents and Boyer, for all his experience, fell for it. Boyer put his foot under the ball and flicked it deliberately over Currie's head so he couldn't take the free kick. Mr Grey rushed up and I was staggered to see him show Boyer the red card. Technically he was right. It was Boyer's second offence but it meant he would miss our next match which might well be the second leg. Mr Grey refereed the match sensibly but it was the old story, the player who offends last is the one to be punished more severely. Bally tried to tell the referee that Currie had provoked Boyer but was ignored.

As the teams were leaving the pitch, John McGrath went up to Currie and said, 'You got Boyer sent off.' They argued heatedly and Hankin stepped in. I pulled McGrath away and in the dressing room he apologized. I said he shouldn't get carried away. The match was only at half-time. There was still another ninety minutes to go. Boyer mumbled an apology. It was not the first time he had been sent off.

After the television and press interviews I went to the players' room to see Jack Charlton, Ian St John, Maurice Setters and a few other friends. When Leeds beat us 4–0 their players stayed on a long time but now they were the first out. The result was a bad one for them. I was elated. We had a chance of showing the whole nation on television what we could do. It was a great comeback and a fine tribute to the character of my players.

Thursday, 25 January.

I asked Lew how the players had celebrated. Most teams would have been up late drinking. It's the habit in the game. Players can't sleep anyway because they're excited and few managers insist on a curfew in such circumstances. 'I found seven of them playing one of those TV games in Chris Nicholl's room,' said Lew. That was typical of my team. Lew had ordered three bottles of wine with their after-match meal and they hadn't finished it. They just weren't drinkers, which was good for me. It meant fewer problems.

But Bally had gone out with Curran and obviously had had a long night. And Peachy, who had a bad ankle, went out for a drink with Boyer. As we were due to meet Preston in the Fourth Round of the FA Cup on Saturday, we stayed in the North and the coach took us on to Blackpool where we made our base at the Norbeck Castle, a big hotel frequently used by football clubs. Stoke City were leaving as we arrived. The hotel had a pool and plenty to occupy the players but the food was nondescript. The staff and I ate out. I arranged for Sealy and Tim Coak to be sent up to replace the injured Peach and Boyer who would be ineligible if the game took place. Boyer never likes being away.

The England Under 21 team was announced and Williams wasn't in it which was a vindication of what I had been saying to him. I knew he would be disappointed because he had never let the Under 21s down.

Friday, 26 January.

The prospects of play at Preston were grim and I alerted the coach driver that we would be going back to Southampton. The M6 was blocked by heavy overnight snow and he didn't appear to have much idea of what he should do. I called British Rail and found there was a train at half past eleven at Preston which would take us to London and we managed to catch it. I was taking a chance because the game hadn't been called off but I phoned Deepdale from the station and Alan Kelly, Nobby Stiles's assistant, said it was now definitely off.

There were lots of letters for me at the office, most praising our performances. One contained cuttings from a local newspaper: 'McMenemy fed his players raw meat at half-time,' one line read and we were called 'brutal' and 'physical'. It is easy for local reporters to become biased. If their team fails to get into Europe they suffer as well. I smiled when I read that Currie, Flynn and Paul Hart were all supposed to be injured. I hadn't said anything about our injuries, Peach, Golac and Ball, but I was sure the Leeds trio would play in the second leg.

Saturday, 27 January.

I had the problem of replacing Boyer in Tuesday's second leg. There were a number of alternative players but they were all young and inexperienced. Leeds had a squad of internationals. That was the difference.

I went to Oxford to see the nearest game that was still on, and saw United draw 1–1 with Watford. Luther Blissett, the Jamaica-born striker just capped by England at Under 21 level, did little but I'd seen him before and knew he was a player of vast potential.

At night I saw Manchester City go out of the FA Cup at Shrewsbury on 'Match of the Day' and it was a reminder that no-one is secure in professional football. Before we beat them in the League, City were one of the fancied teams but we beat them in the League Cup and, despite Malcolm Allison's arrival, they were now out of the FA Cup. The attitude of the players was wrong, as Allison said on television, but I also agreed with Jimmy Hill that City's tactics were at fault.

Monday, 29 January.

I told Bally my plan that Manny Andruszewski would replace Boyer. Bally was impressed and I told him not to tell anyone. Andruszewski was delighted. 'Get yourself in the right frame of mind,' I said.

In a general talk with the players, who hadn't been told the line-up, I brought up the Golac business. Looking straight at him, I said, 'You'll have to be sure your attitude is better than it was last time. You used your injury as an excuse.' His face changed colour and immediately I felt some remorse because after the game the doctor had told me that his shoulder was sprung: there was definitely a bump there. But I'd got the point over.

There were plenty of other things to do to take my mind off the game: the presenting of a Queen's Scout award in the dressing room; the recording of a thirty-second slot for a Fred Pontin advert and the topping-out ceremony of the new house. I climbed a ladder, laid the last brick and stuck a flag on it. Then I said a few words and Anne and I had a drink with the builder, Brian Hunt, the architect, Norman Woodford and the twenty workers.

Tuesday, 30 January.

Some ice still remained on the pitch but it didn't worry Clive Thomas when he made his nine o'clock inspection. 'Get that broken up and we'll be all right,' he said. I suppose I am as close to Clive as any manager but he never does me any favours. He is his own man, very positive. Jimmy Adamson was there and when Clive went off to do some training we had a cup of tea.

I kept busy because if I stopped the enormity of it would affect me: ninety minutes away from another Wembley appearance. Most managers are lucky if they get there once in their career. I was on the verge of a second visit in three years. Players tend to sit around on a match day and that only increases the tension. They go to bed in the afternoons but they don't sleep. I did a few laps and it made me more relaxed.

When we arrived at the Royal Hotel for the pre-match meal, we discovered that we were being moved to another room which was upsetting. Footballers are superstitious and don't like a change of routine. One or two chewed off the waitresses, a sign of increasing tension.

In the team talk, I spoke about how I wanted Manny to play against Currie, not too tight. I used the tactics board to illustrate what I wanted. With no Boyer it meant that the midfield men would have to support more and take the half chance.

The only goal of the game, the one that got us to Wembley, was a bit lucky though I thought we did enough in both matches to deserve victory. Bally, Holmes and Hebberd worked a nice movement up the left and, as Hebberd's cross came in just behind Frank Gray, Curran had time for the ball to bounce off one leg, hit the other and finish up high in the roof of the net as he struck it. If he had been another foot or two further out it would have gone over the bar.

Charlie George made the best crack afterwards. 'I thought the ref. was going to blow up for three touches,' he said. That was a reference to the one- and two-touch training games we play in practice. If a player touches the ball three times, it's a free kick. Curran's goal, his first for the club, wasn't in the Boyer or MacDougall class but it was enough.

We were beginning to lose it by the interval and at half-time I had to work hard. Some players wanted to change the way we were playing but the only alteration I made was to tell Steve Williams to go further forward. Ideally Bally would have been better but he didn't have the legs.

The longer the second half went on, the more convinced I was that Leeds wouldn't score. The crowd were noisy and inspiring, but in the final minutes I sensed they were losing it too, as though they were so nervous about the team conceding a goal that they daren't shout any more. I got out of the box, turned to the stand and waved my arms like André Previn at the Albert Hall. It served to lift the crowd off again. As Clive Thomas jerked his arm forward and blew for the last time, I was engulfed. It was the moment a manager savours most and there was a television cameraman there to record it.

It was some time before I was able to struggle my way into the dressing room and the first person to embrace me was MacDougall. It was a genuine feeling of elation by him, as though he was part of it. Well, he had been.

Golac was in an emotional state. 'At last I am at Wembley,' he said. Peter Rodrigues, captain of the 1976 side, was in the room and he said, 'You've got to win it yet.' I wasn't happy at his remark. Right after a semi-final is a time for pros to enjoy it, not worry about the next one. His comment was out of keeping with the mood of the players. It was a fairy tale for Golac whose life ambition was to go to Wembley, and also for Bally who was crowning a glorious career with yet another Wembley appearance. But for me, the outstanding player on the night was someone who wasn't mentioned in any newspaper, Malcolm Waldron. A local lad, he had developed into a very proficient defender but if I had signed Colin Todd he wouldn't have been in the side.

I used the press interviews afterwards to talk about the need to build a new stadium and I had a go at the inadequate coverage in the *Echo* of the match. I wasn't criticizing individuals but it was an example of the small-town outlook in Southampton that the only daily paper in the area had only eight paragraphs about the game on the back page, less than it had about Aldershot playing Shrewsbury on the inside. If I didn't continue to fight that attitude the club would sink back.

My office was full of journalists, friends and staff. Clive Thomas was there too as we celebrated with champagne before going on to an Italian restaurant. Anne went home early with Alison and Sean and it was well after three when I arrived back at the house. Anne was still awake. On these occasions, the manager's wife can't sleep either. We sat chatting for some time.

Wednesday, 31 January.

I was up early to take Alison to school. When I returned, Bally, who hadn't got home until five, was there to talk over the game. At the ground the messages of congratulation were pouring in, one from Alan Mullery along the South Coast at Brighton. It was a big thing for the South Coast. Brian Clough also rang to congratulate me and we talked about what colours the teams would wear at Wembley. As we both played in red, one club would have to change.

I said I didn't mind changing colours as long as we had first choice of dressing room. I wanted the room we had last time. Clough agreed to let us have first choice with Forest using their normal strip, so that meant we could have the yellow shirts and blue shorts we had worn three years before.

Very tired, I could have done with an early night but we were invited to present a plaque for Guide Dogs for the Blind at a jazz club in Eastleigh and it was midnight before we left. The music was relaxing and the audience, 1920s style, didn't pester me. I enjoyed it.

Thursday, 1 February.

A backlash feeling was setting in. We should have been thinking of Saturday's game against Derby but the players were still walking on air. Curran was strutting around as though he'd finally made the big time. We could do with the game being called off.

Boyer was informed by the FA that no extra disciplinary points were added to his total of eleven for being sent off at Leeds, and that pleased him. If the customary twelve points had been added that would take him past twenty and mean a suspension. He would play on Saturday and Andruszewski, who had taken a couple of knocks, was dropped.

At the board meeting, Sir George Meyrick said, 'I was at both games against Leeds and if ever a manager did more than the players to get this result, this was the occasion.' Ted Bates said afterwards that that was praise indeed.

In the afternoon Golac arrived with Charlie George to shift the rest of his furniture. 'When I move into my house, I will get better as a player,' he said. If he did that would make him the buy of the century. Charlie, who had befriended him at the hotel where they were both staying, impressed me by taking charge. He was nothing like the image some people have of him. He was very humorous, sensible and responsible.

There was no chance of an early night because we were invited to dinner by the Chief Constable of Hampshire, John Duke, at his country home at Ovington to talk with the local vicar, the Rev. George Beachey. He wanted me to deliver a lecture at his church on 11 March, the Sunday before the League Cup Final. I agreed to do it. We could get the congregation to say a few prayers for us.

Friday, 2 February.

The requests for tickets were coming in but it wouldn't be as bad as before the FA Cup Final. The allocation per club in the FA Cup is 25,000 compared with 30,000 in the League Cup. As we had an average of 21,000 at the Dell, few of our genuine supporters would be disappointed. We arranged for a temporary secretary to be hired to help with the letters. A man and a woman had an appointment about making a record for Wembley and, though I was sceptical, Malcolm Price said we couldn't lose on the deal they were offering. The man from the local bus company called about hiring us his executive coach but he was a hard bargainer. He didn't take my point that having his coach at Wembley was worth a lot to him in publicity.

Keith Hollingsworth of Southern Television asked me to do the Friday night sports slot on 'Day by Day' just for the one night. I was pleased to do it although it meant reading from a script whereas I prefer ad libbing. In the evening, the third late one in a row, I spoke at an FA coaches meeting at Bournemouth. Alec Stock was there after his first day with the Bournemouth players. 'I'm short of ability,' he said, talking of his new team. 'When I went into the dressing room I wasn't too impressed. Too many beards. Not many pros.'

Saturday, 3 February.

What I feared happened. We were dead against Derby and lost 2–1. Curran was so bad I had to pull him off. Nine out of ten of his crosses had finished in the terraces and no first-class winger should be that wasteful. Jack Charlton had been on the phone about him. During the game Bally came over to the bench and said, 'What about that bugger Curran, boss?' Tommy Docherty heard us and shouted, 'Don't you take him off!'

Charlie George might have lifted us against his old club but he wasn't quite fit. I was asked a question about George in the press room and was rather curt. 'I'll let you know when he's fit to play,' I said to a reporter from the *Daily Express*. I should have been more receptive; it was a legitimate question.

Everyone went home early. There was no-one in my office. The board room was empty. It was a further reminder that yesterday's success doesn't count today. We were a side that had to be flat out if we were going to pick up points. I had won the Bell's Divisional Manager of the Month award, my sixth award, but was feeling dispirited. I thought about Leeds and Sunderland and how much more I could achieve with more quality players. I hadn't felt that way for weeks. I was helped out of the 'low' by a non-football dinner with Malcolm Price, his wife and some friends and even missed seeing 'Match of the Day'.

9. We've been supporting you since 1929

Reaching a Cup Final is exhilarating for a manager. Only four managers out of ninety-two do it every season. But it also brings problems, especially if the team is in the lower half of the table. In the seven weeks between the semi-final and the Final the players begin to think about ensuring their fitness for Wembley. League form suffers.

In Southampton's case the reaction set in straight away and McMenemy had to jump on his players very early on in the preparations for the Forest match. 'By the time we meet Forest I want a cushion of thirty points to make certain we don't have to scuffle about over Easter to get the points to stay up,' he said.

There was also a new role for him to perform – ticket agent. Thousands of Southampton supporters all over the country were wanting tickets for the big day.

Monday, 5 February.

The applications for tickets were pouring in. I had to decide which ones were genuine and I used the system we employed in 1976: divide the letters into three categories, the try-ons, who received a polite letter back thanking the writer for his congratulations, the ones we knew vaguely who would stand a good chance of receiving a ticket, and people in the game, friends and colleagues, who would go down on the approved list.

The allocation for each Finalist was 30,000 so with an average gate of just over 20,000, none of our regular supporters ought to be disappointed. The snag was that only 14,000 were seats and everyone wanted a seat. Priority would go to supporters who could supply the vouchers we had marked out in the programmes of certain matches. One of these matches was the first leg semi-final at Leeds when about five hundred of our hardiest supporters made the trip. They deserved some reward.

The first team squad were entitled to twenty-four tickets each for which they pay face value and the rest of the players were asked to fill in a list. I warned them: 'Every ticket you get will have a name and address on it and anyone caught selling one on the black market could have his contract cancelled.'

Tuesday, 6 February.

Lunch with Sidney Perry of Southern TV about the increased coverage they were planning. The restaurant was full of businessmen tucking into big meals and drinking wine. It's not for me. I don't know how they manage to do any work afterwards!

Jack Charlton wanted to see our reserve game and arranged to stay with us. When I arrived back at the office he was there and he sat quietly while I dealt with the correspondence. 'You're barmy,' he said. 'I leave all that to my secretary.'

The phone rang and it was Ron Atkinson from the Polygon Hotel where Albion were staying the night before playing a friendly at Portsmouth. When I finished speaking, I said to Jack: 'Let's go round and give him a surprise.'

Ron was in his hotel room with his assistant Colin Addison drinking champagne and orange. Addison said, 'Well done on reaching Wembley.' And Ron said: 'I was going to send you a telegram but I forgot. I wish it was us. I'm as jealous as hell.'

The reserve match on a bleak, cold night ended in a 2–0 victory for Plymouth Reserves, our third loss on the trot. Some of the players were becoming frustrated at not getting into the first team. On the way home, Jack and I popped back to the Polygon to see what Atkinson was doing but he wasn't there. Some of the Albion players were waiting for a taxi. It was raining too heavily to walk.

I offered some of them a lift. David Mills, Albion's £516,000 signing from Middlesbrough, was one who accepted. He is such a nice person that being Britain's costliest reserve didn't appear to worry him. I'm sure if it had been Charlie George in that position, he would have been banging my door down. Which is the right attitude, I suppose. Ron was lucky to have someone like Mills. Jack and I were home by midnight but it was 3 am before we went to bed.

Wednesday, 7 February.

Up early because Chris had to be on the 9.10 train for a Youth Cup tie at Middlesbrough. The week before he was one of eight apprentices who went on a self-reliance course at the Outward Bound School at Rhowniar on the Welsh Coast.

When I heard about the course, I thought it was a good idea to send some of the lads to see what they were made of and also to show them some discipline which is lacking in life these days. To survive the course, you needed character, guts and discipline – qualities that are essential in football.

Anne was petrified. It meant the lads had to sleep a night out on a mountain in the snow, jump down a rope into a pitch black quarry, dive fully clothed into a freezing cold river and perform one of two other endurance tests only encountered normally by commandos. She was ready to fly up there to rescue Chris at any time. But the course was a success. It taught them the value of team work and comradeship and they will be better for it.

In the rush to get Chris to the station, I forgot that Ted Bates had volunteered to travel with the team and I was supposed to pick him up. I rang to apologize and suggest he could catch them up by taking a later train. He was very angry. 'I've been sitting here since 7.30 waiting and you forgot,' he said. 'I'm not very happy about it.' And he slammed the phone down.

I asked Fred Scott to call him back but Ted said: 'I don't want to talk to you or him', and put the phone back on the receiver!

Anne and I were invited to the pre-match meal at the Wembley Conference Centre before England's European Championship match against Northern Ireland and on the way we picked up Jock Stein at London Airport. On our table were Ron Atkinson and his wife, Jock and Jack Charlton. Jack was his usual undiplomatic self. Introduced to Ron's wife, he said: 'That's not your wife, is it?'

He asked Ron if he had bought any more Indians or Pakistanis. Our host at the table was Ranjit Anand, an Indian! Ron was nervous. He was giving the expert comments on TV, the first time he had done it. He asked me what he should do. 'Just look at the cameras and don't think of the people at home,' I said. 'Be yourself.' Later when I saw him he said it went well and he enjoyed it.

I did the comments for BBC radio. It was a good feeling as I walked in the dark from the centre to the stadium. The excitement of the occasion catches you, though it's not your team that's playing. And it's too dark for many people to recognize you. Kevin Keegan was a revelation in England's 4–0 victory. His game has improved so much since going to play for Hamburg. But Pat Jennings had one of his poorest games for his country. He was made captain because it was his seventy-fifth international and he appeared to be doing too much.

The usual group of football people were crowded into the Centre restaurant afterwards. I had a long chat with Bobby Moore. He seemed a nice man. He has more presence than most footballers. He said he wasn't missing football because he was so busy with his pubs.

I was told the outcome of our Youth Cup match: a 1–0 victory. That was a great result because Boro had a good record in the competition at Ayresome Park. I sent the team up on first-class tickets and they had repaid me by reaching the last eight.

Thursday, 8 February.

We stayed overnight at the Esso and the lobby was full of journalists there for a Ron Greenwood press conference. Monte Fresco, the *Daily Mirror* photographer had just been talking to Anne and said: 'That's your strength, your wife. It's the same with Henry Cooper. Albina makes it easy for him.' It was very satisfying to hear him say it.

The board meeting at the club in the afternoon was taken up with arrangements for the League Cup Final. Instead of a banquet we were only having a dinner for the staff. Banquets cost up to £25,000 these days and are simply too expensive. Most clubs have dropped them. In the evening I went to Sean's school, St Mary's College, for the open night. He was lined up for four GCEs, above average for his age, and was working hard. The ribbing he had from the other pupils wasn't affecting his work.

Saturday, 10 February.

After my warning to the players that there might be changes unless their attitude was right in the matches before Wembley, they went out at Ipswich and earned a useful point in a 0–0 draw. The game was played in a swirling wind and on a hard pitch and was uninteresting. Bally had his worst game of the season but he had flu symptoms.

Bobby Robson showed Anne and me the new indoor training area and the club's new executive boxes. While he was conducting us around he talked about his dilemma over an offer he'd had to become Sunderland's manager. At Ipswich he ruled the place and Patrick and John Cobbold, the brothers who had shared the chairmanship in the past twenty years, are two of the nicest, most accommodating people in the game.

Before I left the players, I reminded them not to have a late night because we were playing Preston in the FA Cup two days later. Saturday is the traditional night for footballers to enjoy themselves but I knew I had little to worry about with my lot.

Sunday, 11 February.

As the half-term holiday had started, Anne took Alison and Sean to see her folks in the North East. Chris was going to stay in digs with another apprentice. I wanted to know if the Preston game was still on and when I spoke to Alan Kelly, the former goalkeeper who was Nobby Stiles's assistant, he said: 'No fears Lawrie. It's in good nick. It's hard like it would be at the end of the season. No need for an inspection. We're looking forward to trying our skills against a club from a higher division.'

'You'll have me crying in a minute,' I said. 'I still want the ref. in all the same.' Every small club playing a bigger club at home would want the game on. I didn't want to be caught. I wanted the match referee, Alex Hamill, to give his verdict, not Alan Kelly.

Monday, 12 February.

Alex Hamill said it was playable so we set off, arriving at Euston just in time to see the Inter-City train pulling out. I tried to have it stopped but failed. The Liberal leader, David Steel, had a train stopped for him a few days before but Southampton Football Club weren't worth it!

The next train, two hours later, had no restaurant car but the buffet staff fried up some bacon and eggs which the players ate in their seats. No-one complained, which was a good sign.

The Deepdale pitch was rock hard with a few ruts but I couldn't disagree with the referee. It was just about playable. Preston are an old fashioned club, a bit run down and the hospitality afterwards wasn't what you'd expect, but they have some sound people on the staff – Nobby, a nice, earnest man and his trainer, Harry Hubbick in particular. Harry used to work with Alan Ball senior at Halifax. 'It'll just take a short stud,' he said. He was pleased to talk with me. 'You're not like that bugger from Brighton who was here last week,' he said. 'Him with his big cigar and dark glasses.' He meant Alan Mullery.

The players only had time for an hour's rest and when it came time for the team talk, Bally said : 'Leave me out. I'll not need motivating tonight.' Preston were the club that sacked his father as manager and it still rankled with him.

We won the tie 1–0 and Bally scored the goal. As it went in, he turned to the directors' box and gestured, not offensively, as if to say that's one back.

I left the team to drive to Newcastle to rejoin Anne and it was a nightmarish journey in driving snow across the M62. I stopped at a motorway cafe and it was full of Manchester United fans from Sunderland who had been watching Manchester United beat Fulham 1–0 in the Cup. We exchanged some banter over a plate of chips.

Friday, 16 February.

Heavy snow closed Newcastle Airport the day before and it took me nearly fourteen hours to return to Southampton by rail and road. Everton, our opponents on Saturday, had returned from Majorca at midnight and wanted to know if the game was on. Almost every other match was postponed.

Colin Downey, the referee, passed the pitch at 3 and said providing the weather didn't worsen, the game would go ahead. At 3.20 I told Gordon Lee, the Everton manager, and he said: 'We don't want to go down there on a wild goose chase. It can't be fit surely?'

I said it was and advised him to travel. 'It's too late,' he said. I knew his players had been training at 2, an indication that they thought the match was off. 'You can get a train in time,' I said. 'Yes but it won't have a restaurant car,' he said. He was making every excuse.

Saturday, 17 February.

There was another inspection arranged at 8 am to stop the Everton fans travelling if there had been a deterioration in the conditions. I didn't go. I didn't want to get in a slanging match with Gordon Lee. Later, Brian Truscott, my secretary, rang to say he had been insulted by Lee and he said the Everton manager had raged at the referee.

Some referees might have reported him but Mr Downey stayed calm. Lee had said that if the match went on five or six players could break their legs. Later, he described the pitch as a death trap.

When I arrived, I agreed with the referee. We had covered the pitch with tarpaulins, and it took a short stud. One of Gordon's arguments was that the game was only going on because it was on 'Match of the Day'. Everton had lost only twice up to that point, at Coventry and Wolverhampton, both on hard pitches and both games had been televised.

He seemed to think there was a conspiracy against him. The facts were that the two TV channels alternate each week to have first choice and this week ITV won and chose Leicester *v.* Newcastle, which was certain to go on because of Leicester's hot air balloon.

The BBC chose Brighton *v.* Crystal Palace which had been declared on and our match was second choice. The BBC also had a unit at Plymouth *v.* Carlisle in case we were ruled out. The BBC had asked us because we were likely to play. Their staff were putting up their cameras and offered to help if we needed any labour to work on the pitch. We didn't need it.

Steve Williams' knee was puffy and I said I wouldn't risk him. He didn't like being left out but Graham Baker was a more than adequate replacement. I decided on one other change, Austin Hayes for Hebberd, who hadn't been doing it. The players had been measured for their suits for Wembley and I reminded them that didn't mean they were in the side. 'It's how you play between now and the Final that counts with me,' I said.

I said that the state of the pitch was no excuse. It was hard up the middle but quite soft at the sides and was playable. We played some of our best football of the season and our 3–0 win was a tremendous performance. It was Everton's biggest beating up to then.

In the next dug out, the Everton staff were raving and ranting at their players. They seemed to be suggesting that they should be getting stuck in more, which was surprising if they felt the pitch was as dangerous as was claimed earlier.

When he was a manager of Port Vale, Gordon always said when you arrived that your team would be in for a tough game. They were a very physical side. Since going to Everton, a club that can recruit some of the most skilled players in the country, he's had this phobia that other teams are going to be physical back at his team.

In our case, it was an unjustified fear. We didn't have any physical players. We beat Everton by skill, not intimidation. As the whistle sounded and we got up to go into the tunnel, Gordon was still complaining and I said to his trainer: 'You want to get hold of him.'

Lee was still agitated when he was interviewed afterwards by the press and TV. I was standing just round the corner when I heard him say that five players in his team had been injured. But neither trainer had been on and neither substitute had been used.

'What players?' he was asked. 'Andy King might need an operation,' he said. 'And there's George Wood, Mark Higgins...' He started to tail off. He was carrying the melodrama too far. Everyone could see that the pitch hadn't been dangerous. There were some senior reporters present and they weren't fooled.

The hour after a game is a vital time for a manager to say the right things. Gordon Lee had in my view misjudged the situation. As Bally said, 'He'd given his players an out by condemning the pitch before the game started.' When I was interviewed, I was curt. 'Criticism of the pitch detracts from our fine performance,' I said.

Bob Latchford, Alan Dicks, Danny Blanchflower and Ron Suart all agreed that the pitch was good enough to play on. I asked my players later about King's injury. 'He's had it for a few weeks,' said Steve Williams, who had been talking to the Everton players in the players room. 'It's a cyst that's got to be removed.'

We hadn't any injuries although Hayes was whacked a couple of times. He has a good early touch and had played well in the conditions. When he played like this, no-one mentioned Charlie George, who was moving into a rented house in Cadnam. Charlie's calf muscle injury wasn't coming along as well as expected. But if we had a bad result, people would be asking about him.

Monday, 19 February.

Like the Sunday papers, the Mondays had laid into Gordon Lee and it proved again that it is no use a manager complaining. He has to keep quiet and get on with it. The local radio station carried a report that Southampton were offering nine reserve players for sale and named the players. I hadn't announced it publicly.

What usually happens as the deadline for transfers draws near on 8 March, subsequently put back until 29 March because of the backlog of fixtures, is that managers who want to release players to let others through from lower down send out a circular to other clubs saying they have players available without naming them. But I believe it is better to list the names and ages so interested managers know exactly who is available.

It was annoying that the news had leaked out. One of the players was Hayes but it didn't mean he was no longer wanted. I was testing the market. Peter East said he didn't know how the story got out and further inquiries showed pretty conclusively that someone at Portsmouth Football Club or Bournemouth Football Club had tipped off a local journalist.

I dictated a letter to Jimmy Dickinson, the Portsmouth manager, asking him to investigate it. I considered the affair to be unethical. Circulars of this nature were marked private and confidential. We weren't selling off nine players, but merely finding out which ones we could sell if need be. Reading were interested in Tony Funnell and one or two clubs also fancied Tony Sealy.

Tuesday, 20 February.

Steve Williams wandered into my office in the afternoon and asked if he was playing that night against Bristol City. I said: 'Is your knee all right?'

'Yes, it's 100%,' he replied. 'I'm going to make you sub,' I said. Baker had played well against Everton and I felt it was right to keep the same side. Williams was livid. 'You've got no divine right to be in,' I said.

'I suppose you'll want me to come on and save the game for you if it doesn't work out,' he said angrily.

'You can sit in the back of the stand if you like and try and save it from there,' I said. The prima donna in him was coming out again and I was disappointed. He got up and rushed out the door.

Later, Lew Chatterley rang him at his digs and he said : 'I suppose he's got you to ring me, has he?' Lew put the phone down. I made a note to make Sealy the substitute.

Players react in different ways to being left out. Williams went too far one way just as Trevor Hebberd went too far the other way. When I told Hebberd that he was out and Hayes was playing against Everton, he shrugged his shoulders and said : 'All right.'

Baker combined well with Hayes for the first goal when Hayes beat John Shaw, Bristol's goalkeeper, on the near post and we won 2–0 without being threatened. Gennoe kept another blank sheet. He missed training the day before because of flu and when I asked him if he was going to be fit, he gave me an old fashioned look. With Wembley coming up, some players would continue playing with a broken leg. Gennoe knew if he lost his place to Peter Wells, he might struggle to get it back.

Norman Hunter was unfairly penalized for the free kick which led to the second goal, a brilliantly struck shot from Holmes, and the old 'Bite yer legs' Norman came to the surface soon afterwards when he went rattling into little Hayes, who is six inches shorter and two stone lighter. John Homewood, the referee, showed him the yellow card – a case of retaliation earning the greater punishment.

Afterwards Norman came into our dressing room and we had a laugh and a joke with Bally. 'Norman has only made one mistake in his career,' I said. Bally said : 'Yes, not coming here.' When Hunter was released by Leeds, I went up to see him because I thought he would be an asset to us. But he had a Jewish fellow handling his affairs at the time and we couldn't agree terms. He went to Bristol City instead.

Thursday, 22 February.

Some schoolboy trialists were finishing off their stay with us and I went up to chat to them and watch them train. Ian Branfoot said he'd mentioned it to Bally and Bally turned up on Wednesday morning, the day after a match, and worked with them for two hours. Not many pros would do that. This was a side to Ball's character that never had any publicity. He was also a regular caller at a local approved school, where he coached and talked with the boys on a voluntary basis.

Lew Chatterley said Williams had come up to him yesterday and apologized for his behaviour so that was a good sign. At lunchtime, I cut the tape at the opening ceremony of a new Zenith Windows showroom in the town, a two-way piece of public relations because they would sell our tickets.

In the evening, Anne and I took Alison and two of her friends to see the Southern Theatre production of 'My Fair Lady'. It was a dinner-jacket affair as the civic heads were attending and the ladies enjoyed it. I found it very relaxing. Anne always had a yearning towards the amateur theatre and I could see that Alison was attracted by it, especially when we went back stage and she found that girls of her age were helping with make-up and various other tasks.

Friday, 23 February.

Brian Truscott said that QPR secretary Ron Phillips called to say tomorrow's pitch at Loftus Road was like liquid mud and he was arranging for an early inspection. I told him to ring back and say I would attend the inspection. I was a trifle suspicious. Rangers had just sold their best player, goalkeeper Phil Parkes, to West Ham for £565,000, a world record for a goalkeeper and there was talk of a demonstration by fans.

The deal went through against the wishes of Steve Burtenshaw the Rangers manager and though one doesn't know all the facts I felt that if I had been put in that position I would say to the chairman: 'One of us has got to go.'

The *Echo* were planning an eight-page pull-out for the League Cup Final and wanted us to co-operate. This is always a tricky time for managers because it is traditional for clubs in Finals to set up a pool and share the proceeds among the players. The manager has to avoid appearing to be mercenary but if extra work is involved and someone else is making a profit from it, then he is justified in asking for contributions. Last time I never quoted prices. I left it up to the newspaper or radio or TV station concerned and it worked well.

Manchester United, however, earned some unfavourable publicity with their demands and finished up giving most of their pool to charity as a form of penance. I asked Peter East: 'Are they sticking in a lot of ads?' He said they were and I said: 'Well, I feel the players ought to make something from it.'

I sensed there was still some resentment from my criticism of the *Echo* after the Leeds semi-final victory but we had to live together and help each other and I agreed to a request from Brian Hayward, the sports editor, for a meeting.

The players wouldn't make a lot from the pool, between £2,000 and £5,000 shared among the first team squad. It was a rule that anyone who was approached individually had to put his money in. Bally had just done an article for a Sunday newspaper and chipped in.

Saturday, 24 February.

The pitch was a mixture of rolled mud and sand when it was inspected at 11 am but was playable. I went off for a meeting with Ranjit Anand and his assistant Duncan Revie to discuss hotel arrangements for Wembley. Duncan is an extremely nice person, a qualified solicitor, and from behind it is easy to mistake him for his father, the former England manager.

He is the classic example of a person whose life has been affected by having a famous parent. When we left, Ranjit for Arsenal and me for Loftus Road, he said, 'I'm playing golf.' He doesn't see much football. What happened to his father has soured his love of the game.

I arrived just ahead of the players and bumped into Gerry Francis. Gerry said he was pleased about the bad weather because the lay-off helped his return to fitness. He said he was seeing his contract out at Rangers and would leave at the end of the season.

Rangers strike me as a club that needs a shake up. They have some good players but whether it's the blend, or the changes of manager I don't know, but they never play to their potential. Derek Richardson, Parkes's replacement in goal, couldn't be blamed for his side's 1–0 defeat. Gennoe kept his fifth successive clean sheet, equalling a club record and proving what a good buy he had been at one-twentieth the cost of Parkes.

Three more cautions (Holmes, Peach and Williams) and a sending off (Curran in the eighty-eighth minute) worsened our disciplinary record and according to the *Daily Mail* Fair Play League, we were now bottom. I thought Stan Bowles had a responsibility on two of the bookings. It seemed there was one law for him and another for our players.

When Bowles pushed Bally he wasn't penalized yet Peach was booked for tripping the former England striker and after Bowles brought Holmes down and Holmes half retaliated, it was Holmes who was shown the card. Holmes says little but he was so angry he shouted: 'What?' – and that was probably the reason the referee booked him.

Williams was cautioned for being slow to give the ball back but when Bowles and two other Rangers players chased forty yards after the referee to protest at a decision, no action was taken. Most pressmen thought we should have had a penalty and as the linesman came back to the halfway line I shouted: 'Why didn't you put your flag up?'

He said: 'I did Lawrie.' I said: 'Well you should have kept the bloody thing up.' 'I did,' he replied. 'Didn't you see?'

I didn't defend Curran. Although he denied it, I was sure he struck Ian Gillard, if only half-heartedly, and players who do that must expect to go. It meant he would miss our Fifth Round FA Cup tie and as is our custom, I fined him.

In the Press room afterwards, I thought Steve Burtenshaw went on far too long. If you do that, you run the risk of saying things at the end that can make embarrassing headlines. You should go in, make your points, answer whatever valid questions there are and retire. But Steve seemed to relish it.

As I left the guest room, I met Jim Gregory, the Rangers chairman. We shook hands and I wished him well. He seemed pleasant enough.

Monday, 26 February.

A long drive the other side of Birmingham to see our Fifth Round FA Cup opponents, WBA or Leeds, at the Hawthorns. Albion were 3–1 up and I was thinking about having to take the ticket allocation back for our match with them when Leeds forced extra time and the game ended in a draw. Ron Atkinson was down afterwards. He felt his side should have won it.

I wasn't particularly worried who our opponents were because they would be equally difficult. Leeds were banned from playing FA Cup ties at home so the game would be at the Dell whereas if Albion got through, they were the home side.

Tuesday, 27 February.

The first team squad were invited to a buffet lunch at Vosper-Thorneycroft, the ship builders, and we were shown round the two frigates they were building, the *Nottingham* and the *Southampton*. It was good PR for the club and it enabled the 3,500 workers to talk about something else other than their industrial troubles. A few weeks before one of the vessels had been launched at midnight by the management because the workers were refusing to do it and the men were still sore about it.

Walking around seeing how hard some people have to work for a living was a good experience for the players but by the end I noticed that some had dropped out. Our visit emphasized the importance of a successful football club to a community and I regretted that there were no civic leaders present.

Charlie George and I went off to Bournemouth afterwards for a promotional job with United Biscuits.

Wednesday, 28 February.

I was beginning to think of Saturday's team against Arsenal. Curran was banned and the only other winger on the staff was a twenty-year-old from my hometown Gateshead named Oshor Williams, who cost £4,000. He had been with Middlesbrough and Manchester United as a kid and his father was Nigerian. Golac was appearing at the FA after reaching twenty points and would also be out. That was no problem. Manny Andruszewski could come in and repeat his marking job on Liam Brady.

After training I drove to Aldershot to present the Cup in the Army Cup Final in which the Highland Fusiliers beat the Scots Guards 4–2. When I was doing my National Service in the Coldstream Guards I would turn to jelly if a Colonel or General was in the vicinity yet here I was sitting among a clutch of them.

They thanked me for coming along and mixing with the players afterwards. It was an interesting experience. There was hardly a free kick, no dissent and no swearing or unruly behaviour from the crowd.

Thursday, 1 March.

Charlie George's knee was still puffing up and we had him see the specialist, Bob Jackson, for a third opinion. The previous two experts both agreed that Charlie didn't need an operation and Mr Jackson was of the same opinion, which was a relief. All kinds of rumours were going round about Charlie and I was glad that we could now concentrate on getting him back to fitness without having to rush him. He was a useful reserve to have in the background.

Golac could have been banned for three matches so we asked for a personal hearing at the FA and I drove him there myself. As always, the Commission were very fair and they accepted Ivan's plea that playing in a different kind of football had caused him to be late with some of his tackles. In Yugoslavia, he said, there was always a sweeper to cover the full-back but here no-one used a sweeper as such. Dick Speake, the chairman, announced that it would be a one match suspension – good news.

On the way out I bumped into Ted Croker and we spoke briefly about Alan Ball and his influence over our side. He said it was a pity that Bally had made the admission in his book about Don Revie which had cost him a £3,000 fine. Mr Croker has a frustrating job in the middle of the amateurs of the game on one side and the pros on the other, but does it well and commands respect.

Friday, 2 March.

Golac started to change with the first team and Lew Chatterley said: 'No, you're going with the reserves today.' Golac's face fell. 'No, not me,' he said. 'I go in the gym with the others as usual.'

John McGrath came in. 'Come on Ivan, the bus is waiting,' he shouted. 'I stay,' said Golac. The usual Friday routine was that the first team worked in the gym, which could only take ten at a maximum. There was no room for anyone not in the side.

Golac's pride was hurt but I told him he had to go with the reserves. It was a sharp little reminder to him that he'd been at fault and this was part of the punishment.

The ITV commentator Brian Moore and producer Bob Gardam came down for lunch to discuss the coverage of the League Cup Final which ITV showed exclusively. They asked if they could put a camera in our dressing room before the game and were willing to put a sizeable sum into the players' pool.

'What about Cloughie?' I said. 'Are you going in his dressing room?' They said they were hoping to get in afterwards. 'In other words, you're expecting his lot to win,' I said. I said we would have to think about it and talk to the players. I wasn't too keen on a stranger being with us. A dressing room is a private place before a big match.

WBA beat Leeds 2–0 in the next replay and there were more ticket plans to draw up. I stayed in the office until eight finalizing the League Cup ticket arrangements.

Saturday, 3 March.

We beat Arsenal 2–0, a very satisfying win. Manny kept Brady quiet and I said afterwards that he must be the best marker in Britain. He's never let us down. We had a bad period at the start – Steve Williams was a bit undisciplined – but settled down and played some good football. Austin Hayes scored again and Oshor did reasonably well.

We might have to keep him in. A copy of the referee's report on the Curran sending-off had arrived and the referee was claiming that Curran had called him a bastard. The FA were thinking of charging Curran with bringing the game into disrepute. I couldn't defend him if that was true.

Before the game, I received a gallon of whisky from Bell's as the First Division Manager of the Month and Eric Morley presented me with a plaque for staging a Variety Club charity match.

10. The League Cup Final

Five successive victories had put Southampton's players in a confident mood for the fifth round FA Cup tie at WBA the following Saturday and the League Cup the Saturday after that. A vision of being the first club to appear in both the FA and League Cup Finals in the same season was appearing in front of them.

McMenemy was able to field a settled side and things were looking good for him. But pressure was building up around the players and most of them were new to it.

Monday, 5 March.

Flew up to Liverpool for an Emlyn Hughes testimonial dinner. His committee had invited me to speak with Max Boyce, the rugby comedian and this was the only date we could fit it. Emlyn had to leave when the meal was over because Liverpool were playing the following night. As he left his seat, Max Boyce occupied it and in his 'I was there' speech said: 'I shall tell them, I took Emlyn Hughes's place at Liverpool.'

Some distinguished football people were there, Nat Lofthouse, Bill Shankly and Joe Mercer among them and Jim Mills from Widnes Rugby League Club. I'd never met Mills before but was told that he had been sent off twenty times. When interviewed on the last occasion, he said: 'I'm being victimized!'

Emlyn was expected to gross £100,000 from his year-long testimonial. It was a costly trip for me but I had made a promise to him.

Wednesday, 7 March.

I wanted to see Nottingham Forest *v*. Grasshoppers but was committed to attending a dinner of the BBC Governors at the Post House Hotel, Southampton. I was on the same table as Sir Michael Swan, the Chairman of the BBC and Alisdair Milne, the Director-General. Also on it was a woman underwater archaeologist who was engaged in the restoration of the *Mary Rose*, a 450-year-old vessel at the bottom of the sea at Portsmouth. The BBC people were interested in my views about televised football and the presentation of 'Match of the Day'. Peter Terson, the playwright who wrote *Zigger-Zagger*, came up for a chat and Clare Francis was there too.

Thursday, 8 March.

Some of the players came with me for a signing session to help the sales of the club Wembley brochure at a newsagents in the town. The excitement of being in another Cup Final was building up and Southern TV were filming a documentary for a programme to go out on the eve of Wembley. I noticed Ivan Golac was particularly popular.

Back at the ground Mr Woodford arrived to talk about the offers we had had for Tony Funnell, the reserve striker. Reading, Brentford, Walsall and Gillingham had all been in contact and the best offer so far was for £25,000. I was open to offers at £40,000 and was hoping to knock it up to £50,000. Prices of footballers are governed by supply and demand and the final price is usually the highest the selling manager thinks he can get.

Mr Woodford wasn't too impressed. The directors had talked about it and apparently two of them thought Funnell was worth more than £40,000. Ted Bates would know that this was a good price for an untried reserve but the directors, who didn't know the game so well, wouldn't know that. I was disappointed that the directors weren't accepting my advice and letting me get on with it. They knew we had to release some reserves to let the next class of players through. If we didn't sell some now we would finish up giving some of them away.

The fact that the directors met without telling me was annoying. They might be thinking I was getting too strong and there ought

to be more democracy. My answer to that was I was paid to make
these decisions.

Friday, 8 March.

Normally we would stay at the Europa Lodge before the Fifth
Round tie at WBA tomorrow but that was now a Ron Atkinson hotel.
He was always there and the staff would be pro-Albion. I didn't
want my players subjected to any pressures so we switched to the
Penns Hall at Sutton Coldfield, a hotel I remembered from my days
at Sheffield Wednesday.

Gary Newbon of ATV was there to interview me with some of
the players and when that was finished I was interviewed by Cathy
Cozens of the *Daily Star*. I was very reticent when she first rang.
The *Sun* once caught me with the woman's angle interview and the
end product was embarrassing, how many letters you get from
women, do you kiss female admirers and titbits like that.

I'd never read the *Star*, a new national daily, and didn't know
Miss Cozens' work. But she was quite smart and did the job well
and I was more relaxed, especially when I dragged Bally into it.

Saturday, 9 March.

We drew 1–1 and I was delighted to get them back to the Dell for
a replay. We scored first, a good goal from Phil Boyer and though
they did most of the attacking in the second half, their goal was
a little lucky. As Cyrille Regis shot the ball caught Malcolm Waldron's foot and lobbed into the air for Ally Brown to head past Terry
Gennoe.

Sunday, 10 March.

When I dined some time before with John Duke, the Hampshire
Chief Constable, I promised one of his guests, Canon George Beachey, that I would give the sermon at his church John the Baptist
at Alresford on a mutually agreeable date. This was the day. I was
in no mood to enjoy it. There was a large congregation and a big
choir and for someone used to standing up and making mainly
impromptu speeches it was an intimidating occasion.

If you start with a funny line in a speech the audience laughs and your apprehension disappears. But there are no laughs to be gained from a serious sermon in a sombre church. There was no feedback and I was literally shaking despite all my experience at public speaking. I took as my theme 'aim high, nothing is impossible'.

I spoke about the crippled children we had coming in at the ground occasionally and mentioned there was an eighteen-year-old girl in the congregation, Mary Corbett, the daughter of one of our directors John Corbett, who had no fingers on one hand but could play the organ. I also said the hardest bit about being a Christian was standing up and declaring that you were one. It was the same in football when you had to preach what you believed in, not hide.

Monday, 12 March.

Ron Atkinson was on the phone early asking if I had any spare tickets for tonight's replay. 'You've got too many friends,' I said. He also asked if he could borrow our bus to go home after the game and I agreed.

There were big queues outside the ground long before the start and thousands were locked out. Afterwards, there were scores of complaints from fans who hadn't been able to see the game properly. The Dell wasn't equipped for a capacity attendance, even with a reduced 26,000 capacity.

Albion scored first through Laurie Cunningham and we equalized in the seventy-seventh minute from a David Peach spot-kick after referee Kevin McNally awarded a penalty for Alastair Robertson holding Curran back. At the time it didn't look a good penalty but it appeared worse on TV. As a high ball came over, Robertson put out an arm and dragged Curran back. He should have known that Curran has hardly ever headed a ball straight in his life.

I didn't feel too bad about it because we could have had four more penalties, two trips and two hand balls. At the end of normal time it was still 1–1 and I gathered the players round me and told them they were battling hard enough and that Albion could not match the pace we were setting. Curran kept trying to interrupt. He is not the wisest of players tactically and feeling that he would have little to contribute that would help us, I ignored him. 'Excuse me boss,' he said holding his hand up. Exasperated, I said: 'What is it then?' 'Can I go to the toilet?' he said. The other players dissolved in laughter. The crowd must have thought he was being sent off as he ran back to the dressing room. We were much stronger in extra time and Phil Boyer's goal earned us a sixth-round home tie against Arsenal the following Monday. It was a deserved success.

Ron Atkinson took defeat sportingly, handling the press well. I jotted down a note to write and thank him. Some managers can be ungenerous when they lose a close game and search for excuses. Ron didn't even bother to argue about the penalty.

Tuesday, 13 March.

I called the FA and the Football League to seek permission to postpone the Arsenal game from Monday to Tuesday to give my players twenty-four hours more rest after the League Cup Final. Both organizations said they were agreeable providing Arsenal accepted the change. When I first spoke to Ken Frair, the Arsenal secretary, he wasn't against the idea.

Half an hour later it was a different story when Ken had spoken to Terry Neill. He said he couldn't agree to switch as Arsenal were playing at Chelsea on the Wednesday. I felt that game could be put back. He wasn't prepared to help us.

Wednesday, 14 March.

Before our FA Cup Final appearance in 1976 we stayed at the Selsdon Park Hotel, a palatial country mansion style building sixteen miles from central London in Surrey and we decided to follow the same plan this time. The traffic was heavy and it was later than I'd expected when we arrived. A week before Brian Clough had rung John Bond and asked if he wanted to fix their postponed game against Norwich before the League Cup Final. No other manager would volunteer to play a match four days before a Wembley Final but Clough is always different.

Bondy was agreeable and the game was on. It was a good chance to see Forest and I'd planned to go. By late afternoon, however, it was obvious we would never make it by road and the hotel manager said he could contact a helicopter firm if I wished it. He made the call and one was available at a cost of £450. It was nearly 5 pm when I rang the Dell to get my secretary to ring the chairman so that he knew about the flight before reading about it in the papers next morning. Val said: 'Mr McMenemy, have you been drinking?'

Several newspaper reporters were at the hotel and hoping to offset the cost, I asked them if their papers would be willing to let them make the trip with me. Kevin Moseley of the *Daily Mirror*, who was detailed to write a pre-Wembley diary about me, agreed to chip in £150 but the *Sun* man Alex Montgomery had to turn it down when his office said no. That left the local man, Peter East. He took a deep breath and said: 'All right, count me in.' It was a big decision for him to make on his own and I was pleased that he had shown initiative to match the Fleet Street man.

None of us had ever flown in a helicopter before. It was snowing as the hotel tannoy broadcast an announcement asking guests to vacate the lawns because a helicopter was arriving – not that there were any outside in that weather.

The helicopter was quite small, and you could see London below us through the Perspex as we zoomed across the capital at 125 mph. Lew Chatterley held his head in his hands and Peter East sat shivering without a coat. Lew asked him why he didn't bring a coat. 'I was afraid you'd go off without me,' he said.

I noticed a sign saying 'heater failed' and watched what the pilot was doing in case he failed too. We were in Nottingham so early that we had time for a drink at the Bridgford Hotel. Norwich were very defensive and it was a terrible game. Forest won 1–0. The helicopter put us down at Brooklands – it couldn't make the hotel this time because there were no landing lights – and I was at the hotel in time to see the interview which Brian Moore recorded earlier in the day.

Thursday, 15 March.

Following the 1976 pattern, we laid on a buffet lunch for the press and allowed them to talk to all the players. Cloughie doesn't let his players talk but after what happened with our free for all I think he is wise to keep a check on what is said and written. Bally was interviewed about Forest and in his usual frank way, said, 'At times they can be negative.' He continued: 'They get a lot of players behind the ball and play a kind of 4–4–2. They were a bit negative at our place earlier in the season when they drew 0–0.'

When that appeared I realized straight away it could provide

Clough and Taylor with motivation. I didn't say anything to Bally though. I took a hired car to London Airport for the flight to Newcastle for the much-postponed ITV debate with Clough at the Neon Social Club in Jarrow, a Batley Variety club type of place in the middle of a council estate. Some five hundred people paid £1 each to be present. Cloughie was with Mike Keeling, a former Derby director who often accompanies him, and was as relaxed as I have ever seen him.

The questions were interesting and often funny and it was an entertaining night. There was no attempt to outwit each other. We were both on home territory, amongst friends, and enjoying ourselves. The reaction from the audience was very enthusiastic.

Friday, 16 March.

I caught the 7 am flight to London and was supervising the training at the Crystal Palace National Recreation Centre at 10.30. I called the four possible substitutes together – I'd already named the side that beat WBA – and told the four of them, Manny Andruszewski, Trevor Hebberd, Graham Baker and Tony Sealy that Sealy would wear the number 12 shirt. He couldn't believe his luck. Another Geordie at Wembley!

In the afternoon I went to Lime Grove for a 'Nationwide' interview with John Motson. They showed some film of me when I was at Grimsby and asked me how I had changed. I said my ideas were still the same. No-one got anywhere in the game without hard graft and people in places like Grimsby and Doncaster who worked in hard jobs appreciated that. I didn't think the interview went over too well.

By the time I had finished dinner at the hotel with the staff, the players were drifting off to bed from 9.30 onwards. Some sat in their rooms watching TV, others went straight to sleep and some needed sleeping tablets. David Peach said it didn't seem like a Cup Final next day. 'It seems like another game to me,' he said. I felt the same way. Once you've been to Wembley it's never the same again.

Saturday, 17 March.

The sun was shining when I woke up. The snow was still on the trees and lawns and the view from my window was like a Christmas card. The telephone kept ringing, mostly friends with good wishes. Ted MacDougall was almost in tears. He intended to be at our after-match dinner but was playing at Torquay and would never get there in time.

Another call was from Freddie Starr, the comedian, whom I'd never met. He rang me on the morning of the 1976 Final and said he would come along to see us but never showed up. He said he would drive over but I expected that we wouldn't see him, as last time.

I went round talking to the players who were wearing their new suits. Athletes always look smart in suits. Ivan Golac wore his own tie. He didn't like the club one. And Chris Nicholl had his favourite £8.95 Parka hooded jacket in his hand. It was a joke with the players. His ambition was to be a mountain climber in Canada and he always seemed dressed ready for the part. He was the only one with brown shoes with his dark suit. 'You look great,' the others told him.

Surprisingly, Freddie Starr did turn up and had the players laughing with his impersonation of Alan Ball. After a light lunch, I took the players to a room for my team talk. I told Curran to keep close to me because I suspected that Clough, his ex-manager, would try to psyche him.

At the end of my talk I said to Curran: 'What have you got to do?' He replied: 'Stick with you boss.' The other players were amused. There was no sign of tension.

The hotel staff lined up to wave good-bye. When I stepped on the coach I noticed Freddie Starr sitting at the back, uninvited, talking to the players. It was 1.15, rather late, and I decided to let him stay.

We should have left earlier because it was 2.10 when we arrived at Wembley, even with our police escort. The attendants made no attempt to ask Freddie Starr for his ticket. In view of the time, we walked straight up the tunnel out on the pitch to test it. Starr came with us and marched in front of the band waving his arms about. I was surprised no-one went to him and asked who he was. He'd struck me as being a complex character, funny but zany.

Curran was a foot away from me all the time as we walked over the pitch, which was on the heavy side. The thousands of Southampton fans standing on the terraces at the tunnel end kept chanting: 'Give us a wave', and I shook my head, geeing them up to make more noise. Finally I waved and there was a loud roar. Starr was showing more signs of excitement than the players.

In the dressing room a Wembley employee came in with a sheet for me to sign – a bill for the bottles of beer and orange that we had ordered. Receipts for the match were a record £430,000 and they bother about claiming a few quid back from the two clubs that made it all possible!

Another employee was fidgeting about nervously. 'Come on, it's time to come out,' he said. I told him to wait. We weren't going to rush out and have to stand in the tunnel waiting for Forest. As it turned out, Forest were out first and had to wait for us.

Peter Taylor, not Clough, was leading Forest and as we walked across the muddy pitch I said: 'Where's Cloughie then?' He shrugged and made no reply. On reflection, I was unwise to speak to him. He was affected by the occasion. It was my third time and I was blasé about it. I thought about managers like Bill Shankly and Bob Paisley who were always leading teams out at Wembley and whether it still got through to them or was just another match.

I looked up to the seats behind the Royal Box and picked Anne out immediately. She was right at the back which didn't please me. There was a private box nearer the front but they wouldn't let the children in, only her and she wanted to be with them.

As the teams lined up I noticed Alan Hardaker look at the new red and white ball which was being used for the first time and rub his fingers as if to say it was worth money to the clubs. Both teams kicked in with three of the balls and I wanted to keep them but they were claimed back. I thought the match ball was soft and so did the players. The idea was that it should be more easily identifiable but you couldn't see it as well as the black and white balls used in the World Cup Finals.

As we sat down on the front bench, Clough and Peter Taylor and his trainer Jimmy Gordon at one end and Lew Chatterley and Don Taylor and myself at the other, I spotted Freddie Starr sitting behind us! He'd gate crashed right to the best seats in the stadium.

When the game started, Bally made a bad pass, then another. I felt he was trying to do too much. But in the seventeenth minute he laid a brilliant ball in for David Peach to run on to and take round Peter Shilton to put us ahead. The players ran towards our side of the pitch. Bally's face bore a twisted look, like a mask and I sensed straight away what was in his mind. He was coming over to Clough as if to say, 'There, that shows you I can play.' It went back to their clash in a hotel at Torremolinos a few years before. I don't believe Clough cared whether Bally could play or not. Managers don't care about other manager's players, only their own.

I jumped up and raced to the fence. 'Hey you,' I said, waving my arm at Bally. 'Settle yourself down.' His expression changed and he turned away and walked back to his position for the restart. For much of the first half we played the better football and Forest weren't in it. Shilton made a brave, head-first dive as Boyer and Holmes were about to shoot and a Boyer shot struck someone on the back. Then we started slowing it down as though it was late in the second half. We should have kept the pressure on, I told them at half-time.

'That fellow over there is going to gee them up and they're going to come tearing out in the second half,' I said. 'You've got to battle to compete with them.' But as Charlie George said afterwards: 'Cloughie's lot did what he told them. Yours didn't listen.'

Clough's last words, apparently, were 'Run out there and be positive', and that's what the Forest players did, they sprinted back on to the pitch. As I emerged into the sunlight from the tunnel, I was disappointed to see that not one of the many divots had been put back. It was a difficult enough surface to play on without that.

Forest, predictably, were a different team. They came at us like a swarm of bees. In the fiftieth minute Nick Holmes tried a back pass under pressure and the ball went to John Robertson. Robertson crossed and Chris Nicholl stopped it with Terry Gennoe behind him and made no effort to hit it behind for a corner as he should have done. Gary Birtles took it off him, went to his left and fired into the roof of the net.

Birtles outpaced Nicholl again for the second goal and I knew that was it. Nicholl had been disappointing and his indecision spread to some of the other defenders. Archie Gemmill kept getting in behind Golac on the left. Only Peachy had a fine game. Steve Williams had a nightmare. Bally too had an off day. Near the end I told Sealy to get his track suit off. It wasn't tactical. As I sent him on for Austin Hayes, I said: 'Show your Mum what you can do.'

The difference between the teams was that they got sharper as we became more sluggish. They started playing balls into the channels alongside our centre-backs, pulling Waldron and Nicholl out of position and Birtles and Woodcock were quick enough to get to them and turn before they were challenged. From one of these passes, from Gemmill, Woodcock scored the third goal. Forest's lead was deserved – they could have had more – but on the TV replay later I noticed that Gennoe had spread himself well and the ball bobbled and bounced over his body.

Nick Holmes made it 3–2 near the end with a cracking left-foot volley. We were well beaten but at least we'd scored two of the best goals at Wembley for some time. There aren't many goals in League Cup Finals. This game was an exception. When Peter Reeves, the referee, blew the whistle for the last time I shook hands with Clough and Taylor and told them: 'You deserved it.'

You stand there surrounded by people but suddenly you feel lonely. I looked at the faces of the players. Sealy, who'd been on only a few minutes, was crouching and holding his head as though he'd just been pulled out of a crashed airplane. It struck me that perhaps we take defeat too seriously in professional football. Williams had tears in his eyes and when the players came back from the Royal Box with their medal and tankard he didn't want to go on the lap of honour.

I grabbed him. 'Your mother has come out of hospital to see you,' I said. 'Get round there!' His mother suffered from multiple sclerosis and we'd arranged with the hospital to bring her by ambulance.

I shook hands with the players of both sides and congratulated the Forest team. I was particularly pleased that Frank Clark, whom Clough later said was the best player on the pitch, had received another medal at thirty-five. He'd been a credit to the game and if I hadn't just bought David Peach when I first came to Southampton, I would have been in there competing with Clough to sign him on a free transfer from Newcastle.

I was about to depart for the dressing room when I heard Clough shouting: 'Hey, come here.' I looked round. 'You're coming up those steps with me,' he said. He pointed towards the Royal Box. I said: 'No.' 'You are,' he said. 'We're not going without you.' He took my arm and we went up together.

Clough was presented with a medal and a tankard by Dr Artemio Franchi, the President of UEFA but when it was my turn, Alan Hardaker looked perplexed because there was nothing for me. As I was walking away some supporters pointed behind me and I turned and saw they'd come up with a medal to give me. Later I was given a tankard in the dressing room.

When we were all back inside the dressing room I said to the players: 'I know you are disappointed but you've done great. You haven't let anyone down. Now go and have a bath and if anyone has a miserable face afterwards it will be a slap in the face for me personally.' I went outside to say a few words to the press and then went to find Anne. ITV were wanting me to be interviewed but couldn't find me in time and Brian Moore spoke to Bally instead.

We turned the dinner at the Royal Garden Hotel into a celebration party. Mr Woodford congratulated me and I asked the players to stand up to receive the applause of the company. I said I wanted to make three points, the clock goes forward an hour tonight, we leave at 11.30 am tomorrow morning and I'll fine anyone who looks miserable. We didn't have time to dwell on defeat. Our thoughts tomorrow had to be on the Arsenal game and before that, let's enjoy ourselves. Jimmy Tarbuck did a short turn and it was an enjoyable affair.

We were paying silly prices in one of London's most expensive hotels but the players deserved a treat. Our four days in London cost about £10,000 and when bonuses and other expenses were paid, we would be lucky to make £100,000 from the Final. But it was worth it. We'd got there ... ninety others hadn't.

11. Out of everything

The football season lasts nearly ten months but in terms of winning trophies it can end for some clubs in as many days, even less. In Southampton's case it was exactly five days, the time between losing the League Cup Final and the sixth-round FA Cup replay against Arsenal the following Wednesday.

On the Friday the players were happy and excited. The atmosphere was relaxed and jokey. But by 9.11 on Wednesday, 21 March the mood had changed to one of deep depression.

McMenemy now had to assume another of his roles, that of psychiatrist. There were still thirteen League matches remaining, almost a third of the programme, including two games against Liverpool, an away game at Nottingham Forest and home games against Leeds, WBA and Manchester United. The players might think that their season was over but it wasn't.

Monday, 19 March.

The ticket touts were down from London and it was clear that we were going to have a full house for the Arsenal tie. In my team talk I praised the players again for getting us to Wembley and impressed on younger ones like Austin Hayes that the experience should give them more confidence. I said he ought to be thinking about turning on the ball more instead of laying it off all the time, especially as he was up against Willie Young, a big man who wouldn't like that.

Austin had a fine game and scored our goal in the 1-1 draw. It was a tremendous tie and I thought we were the better side. But Arsenal were let back into it by a ghastly mistake by Gennoe. He was under no pressure as a corner came over but flapped at the ball and it went to David Price at the far post who chested it in. The players were stunned in the dressing room afterwards but I didn't say anything to Gennoe. He'd got us that far with some magnificent performances. It was a carry over from Wembley. He had the wobbles from the time Forest scored their first goal. I decided then that I would bring Peter Wells back for the replay on Wednesday.

Gennoe was full of apologies. Later on I said: 'You would have swallowed that ninety-nine times out of a hundred,' and he replied, 'I know I would.' Charlie George came in. 'Lucky buggers,' he said about his old club. I got him in a corner out of hearing of the other players and said: 'I'm thinking of playing you at Highbury.' A look of astonishment came over his face. We needed something to lift us, a new face.

Outside the press were waiting at the entrance of their room next to the referee's room. Terry Neill hadn't seemed keen to talk with them. 'It's only half-time,' he had said. Then in what I took to be a veiled reference to a comment I had made about Arsenal's refusal to delay the match by twenty-four hours, he said: 'Someone does enough talking, see him.'

Tuesday, 20 March.

Peachy was injured and wouldn't play tomorrow and when I went to the training ground to see how Charlie was shaping one of the trainers told me: 'His wife has just rung to say he's got a migraine.' I thought, 'here we go'. Charlie hadn't played for three months. Perhaps he didn't fancy it.

But at the Dell at midday he was there and he apologized for not coming in earlier. 'I'll train after lunch and see how it goes,' he said. I had already made my mind up that he would have to play.

Wednesday, 21 March.

At the hotel I went to Gennoe's room to tell him he was out. He looked shocked. I said: 'It's a hard decision for me and it's even harder to have to tell you.' I noticed that some of the critics were already writing about his mistakes. The press build you up but they can soon knock you down. I also told Curran that he would be the one to drop out for Charlie. He was hurt but took it better than Gennoe. Sheffield Wednesday had offered £70,000 for him but he was still a useful player to us. It would cost far more than that to replace him.

Wells was delighted that he was back for the first time since early September. I decided to retain Manny to mark Brady. The game was a miserable affair, only redeemed by a smashing goal by Alan Sunderland, who scored both goals in Arsenal's 2–0 victory. Malcolm Waldron was too close to him and he got away and shot past Wells from outside the box.

Waldron lunged at Brady and brought him down and I regretted that Brady injured a knee in the collision. It put him out of the semi-final. It hadn't been intentional but you don't like to see a player of Brady's class injured. He's priceless.

I pushed Charlie further forward in the second half but it didn't come off. In the dressing room afterwards hardly a word was spoken. Bally sat looking like a man of fifty, his face grey and sunken. I sat next to him and put my arm round him. We'd been pictured together like that smiling in countless newspaper pictures in the past week or two. If a photographer had been allowed in his picture would show as never shown before the effect defeat can have on a man like Bally.

This was the football life in a nutshell – one minute you are up, the next you're in the depths of despair. I thought ahead to the next game, at Bolton on Saturday. The last place we'd want to go to after this. Mr Woodford came in and congratulated the players, which was a commendable gesture on his part.

There was a knock at the door. A commissionaire said: 'Mr Neill says can you come to the press room with him.' I said he hadn't said anything at the Dell on Monday night. Let him do the talking now.

Neill was in the corridor. He said: 'Are you coming?' 'You said last time that I did all the talking, it's your turn now,' I said. I was slightly niggled because I had to go out and face the press at Southampton when it was a bad result for us and a good one for him and I bailed him out a bit.

He said: 'I didn't say that.' 'Well I saw it quoted in the North East papers,' I said. Turning back into the dressing room, I said: 'I can't go. I've got a lifting job to do in here.' I didn't go to the press room but later I spoke to half a dozen reporters in the main entrance.

Thursday, 22 March.

I told the players they could have the day off and was driven to London Airport for a flight to Liverpool to attend a dinner at Tranmere Rovers hosted by the Rovers chairman Bill Bothwell, who is also a BBC broadcaster. There were two hundred people there and they asked some sound questions. Everyone said how sorry they were for me but I said: 'I don't feel any sorrow. I hope it happens to us again next year!'

Friday, 23 March.

Bill is also PRO for Vauxhall's and he asked me to meet the men in the canteens at Vauxhall's factory at Ellesmere Port. Once again, the questions dug in deep and I relished it. They know their football on Merseyside. Afterwards I was driven to the Mottram Hall Hotel at Wilmslow where the team joined me. There was no sparkle about any of the players and I realized I would have to do a massive lifting job on them before the game at Bolton.

Macclesfield Cricket Club were having their annual dinner in the hotel and as Colin Ingleby-Mackenzie, the former Hampshire captain, hadn't been able to attend, I was asked to speak on behalf of Hampshire, which I did. We had a few laughs.

Saturday, 24 March.

I popped down to the town to buy a present in Mothercare for Jim McCalliog's first child. Anne and I had been invited to the christening at Lytham. It was heartening that an ex-player should invite you to be a godparent. I liked Jim. He was a better player than some people thought he was and since returning from America he'd rung me a number of times about going into management. He had just been paid up at Lincoln, where he was player coach after falling out with the manager Colin Murphy.

I bought an outfit for the baby, who was named Mark James, and a huge Humpty Dumpty which I took back to the hotel and told the players was my new signing. I left Hayes out to let Curran back in. Austin had played a lot of football in a short space of time. It had nothing to do with the way he was playing. I also kept Charlie in.

In my talk, I spoke about the need for showing character and pride and they certainly showed both qualities in the first half. We played as well as at any time in the season and had enough chances to take a winning lead. The best fell to Charlie but he headed wide from six yards. It would take him some time to get match fit again. His timing was off.

We fell away in the second half and Alan Gowling scored two goals for Bolton who won 2–0. Ian Greaves was delighted. Bolton's win ended a bad run. It was quite a managerial gathering afterwards with Greaves, Harry Catterick, Tony Waddington and Jimmy Armfield, who reported the game for the *Daily Express*, all in the tea room.

Sunday, 25 March.

The weather was good and Anne and I went for a walk in the hotel grounds before lunch. It was a relaxing way of starting Mother's Day – no lunch to cook. She'd brought the car up and we drove to Lytham for the christening. There were only a dozen guests but half a dozen photographers. I was surprised by the turn out of pressmen. Jim said he didn't know how they knew about it.

A local freelance asked me all the details. 'Now you bought Jim from which club. . . .' 'And he played in the Cup Final when. . . .' His next question floored me. 'And where was that played . . . ?'

Jim was unlike most footballers. He married late in his career, to a lovely lass and I was pleased for him. His mother had died and his father had been ill and his life needed the pick up that a happy marriage and children can bring.

It took us five hours to drive home from Lancashire. The day's total mileage was about 305 and we fell into bed exhausted.

Monday, 26 March.

We now had the problem of finding somewhere to live again. The new house still wasn't ready and the house we were in was wanted in two weeks by the nineteen-year-old son of the owners who were abroad. He was down from Oxford University and had invited his friends to stay. It would be a miserable few days for Anne as she packed the household effects once more.

The transfer deadline was on Thursday and managers were

ringing about players we had available. Maurice Evans of Reading wanted Tony Funnell and I arranged for him to meet Funnell. Frank Sibley of Walsall wanted Tony Sealy. Neither player was keen to go and Funnell turned down Reading's offer.

I rang Funnell and warned him that it might be in his best interests to go because he would be struggling to get in the reserves the following season. He said he would think about it.

Tuesday, 27 March.

Chris had injured his ankle and the doctor advised that it should be immobilized for several days. His foot was strapped up and he was put on crutches. Anne had to run him home again . . . another aggravation that had cropped up at the worst possible time.

A lady from the BBC had invited me to make a TV appeal on behalf of the students of the Wessex Rehabilitation Association and I went to the University to record it. The Association needed money to build a lift in the building, Clarkson House, which was shared by able-bodied and handicapped students. The British public will contribute to appeals on behalf of animals but won't contribute when it is for students. The recording, which I ad libbed, went well and was scheduled to go out on a Sunday in April.

12. Sale time

As it was most unlikely that Southampton would be relegated, McMenemy now had to think about the following season. He didn't need to buy players – the staff was already too big – but he had to sell some. His role was now that of a salesman intent on making as much money for his club as he could.

The traffic in footballers from club to club leaves no room for sentiment. Two of the five players to be released were George Shipley and Tony Sealy, two Geordies who were the first apprentices he signed five years previously. He liked them and had almost been a father to them but they had to go. Three other players, Forbes Phillipson-Masters, Tony Funnell and Terry Curran also went and the proceeds of £200,000 meant that Southampton finished the financial year in profit despite paying out £350,000 for Charlie George.

Wednesday, 28 March.

I intended to leave at 10.30 with the team for the match against Tottenham Hotspur at White Hart Lane but had to stay behind to take calls from prospective buyers. Maurice Evans, who had signed George Shipley from us on loan, was disappointed that Funnell didn't want to join Reading but I wasn't too concerned because Gerry Summers of Gillingham was now interested.

Gerry had a bid in for Steve Perrin of Plymouth and rang back to say that he wouldn't want Funnell. Later he called again and said that he'd changed his mind – the Perrin deal had obviously fallen through. Evans now wanted Trevor Hebberd and I arranged for Hebberd to go and see him.

David Pleat of Luton asked if Chris Nicholl was available, an ex-Luton player. He explained that Chris Turner, whom Luton had bought for £100,000 from Peterborough, wasn't doing it for him and New England Tea Men wanted him. Noel Cantwell, the Tea Men manager, was Peterborough's manager at one time.

I said: 'We're not ready to let him go, he's still doing reasonably well for us. How much were you thinking about?' Pleat said £60–£70,000. 'That's ridiculous,' I said. 'He's a current international.'

I asked him what went wrong with Turner. 'He's spent too long in the Third Division and he wants to go to America,' he said. 'But they're not offering the same money we paid.' David is a nice, honest man who hasn't been in management long; it was his first season, and he was still thinking that if you were open and straight with people they would treat you the same way. But football is not like that. Sometimes you have to get tough with players and this seemed a typical case.

When I arrived at the hotel in London, I spoke to him again and arranged to loan him Forbes Phillipson-Masters, our reserve centre-half who had been on loan before to Exeter and Bournemouth. It would give the lad some experience of the Second Division and would help both clubs.

Just before I left the hotel, Curran rang me from Southampton. 'I want to go,' he said. I thought he meant go to the game at Spurs. He was suspended for one game and this was it. 'No, I want a transfer,' he said. 'You said you'd fit me up somewhere before Christmas.'

I asked him why he hadn't come in the day before when I had more time. I was in the middle of several deals and had no time. 'I had some business to do,' he said. I guessed what business it was – at the races. I put him down. He was a good-hearted Yorkshire lad, perfectly harmless, but had picked up some expensive habits with his new racing friends and probably needed the money from a transfer.

I suspected that Jack Charlton had rung him direct and this was the outcome. Curran said he wanted to go back North. He had no children and all his relatives were up there. 'You've no money from week to week,' I said. 'You've got it made here, why do you want to join a Third Division club?'

He said he knew that it was the best club he'd been with and he became emotional. 'Okay,' I said. 'I'll speak to Jack.' Jack had only seen him play once. As he was a friend, I'd go through with it, but not at £60,000, his first offer.

Curran had used me and I had used him. He'd scored the goal against Leeds in the League Cup semi-final and now he was opting to become a bigger fish in a smaller pool. When I spoke to Jack later, we agreed on one payment plus another payment after he had played ten games. That would spread it over until the following season and help his cash flow.

Terry Venables, the Crystal Palace manager, also called and asked whether he could see me about buying a striker after the game at Tottenham. He said he had been let down over a deal. I discovered later that it was Don Givens of Birmingham.

The Spurs game ended 0–0, which was disappointing for their fans and the London press, who knocked the home team but I thought we played quite well and deserved better notices. Phil Boyer could have scored twice and Charlie George had a tremendous shot stopped on the line by Steve Perryman. Charlie did nothing in the first half and at half time he held his hand up and said: 'Don't say anything. I know how bad I am.' The confidence had totally drained out of him. 'Forget it,' I said. 'I know you can play. It will come.'

Early in the second half he forgot about his knee and swung his leg at a corner. It was a perfectly struck volley which almost knocked Perryman into the back of the net but it jarred his knee and though he wanted to stay on, I replaced him with Austin Hayes. Osvaldo Ardiles, played in attack, hadn't been effective and nor had Ricardo Villa.

Terry Venables had been speaking to Bobby Robson, who was also at White Hart Lane, about buying either Alan Brazil or David Geddis but Robson delayed making a decision. He didn't really want to let either player go. Terry wanted somewhere private to talk and suggested the Chanticleer Restaurant the other side of the ground. We were shown to a corner table and were about to order when a waiter came up and said: 'Would you like a bottle of champagne with the compliments of the gentleman over there?'

It was Charlie George, who was in the restaurant with his wife. We ordered some orange with it and settled down for a long talk. I like Terry. He's opposite to me in many ways. Supporters kept coming up and one old lady said we were the first managers she had ever seen in the place after a match. She congratulated me on coming in ... as though I would normally keep my team waiting while sitting down to enjoy champagne. The coach had already left and I had my car. We were very late home.

Thursday, 29 March.

All the outstanding transfers had to be completed before the deadline at five pm. Gerry Summers was on the line again about Funnell and we agreed a fee of £50,000. I had sent Funnell up to see him and this time there were no problems. Hebberd returned from Reading and said he was only willing to go on loan, not a permanent transfer. I told him he wasn't going on loan.

Venables, meanwhile, had been turned down by Ipswich and was now in with a £50,000 offer for Tony Sealy. I accepted on condition that we could buy him back and we signed letters to that effect.

Sealy was an unknown quality. He could develop into a good player and if so, I would want him back with us. A few games with Palace would help him. Funnell came in to thank me for what I had done for him and that was very satisfying.

Manny Andruszewski complained about being left out at Spurs and said: 'I feel I am being totally used.' I said: 'You are.' I explained that if I could have fixed him up with an American club I would but I had been very busy getting some other players to new clubs.

Manny is one of the nicest people in the game but he said: 'I'm not bothered about other players, only me.' It's a game that breeds selfishness. You try to encourage team work and selflessness but in the end the professional is only in it for himself and what he can make out of it. The system, the money, the bonuses all make players think of their own interests first.

The club offices had been broken into during the night but fortunately my office escaped. At the directors' meeting, I related how I had managed to raise £200,000 by selling players and the directors were delighted. I mentioned too that I was due to move out of our house at the weekend and still hadn't found anywhere. Football clubs find houses for new players but not for well established managers, I said. I think they were embarrassed.

Friday, 30 March.

Most of the houses Anne had been shown by estate agents were unsuitable, usually on estates where we would be pestered all the time. But Brian Hunt, the builder of our new house, came on and said we could have his mother's two bedroom bungalow for a time. I thought it would be too small but when we saw it, we were impressed. It was spotlessly clean and had character, unlike the house we were leaving which would fetch £60,000 but which we hadn't liked.

It would mean that Chris would have to go into digs but he was a sensible lad and it appealed to him that he would be on the same footing as the other younger players who were in digs. Once again Anne was burdened with most of the packing and disposal of our effects. It was our fourth move in three months.

Saturday, 31 March.

She had spent all the morning packing and cleaning up but still managed to get to the Dell to see our 2–2 draw with Leeds. Leeds scored first and for the next seventy minutes produced some of the old Leeds cynical stuff, which upset the crowd. Malcolm Waldron, who had only scored twice all the season, now scored two in as many minutes to put us ahead. If we had been professional in the final minutes we would have repeated our League Cup win but Golac went charging up the wing and the ball was played back down his side and John Hawley equalized.

Arsenal had beaten Wolves 2–0 in the FA Cup semi-final. I couldn't help thinking that but for a single mistake in the game at the Dell against Arsenal that could have been us qualifying for the FA Cup Final.

In the board room, Mr Woodford asked if we had got accommodation. 'This looks nice, I think we'll bed down here,' I said. The players, particularly Bally, were tired and once I heard that our game the following Tuesday against Manchester United was postponed because of their FA Cup semi-final replay against Liverpool, I decided to fix a trip abroad to recuperate.

We'd had Charlie's knee looked at again and the advice was that it wasn't a cartilage. The knee was slightly swollen and I sensed that Charlie didn't want to play so I left him out for Austin Hayes.

The reserves were depleted with so many players being transferred but achieved a fine result at Norwich, 1–1, and the third team, composed mainly of schoolboys, drew 0–0 with Havant. Ian Branfoot, the 'A' team trainer, told me that the boys had been kicked and shoved and the coloured ones scoffed at but to their credit, no-one had tried to retaliate. I can never understand why grown men, semi-pros, should descend to such tactics against boys. It was the red and white shirt of Southampton. They wanted to do us down.

When Anne and I arrived at the temporary bungalow we had supper out of newspapers with the children. The public imagine leading managers being wined and dined at expensive restaurants all the time. But it's not often like that. Even Cloughie is often a fish-and-chip man at home on a Saturday night.

13. Testimonial

With Southampton in a safe mid-table position, there was none of the usual end-of-season pressure on McMenemy. But there was still much to be done, including the arranging of his testimonial match. Managers are often scurvily treated when they are sacked so you can't blame them when they try to make money when the going is good. Brian Clough set a precedent in having a testimonial for himself and Peter Taylor and McMenemy invited him to bring his team to the Dell for his own game.

Monday, 2 April.

Tommy Lawrence spent the weekend trying to fix a short holiday for the players and came up with a four day trip to Cannes. It would cost about £3,000 but I felt it was worth it. Golac and Boyer didn't want to go, as expected, I didn't make them.

I stayed behind to catch up with some outstanding items like a mortgage for the new house and buying new furniture. Bob Gardham of LWT called to say ITV wanted me to join Cloughie in their team of analysts and the contracts would go beyond the 1982 World Cup. I said I had a verbal agreement with Alan Hart, the BBC Head of Sport, to work for the BBC during the 1979 FA Cup Final and the home championship and would have to speak to him first. I wanted to play it fair.

I called Clough later to discuss ITV's plans and while we were talking, I mentioned I would like him to bring his side to the Dell to play in my testimonial match. The proposed date was 11 May, the Friday before the Cup Final. To my surprise, he agreed. Forest had more games left than almost any other side in the country.

I had no qualms about staging my own testimonial. Normally only players have them – after ten years service with a club – but Clough and Peter Taylor set a precedent by having one themselves and I felt the same way as they did, that managers were just as entitled to these benefits as players. I had eleven successful years in management and the directors sanctioned a testimonial when I gained promotion the previous season.

A testimonial doesn't cost anything. The club only loans the ground. The beneficiary pays all expenses. The public decide whether it is worth supporting. If they like you, you make money. If they don't no-one has lost money.

Wednesday, 14 April.

Anne and I spent the day in London shopping for the new house in Harrods and buying clothes in the Kings Road. In the evening we went to an Elton John concert which I found fascinating. It was a pleasant change from routine.

Friday, 6 April.

I met the players at Heathrow and took them straight on to Birmingham for the next day's match. They were in good spirits and I was surprised to find that most of them had tans. Lew Chatterley said it was so expensive in Cannes that there had been hardly any drinking. Bally found a good way to deter hangers-on. A man in the hotel shouted: 'Hey Bally, do you want a drink?' and Bally replied, 'Yes please, four lagers.' The bill was so hefty that the man soon disappeared.

Nicholl stayed behind to have an operation on his nose but it still wasn't right and he couldn't play at Birmingham. After his mistake against Leeds, I was determined to speak to Golac and took him aside at the first opportunity.

'You've changed,' I said. 'When you first came it was all about pride and how you liked our football. Now you are thinking too much about money and what the other players are earning. You're blaming other players. No-one else at this club did as well as you did financially when you came. Have you got something on your mind?'

His head dropped. He is a sensible, adult person and he didn't try to argue back. 'You are right,' he said. 'But I want to play tomorrow. Let me play.' I was going to leave him out but decided against it. My talk with him had the desired effect. I told him he had to stop feeling hard done by.

Saturday, 7 April.

St Andrews had a depressed air about it. Even the doormen seemed gloomy about the club's predicament. We played the better football in the first half but a mistake by Andruszewski, deputizing at centre-half for Nicholl, let Stuart Barrowclough in to put Birmingham ahead. We were 2–1 up near the end when the referee gave one of the silliest penalties I've seen. The ball was out of play as two defenders sandwiched one of their forwards and the forward wasn't in possession of the ball. Birmingham scored from the penalty and the match was drawn 2–2.

In the press room I stood up for Jim Smith. I was asked how Birmingham would get on in the Second Division and I replied: 'You need battlers there and Jim is a battler.'

Sunday, 8 April.

John Bond's meeting of managers at Bisham Abbey. Bondy had called it because he felt it was about time the managers' voices were heard acting collectively. We spent too much time arguing among ourselves and not enough on trying to put right the wrongs in the game. His view was that we should be more intent on cleaning the game up and improving its image. The Secretaries and Managers Association took over the running of the meeting and one of the committee, Bertie Mee, took the chair with Ken Friar, the secretary, next to him. Bertie had an agenda but Jack Charlton got up at the start and said: 'We don't want any agenda. We want to talk about the points Bondy has raised.'

I'd never seen our profession so militant. There were some strong, solid arguments from people like Bobby Robson, Ron Atkinson, Gordon Lee, Malcolm Allison, Terry Venables, Andy Nelson, Gordon Milne, Danny Blanchflower and Bond himself. Most of the First Division managers were there but notable omissions were Brian Clough and Bob Paisley. And I didn't see Terry Neill either.

There was a feeling that something had to be done about referees and an idea was put forward that half a dozen players who were retiring should be given a crash course each year and put on the League list. Bobby Robson said transfer fees should be paid all at once which would act as a curb on prices. If clubs couldn't have time to pay, fees would be lower.

I was impressed with Mick Brown, the Oxford manager, who was one of the speakers but less impressed with Dario Gradi, the Wimbledon manager. Gradi said he would have to see what eventually came from the meeting before he gave his support. That riled me. Most of us had given up a Sunday to come because we were fighting for managers like him, those in the lower Divisions with little say in the running of the game.

Friday, 13 April.

The start of the Easter programme. Our game against WBA kicked off in the morning and it drew a 22,063 crowd, about 1,000 above average. We prefer playing in the morning on Good Fridays. It was gloriously sunny, cricket weather, and the atmosphere was good.

Waldron, voted Player of the Year by the supporters, put us ahead and we looked to have had it won until Cyrille Regis, who had done little against us in previous matches, scored right at the end to keep Ron Atkinson's title hopes alive. Laurie Cunningham's pass hit him on the back and he spun round and whacked the ball so hard past Peter Wells that it nearly took the netting away.

Ron intended to take in the Reading *v.* Portsmouth game on the way back and I was going too, but he had his own transport arranged. I wanted to see how my player George Shipley was performing in the Fourth Division. George was the best player on the field, I felt. He was playing his bits of football while the others were tearing around.

It was a good opportunity to contrast First Division football with Fourth. In terms of ability, controlling and passing the ball, there is no comparison but I wish more First Division players showed the endeavour of Fourth Division players.

Saturday, 14 April.

Most clubs have little to play for at Easter and you get some unusual results. But as I reminded the players, they needed forty points if they were going to qualify for a further bonus and a win was needed at Chelsea.

Stamford Bridge looked almost as depressed as St Andrews the week before except that the sun was blazing and you couldn't but admire the new stand even if it was half empty.

Before the game Petar Borota, Chelsea's Yugoslav goalkeeper came in to talk to Ivan Golac. They embraced and kissed and one of the players said: 'I wonder who he'll kiss next. He'll go down the line ... until he sees Chris Nicholl.'

Borota is obviously a character and when the referee disallowed his save from David Peach's penalty – he was down at the post before Peachy had kicked the ball – he gestured angrily and turned to the crowd. He was out on the six yard line as Peachy struck his second shot but Peachy chose the other side and it went in. It was clearly a penalty, Ron Harris handling as the ball was about to reach Boyer.

Typical of a team at the bottom, Chelsea had no luck at all. They struck the post in the first minute and put us under pressure early on. Peter Osgood, captain for the day against his old club, stroked the ball around in midfield but his pace and sharpness had gone. Ray Wilkins went through the motions alongside him like an Osgood of ten years ago. It was all very sad. Our second goal was harsh on them. A shot was going wide until it hit a defender and went in.

Garry Stanley came on for Ossie early in the second half and perked his team up. He scored and the game ended 2–1 to us. Bally was disconsolate in the dressing room afterwards. He felt we hadn't played well and I agreed – but we'd collected three out of four points.

Monday, 16 April.

I hadn't insisted that the players go to a hotel overnight and they appreciated the decision. They came straight from their homes to the ground for the Tottenham game and in the first half, played as well as any team I have ever had. We led 3–0 at half-time and it could have been six. Bally was superb.

During the interval I asked: 'Do you think you can keep it up, like Liverpool do?' But the back four started fannying about and we conceded three goals to end 3–3. Ardiles took over from Ball in running the game.

When the match ended, several cans were thrown on the pitch and insults were hurled at the players. It was a salutary reminder that spectators won't put up with anything less than the best. You can be on high one minute and flat on your back forty-five minutes later. As the players sat down, I said: 'You gave me the bloody answer to that question of mine.'

Wednesday, 18 April.

We had 250 young supporters aged between 8 and 16 at the Dell to look around and meet the players. They were members of the junior section of the Supporters Club. What with our family centre and Travel Club, Southampton do as much as any club to make fans feel part of the club but I still don't think it is enough. We are limited by the accommodation.

Along with many people in the game, I felt the problem of hooliganism had declined somewhat but it was still there and I wouldn't be happy until the last vestiges of it were wiped out. Bally, who spoke to the lads along with some of the other players, told me that he never had any fears about bringing his children to the Dell to watch games. 'It's the first club I've been with that I can say that,' he said.

I asked the boys if any of them had experienced any trouble themselves and an eight-year-old made us all laugh when he replied: 'Yes, my seat keeps breaking.'

In the evening I spoke at a meeting of the Travel Club in the Supporters Club and thanked them for their support.

Thursday, 19 April.

Anne and I drove up to Manchester to see Chris playing in the first leg of the Youth Cup semi-final against Manchester City at Maine Road. We lost 1–0 but put up a good show. As the first team was playing Coventry on Saturday, we drove back to Kenilworth and Anne did her shopping there. With no fixed address, we were real nomads!

Friday, 20 April.

Peter East called to say that Austin Hayes had been named in the Eire squad for the following Wednesday's European Championship match against Denmark. It was a surprise to me ... and to Austin. He was born in London and spoke with a broad Cockney accent, but both his parents were born in Limerick.

I remember mentioning that fact to Johnny Giles, the Eire manager, some time before but he hadn't spoken to me since. The players had a lot of fun at Austin's expense. I said to him: 'Now come on Austin, what's it to be, England or Eire? Shall I ring Ron Greenwood for you?' He thought a while and said: 'I'll go for Eire if you don't mind.' At the time, he had only played fifteen first team games.

Saturday, 21 April.

Coventry are like Southampton, a small club that has to work hard for what it gets. They're nice people and I always like going to Highfield Road. Joe Mercer, now a director, always makes a fuss of the family. The game was like the Tottenham fiasco. We played well for a time then fell apart and Ian Wallace, Coventry's Scottish striker, scored a hat-trick in a 4–0 win. That equalled our previous worst defeat, 4–0 at Leeds in November. Once again, the back four were at fault.

Monday, 23 April.

Tampa Bay Rowdies, Gordon Jago's club, wanted Manny Andruszewski, and a representative of theirs called at the ground to meet him and discuss terms. I don't know who had advised Manny but he started to make some outrageous demands. I interrupted and said: 'It's nothing to do with me but you're being greedy. If you don't like it, we'll find someone else.' He signed.

I spent the rest of the morning ringing up suppliers of materials for the new house. There were some tiresome delays and I chivvied them up, reminding them that I had paid in advance. Afterwards I drove to the Winchester Remand Centre to speak to eighty young offenders, some of them football hooligans.

It was a frightening place. I told them I wasn't there to moralize. Two hours later, I found I was still talking. I think they enjoyed it. I thought it was very satisfying. On the way home, I visited the Rising Sun pub in Fair Oak to accept a cheque on behalf of the Mentally Handicapped. People were writing in with cheques after my appeal on BBC which went out on television the previous Sunday.

Tuesday, 24 April.

Liverpool at the Dell. It is always a thrill to be playing against Liverpool. Their strength is their team work, from the managers and coaches through to the players. They are all as important as each other.

They'd come down the day before and had brought their kit round twenty-four hours before they needed to. That's another part of their success formula: they are so professional. For fifteen minutes they outplayed us. Their movement and endeavour threatened to overwhelm us and when David Johnson headed in a free kick with our defenders static I feared we would lose. At the time, Liverpool had only conceded fourteen goals all the season in the League.

But Steve Williams, who had an excellent game, crossed to Holmes and his header beat Ray Clemence to make it a 1–1 draw. Both sides were delighted with the point. Afterwards I told Lew Chatterley and Ian Branfoot to be sure to get the drinks in for Joe Fagan, Ron Moran and the Liverpool staff. Liverpool always entertain us well at Anfield.

Wednesday, 25 April.

The BBC said they were willing to take me across to Cologne for the second leg of the European Cup semi-final between Nottingham Forest and Cologne as I was going to be an analyst in the Final. I accepted readily.

Forest's Ian Bowyer scored the only goal and I was surprised afterwards in the dressing room at the lack of atmosphere. The players were muted and there wasn't a drink to be seen.

Thursday, 26 April.

The Youth side lost the second leg of the Youth Cup semi-final to Manchester City 3–0 but it wasn't the thrashing it appeared. One player was away on tour, another half-fit and two more, Steve Moran and Colin Angoy, had been refused permission to play by the English Schools FA who needed them for a friendly match the following Saturday! I was angry about the refusal of the Schools FA to co-operate but they wouldn't budge. If it hadn't been my insistence that these boys stay on at school to get their 'A' levels, the problem wouldn't have arisen.

I had acted in their interests but the Schools committee declined to help us. We were down to twelve players. Despite our defeat, I felt it had been an achievement to reach the last four. It augured well for the club's future.

Saturday, 28 April.

We beat Manchester City 2–1 in a poor match. City looked disorganized and I was sorry for Tony Book, their manager. The day before I had lunch with him and he appeared more worried than usual. He was in the last year of his contract, the club was in a bad trough, and he had little time to do much about it.

Monday, 30 April.

The last home game: Manchester United, the FA Cup Finalists. Dave Sexton, their manager, was in a relaxed mood, cracking jokes and though he had six of his Cup Final side either injured or on international duty, United put up stout resistance and it was an entertaining match.

Having the younger players in meant that United were more dangerous than they would otherwise have been so close to a Cup Final. Andy Ritchie, in particular played well. Boyer scored his fifteenth goal of the season in a 1–1 draw but missed many more chances. If he had put all his chances away in the season he would have broken the Football League scoring record.

Tuesday, 1 May.

Moving day. The new house wasn't ready but we were determined to get in. Anne had done the necessary packing and it was our fifth move in four months. The inconvenience was worth putting up with because we knew this would be the last move for some time. Unfortunately for the rest of the family, I wasn't there to help. I had to go to the Midlands with the team for tomorrow's League match against Nottingham Forest.

Wednesday, 2 May.

Three matches to go in the League, tonight's, Liverpool at Anfield on Saturday and WBA the following Tuesday at the Hawthorns, the three top clubs in the country! None of our players could complain about having a boring finale to the season.

The Forest match, however, was a nondescript affair. There was a smallish crowd, little atmosphere and neither side seemed in the mood to improve things. Peter Wells, playing against his old club, kept us in the game with some brilliant saves but it was his mistake which cost the goal in a 1–0 defeat.

Thursday, 3 May.

General Election Day but I wasn't able to vote. I was in a hotel in Leicester while the team went on to Southport to prepare for Saturday's match against Liverpool at Anfield. Jack Charlton picked me up and we went on to the second managers' meeting at Coventry.

It was much less productive than the first meeting. There was a bigger turn out but it was mainly a re-run of what we had discussed at Bisham Abbey. Bertie Mee said that there were fifteen applicants for the proposed post of paid secretary and a sub-committee had whittled it down to a short list of four.

Jack Charlton asked who the four were and Bertie replied: 'I am not prepared to divulge that.' Jack was very upset and started to walk out. I shouted to him to come back. We were going to a function in Newcastle that night and I needed a lift!

Eventually, he decided to remain and I proposed that the sub-committee be left to handle the appointment after it had been advertised nationally. The function in Newcastle was for OCS, Clive Thomas's company. Afterwards Jack suggested driving back early for an hour's shooting. I said I preferred to lie in.

Friday, 4 May.

I flew from Newcastle to Manchester for a BBC link up with Bob Wilson for his Saturday morning programme and from there went to a Sportsman's Dinner at Crosby before joining the team at Southport.

Saturday, 5 May.

Every pro likes playing at Anfield even though he's likely to be on the losing side. The place has an aura about it. Steve Williams had a groin strain and with Ivan Golac out injured I knew we would be up against it.

Liverpool put us under immense pressure and it was a splendid spectacle for 'Match of the Day' cameras. Phil Neal scored both goals in Liverpool's 2–0 win. Peter Wells had a fine game. He was back to his best form at last.

Normally we go home by train from Liverpool but this time we were in the coach and to break a long journey we stopped at Ron Atkinson's second home, the Europe Lodge. Inevitably, Ron was there with his wife and he insisted on opening two bottles of champagne before dinner.

Monday, 7 May.

Bank Holiday but there are no holidays in the football season. We were playing at WBA the next day and there was plenty to do before I set off to fly over to Belfast to speak at the Irish Football Writers' annual dinner. Malcolm Brodie invited me and I felt I had to go. It's important for the game over there that we keep up the links. As in previous visits, I saw no disturbances or tension but that's the problem, you don't see it until it hits you.

The managers of the 12 Northern Ireland League clubs were present including Alan Campbell, one of my former players at Grimsby. He was managing Ballymena. The event was sponsored by Guinness and a few pints of Guinness were consumed. It was an enjoyable night and I was glad I went.

Tuesday, 8 May.

Ron Atkinson had promised to meet me at Birmingham Airport. Because it was a Belfast flight, we took a long time to pass through the checks. Ron was waiting outside in a Rolls Royce in his tracksuit and I said: 'What's happened to the Jag?'

'Someone nicked it on Saturday night outside the Europa,' he said. 'There were three Jags together, mine, Jim Smith's and a friend's and they got mine. I've borrowed this from a friend. I'm off to play squash with Jasper.' He meant Jasper Carrott, the Midlands comedian.

Steve Williams was fit but Golac was still out. We have an excellent record at the Hawthorns and it was a good game. Albion won 1-0 through a second half goal from Ally Brown. My players were very weary, especially Alan Ball. This was their third game in seven days – against the top three clubs in the First Division. The public can't understand why players can't keep going full pelt through a season but they would understand if they had followed us around this week.

Wednesday, 9 May.

An offer had come in to play two matches the following week in Cairo and I was keen to accept. The players were tired but they would get some sun and rest and I also felt it would be beneficial for them as people. Not many of us have the chance of a free trip to Egypt to see the Pyramids. Middlesbrough were originally going but that fell through.

While in London for a trip to the BBC TV Centre at Shepherd's Bush I met the agent for the NASL club Philadelphia Fury to discuss Alan Ball's contract to play the summer with them. They wanted me to sign the previous night but I insisted on bringing it back with me to study the small print in the coach.

When I first discussed it with Bally, I said I wasn't keen for him to play throughout the year. He'd had a punishing season and it showed in his face. He looked grey and much older than his years. But I had to think of his career. He was on the last lap and deserved to make as much out of the game as he could.

I agreed to let him go and provided they still wanted him in America, consented to his signing full time after he had played one more season with us. He would then be thirty-five. The Fury club were even paying for a nanny to go out with the family. It was a good deal for Bally.

After the BBC interview with Bobby Robson and Desmond Lineham, I drove back to the Dell because I wanted to see a reserve match. It had been a shattering week and I was so carried away on the M3 that I suddenly realized the car was travelling at 140 mph. It occurred to me that perhaps I was overdoing it in more ways than one!

The reserves won their match but I had the players and staff in for a talk afterwards and told them how concerned I was about their prospects. 'You are the club's future but sometimes I wonder where the next meal is coming from,' I said. I was snapping at people and later when I got home I was no better. The end of the season couldn't come soon enough. Everything was catching up with me. In two days' time my testimonial was due to take place and there were scores of tasks still to be carried out. The Football Writers' dinner was taking place in London the next day and although I have always attended in the past, I sent my apologies this time.

Friday, 11 May.

The end of season tour was lengthened by three days because the organizers wanted a team to go to Dubai to play a match. Most of the 1976 Southampton Cup winning side promised to show up for my testimonial. Mike Channon was playing for us and Hughie Fisher, Jim McCalliog, Ian Turner and Paul Gilchrist came along but there was no Peter Osgood. Ossie had rung Bally and said he would try to make it but I noticed his divorce had gone through the day before.

Nottingham Forest played very competitively and won 4–0. The attendance was just over 14,000 though it looked more to me. That meant, after expenses, I might clear about £15,000. I paid the players' expenses and gave them and the referee, Clive Thomas, and linesmen decanters and bought flowers for all the ladies on the staff. I also arranged a party with a buffet supper for 250 people at the Royal Hotel. I didn't think I had overlooked anyone. So many people had worked hard for me and I wanted to show my gratitude. I am not an ungenerous person.

But two things took the edge off the night. Usually the bus company which provides special buses for our matches receives 26 complimentary tickets for its drivers but as this was a testimonial match with almost everyone supposed to be paying for admission – the charges of £1 and £2 were below our usual and we were playing the European Cup Finalists just before their Final against Malmo in Munich – they weren't allowed any this time.

Before the kick off, I was told the drivers were withdrawing their labour in protest. The head man at the company was embarrassed and I pointed out: 'They have had complimentaries to twenty-seven matches here this season.' I said I wasn't going to be blackmailed. If they had asked me in the right way and not presented me with what amounted to an ultimatum, I would have co-operated.

Having no buses probably cut the gate but I wasn't going to concede. I was slightly disappointed in the attendance. Mike Channon's testimonial in 1976 was a packed house, but that was two days after we had won the FA Cup.

The second discordant note was at half-time and it literally was a note. A representative of a handful of stewards handed me a petition which read: 'We are upset that we haven't been asked to your party. Have a good time.'

I remembered I had invited the car park stewards. At the end of the game I was given a second petition from another group of stewards which said they didn't want to be associated with the first petition! Apparently in the programme I had mentioned 'gatemen and stilemen' and this should have read 'stewards and stilemen'.

Saturday, 12 May.

FA Cup Final day and I was the only panellist on the BBC's programme. When I arrived at Wembley, I met Sir Stanley Matthews who had come over from his home in Malta for the Football Writers' Dinner. He looked incredibly fit for a sixty-four-year-old. He still doesn't drink.

Terry Venables was appearing on ITV and I congratulated him on winning the Second Division championship the night before. The attendance at Selhurst Park was 52,000 which was 4,000 above the police limit. I bet they had no petitions that night!

The rival channels tend to be dismissive of each other but I thought both sides covered the match splendidly. I enjoy working with Jimmy Hill. He is a supreme professional and so is David Coleman who was the link man. I was a little niggled, however, that I didn't have more time before the kick-off to talk about how I expected the game to go. I had barely two minutes but I managed to get a point in about the probable physical outcome. David Coleman picked that up at half-time.

'You said it was going to be a bit physical and it has been,' he said. I explained my thinking. I thought it was a magnificently entertaining Cup Final and summing up Manchester United's pulling back from 2–0 down to 2–2 in the 87th minute before losing to an 88th minute goal, I said: 'It's like a man being reprieved at the Old Bailey and walking out in the street and being knocked over by a car.'

As Arsenal had won, I was asked to stay on at the studio for the 'Match of the Day' programme and it was midnight before I started for home.

Monday, 14 May.

We flew out early in the afternoon for Cairo. The season started on an aeroplane and was finishing on one. It would give me time to reflect on the year and how Southampton had progressed.

I thought of a remark Ted Bates had made some time ago. Ted is good for me because he has been in the game so long and he can step back and see things more clearly than some of us. 'You are so involved in what you are doing that you hurt the people who are closest to you,' he once said.

He was right. Often I was a move or two ahead and my impatience showed. I had a good staff but I suppose I was too short with them on occasions. It made me appreciate more the qualities of my first manager Alan Brown at Sheffield Wednesday. He was so dedicated to his objectives that he didn't have time to explain himself fully to the rest of the staff and his reputation may have suffered. And Alan Brown didn't have the distractions of TV and the myriad other activities which claimed my time.

Football management is like riding a very fast roundabout at a circus. You struggle to climb on and it's even harder to hold on as it whirls round. Then you lose your grip and slip off. The resilient ones fight their way back into the saddle but except for a very select few, it's an up and down life. My family, which is the sane part of the life, the stabilizing factor, come to fear the ups because they know they will inevitably be followed by downs. For all that, it is a fascinating life.

Appendix: Southampton's record 1978–9

DATE	OPPONENTS	VENUE	SCORE	SCORERS	GATE	LEAGUE POSITION
1978						
August						
19	Norwich	A	1–3	MacDougall	21,133	—
22	Bolton	H	2–2	Baker, MacDougall	21,059	—
26	Middlesbrough	H	2–1	Nicholl, Ball	20,691	12
30	B'ham (LC2)	A	5–2	Boyer 2, MacDougall 2, Peach	18,464	—
Sept						
2	Aston Villa	A	1–1	Nicholl	34,067	11
9	Wolves	H	3–2	Boyer, Waldron MacDougall	22,060	7
16	Bristol C	A	1–3	Holmes	21,420	12
23	Derby County	A	1–2	Peach (pen)	21,623	14
30	Ipswich Town	H	1–2	MacDougall	21,764	15
Oct						
3	Derby County (LC3)	H	1–0	Boyer	19,109	—
7	Everton	A	0–0		38,769	18
14	QPR	H	1–1	MacDougall	22,803	16
21	Arsenal	A	0–1		33,074	19
28	Notts F	H	0–0		22,530	17
Nov						
4	Man United	A	1–1	Holmes	46,259	17
8	Reading (LC4)	A	0–0		25,046	
11	Norwich	H	2–2	Nicholl, Holmes	21,183	16
14	Reading (LCrep)	H	2–0	Hebberd, Nicholl	22,829	
18	Middlesbrough	A	0–2		17,169	17
21	Aston Villa	H	2–0	Baker, Holmes	22,080	16
25	Leeds U	A	0–4		23,597	17
Dec						
2	B'ham	H	1–0	Boyer	18,957	15
9	Man C	A	2–1	Viljoen og, Boyer	33,450	12
12	Man C (LC5)	H	2–1	Boyer, Hebberd	21,523	—
16	Coventry	H	4–0	Waldron, Hebberd, Boyer, Baker	19,102	12
26	Chelsea	H	0–0		20,770	12
1979						
Jan						
9	Wimbledon (FA3)	A	2–0	Boyer 2	9,254	—
17	Wolves	A	0–2		15,104	12
24	Leeds (LCsf)	A	2–2	Holmes, Williams	33,415	—
30	Leeds (LCsf)	H	1–0	Curran	23,646	—
Feb						
3	Derby	H	1–2	Peach (pen)	21,109	16
10	Ipswich	A	0–0		19,520	16
12	Preston (FA4)	A	1–0	Ball	20,727	—

17	Everton	H	3–0	Peach (pen), Baker Boyer	20,673	12
20	Bristol City	H	2–0	Hayes, Holmes	19,845	10
24	QPR	A	1–0	Holmes	13,635	8
March						
3	Arsenal	H	2–0	Hayes, Waldron	25,052	8
10	WBA (FA5)	A	1–1	Boyer	30,712	—
12	WBA (FA5 rep)	H	2–1	Peach (pen), Boyer	25,775	—
17	Notts F (LC Final at Wembley)		2–3	Peach, Holmes	100,000	—
19	Arsenal (FA6)	H	1–1	Hayes	24,536	—
21	Arsenal (FA6 rep)	A	0–2		44,820	
24	Bolton	A	0–2		19,879	13
28	Tottenham H	A	0–0		23,570	13
31	Leeds	H	2–2	Waldron 2	21,805	13
April						
7	B'ham	A	2–2	Baker, Hayes	12,145	15
13	WBA	H	1–1	Waldron	22,063	14
14	Chelsea	A	2–1	Peach (pen), Holmes	18,243	11
16	Tottenham H	H	3–3	Peach (pen), Ball (pen), Boyer	22,096	11
21	Coventry	A	0–4		17,750	13
24	Liverpool	H	1–1	Holmes	23,181	13
28	Man City	H	1–0	Hebberd	19,744	12
30	Man United	H	1–1	Boyer	21,616	11
May						
2	Notts F	A	0–1		20,388	11
5	Liverpool	A	0–2		46,687	13
8	WBA	A	0–1		17,302	13

FINAL LEAGUE RECORD (LEAGUE POSITION: 14TH)

P	W	D	L	F	A	Pts
42	12	16	14	48	53	40

League Cup	Second Round	B'ham	(a)	5–2
	Third Round	Derby	(h)	1–0
	Fourth Round	Reading	(a)	0–0
			(h)	2–0
	Fifth Round	Man C	(h)	2–1
	Semi-final	Leeds	(a)	2–2
			(h)	1–0
	Final	Notts F		2–3
FA Cup	Third Round	Wimbledon	(a)	2–0
	Fourth Round	Preston	(a)	1–0
	Fifth Round	WBA	(a)	1–1
			(h)	2–1
	Sixth Round	Arsenal	(h)	1–1
			(a)	0–2

GOALSCORERS

(League, FA Cup and League Cup): Boyer 15, Holmes 10, Peach 8, MacDougall 7, Waldron 6, Baker and Nicholl 5, Hayes and Hebberd 4, Ball 3, Curran and Williams 1, Viljoen og.
TOTAL: 70.